Foundations for a Philosophy of Education

'Tis written, "In the beginning was the *Word.*"
Yet here I falter. Who can help me on?
Upon this word I shrink to place such high esteem.
It must be rendered otherwise
If the Spirit lights me with resplendency.
'Tis written, "In the beginning was the *Thought.*"
Reflect upon this opening line,
Lest in rash haste your pen speed on.
Is it thought that all with form and being endows?
'Tis better, "In the beginning was the *Power.*"
But as I write the very word
A fretful doubt assails conviction.
The Spirit aids me and at once the truth is manifest.
I write assured, "In the beginning was the *Deed.*"

GOETHE's *Faust,* Act I, scene 3

Frederick C. Gruber
UNIVERSITY OF PENNSYLVANIA

FOUNDATIONS FOR A PHILOSOPHY OF EDUCATION

Thomas Y. Crowell Company New York
ESTABLISHED 1834

To the Memory of My Mother

Library of Congress Catalog Card Number: 61-7951

Designed by Edwin Kaplin

Manufactured in the United States of America
by Vail-Ballou Press, Inc., Binghamton, N.Y.

Preface

In *Goals for Americans,* "The Report of the President's Commission on National Goals," John W. Gardner, President of the Carnegie Foundation, writes: "In terms of our national future, teaching is the most important profession." In the light of the vast changes that have come about in the last half century in the social and economic fabric of American life, and of our nation's important role in world affairs, the training of those who will educate our young takes on added significance.

An examination of courses in pedagogics at the turn of the century, even at outstanding universities, finds them concerned with problems of classroom management and the techniques of teaching the traditional school subjects. Even such a distinguished national committee as The Committee of Ten which reported in 1892 was concerned exclusively with secondary-school subjects, their selection and arrangement in the curriculum.

Although Herbert Spencer's great book entitled *Education* appeared in 1861, it took over a half century until the Committee on the Reorganization of Secondary Education set down the *cardinal principles* clearly derived from Spencer's five objectives.

Philosophy of education was generally included in courses in the history of education and scarcely existed as a separate subject. Such dissertations on the philosophy of education that came out of American universities were biographies of leading educators or aphorisms and collections of quotations bearing on education from the writings of the world's great thinkers. The century was well advanced before such studies as Raup's dissertation on "Complacency" began to appear.

The first substantial textbook on educational theory written by a philosopher was John Dewey's *Democracy and Education* published in 1916. On the whole this book was badly misread and badly interpreted, but it did stir up a revolt against the traditional subject-matter-centered and teacher-controlled classroom. I believe that much of the gross misrepresentation of Dewey on the part of the "progressives" was due to their lack of background for understanding the intellectual implications of Dewey's instrumentalism, and their impatience to get on to something new which did not require the mental discipline which the subject-matter approach demanded of the teacher. The pupil was now to do all the learning and growing for himself. As a young pedagogue I was told that one did not need to know a subject to teach it; all that was required was the right method.

Essentialists, of whom William Bagley is an outstanding example, wrote vigorously in defense of the schools as transmitters of the cultural heritage. At the same time the very significant movement toward developing a *science* of education was being advanced with great vigor. On the assumption that whatever exists, exists in some measurable quantity, jobs and activities were analyzed and a multitude of data was collected and submitted to elaborate statistical analysis.

During the thirties a number of books appeared bearing such titles as "The Philosophy of American Education." For most teachers' colleges this sort of text seemed to be sufficient, and many normal-school graduates seemed not to know that there were points of view other than the one into which they had been indoctrinated. R. R. Rusk and William Hocking did notable work in presenting concise expositions of different "philosophies," but possibly the most outstanding work in the field of comparative philosophy of education was done by John S. Brubacher. The *Forty-first Yearbook of the National Society for the Study of Education*, which he edited, is a notable milestone. A decade later, J. Donald Butler, Theodore Brameld, and others made significant contributions.

An important development since World War II has been the attention given to philosophical analysis. This movement reflects the interest of educational theorists whose basic training has been in philosophy rather than in education. Israel Scheffler of Harvard represents this group especially in his latest work *The Language of Education*.

Brubacher, in editing the *Fifty-fourth Yearbook of the N.S.S.E.*, to which we shall pay much attention later, recognized the important contribution philosophy could bring to education, not by building new systems which could be adopted by majority vote of school boards or committees of administrators, but through analysis of educational concepts and a comparative study of varying points of view.

A recent trend in teacher training is to place the professional preparation of teachers on the graduate level or in the last years of the undergraduate college. The young teacher needs a substantial basis of fundamental or general education and a thorough grounding in the subject he will teach, a knowledge of the nature of the student and the psychology of learning, and above all an orientation to the philosophical, social, political, and economic setting in which American education takes place.

It is my purpose to give the student the foundation for building a philosophy of education for himself by giving him a working knowledge of the language of philosophy, by presenting a brief comparative study of some contemporary views on education, by acquainting him with the main currents of educational thought over the last twenty-five hundred years, and by giving him an insight into the nature of man, the relation of the citizen to the state, and the ways in which value systems can be formulated.

Only a well-informed and intellectually well-disciplined group of professional educators can deal with the problems of education as they confront us at the present time. In the following pages I hope to set forth the background for forming such an understanding.

In writing a study upon which a philosophy of American education can be based, the most serious problem an author faces is what to leave out. The present volume is the fruit of many years of experience in teaching courses in Philosophy of Education to students at the University of Pennsylvania. I offer this book as a first book to students who are relatively unfamiliar with philosophy as an academic discipline or with the history of educational theories, and who are seeking a background against which they can construct their own theories and practices.

Thanks are due to my classes upon whom I have tested many portions of the manuscript, to individual students, notably Doreen Steg and Herman von Helmold for inspiration and valuable suggestions, to my assistant John Cabry for his critical reading of the text and for valuable work in constructing the bibliography, and to my colleagues Professors Flower and Hammock and my wife Alma Hellwege Gruber for valuable suggestions and criticisms: Thanks are also due to Miss Paulette Mitchell for typing the manuscript, and also to Herman Makler for his excellent suggestions, editorial work, and attention to many technical details. Whatever faults or shortcomings are found in the work are my own.

Acknowledgment is gratefully made to authors and publishers for permission to quote from their works and to all who have had a hand in seeing the manuscript through the press.

If the book can raise more questions than it answers, and stimulate the reader to a lifetime of study to solve the riddles which the theory and practice of American education pose, the author will feel amply rewarded, and to such he says, "Welcome fellow pilgrim," or as those who first stepped on Plymouth Rock might have said, "Welcome fellow Seeker."

Philadelphia, Pa. FREDERICK C. GRUBER

Contents

Chapter IX Society and the Individual

Chapter X Education and Value

APPENDICES

Charts and Maps

Part I

FOUNDATIONS

Chapter I

The Nature of Philosophy

PREVIEW

From earliest times, some of the greatest minds have been concerned with the problems of education, for basic to the perpetuation and welfare of any society is the initiation of its young into its traditions, knowledge, beliefs, and activities. Philosophy provides the theory for education and the technical study of the educationist directs its practice. Philosophizing about education must be based as much as possible upon that which can be empirically or logically verified. On the other hand, the application of techniques and procedures will be aimless, and perhaps even harmful, unless they are built upon a solid foundation of educational theory. Thus we see that an understanding of both the theory and practice of education is necessary for professional education.

The purpose of this introductory chapter is to provide the student who is beginning a study of the philosophy of education with a knowledge of the divisions and method of philosophy as a basis for understanding current philosophies of education. Philosophy is an over-all view of existence, knowledge, and value and their interrelationships. The study of philosophy is usually divided into metaphysics, epistemology, logic, and axiology. The remainder of this chapter discusses these four divisions in some detail. The student will find it interesting to note how each of the basic philosophies, together with the systems derived from them, emphasizes one or the other of these divisions as fundamental to its own world view.

THE DIVISIONS OF PHILOSOPHY

METAPHYSICS

Theories regarding reality make up the body of philosophy known as metaphysics; that is, what is above or beyond ("meta") nature ("physics"). It is concerned with such topics as the nature of the universe, how it came into being, and the relation of time and space to eternity and infinity. These topics dealing with the nature of the universe (cosmos) are known collectively as cosmology. For example, whether the world came into existence by chance or by divine command is a cosmological problem.

Cosmology is also concerned with the stuff or substance of reality. Is reality mind or matter? Are there other substances, or is there a combination of these? Those who hold that the world is composed of only one substance, for example, matter, are called monists from a Greek word meaning single or alone. Those who believe reality to be made of two substances, spirit and matter, for example, are called dualists from the Greek word for two. Those philosophers who hold that there are more than two substances composing reality are called pluralists from a Latin word meaning more.

Those who believe that reality consists only of spirit or ideas are known as idealists (the term should be idea-ists); those who hold to the theory that reality consists of matter are called materialists or naturalists. Those holding a dualistic or pluralistic concept of reality are often realists or pragmatists.

The Nature of Man

Metaphysics is also concerned with the nature of man and his relation to other living creatures. Whether he has been specially created or has evolved from lower forms is a metaphysical issue. The nature of man also considers his makeup, whether he be only mind or made up of other substances. If the nature of man is made of several substances then the question arises, "How do these substances interact with one another, or do they react at all?" For example, if we accept the notion that a table is a material thing, that man's sense organs are also material, but that his mind is spiritual, and I see the table, what do I have in my mind? Certainly not the wood and metal of which the table is composed. We shall see later how philosophers have tried to answer this question.

Then there is the question of the relationship between the various substances of which reality is composed. Which is the greater—mind or matter? Which influences which; as in William James' illustration, do I run because I am afraid, or am I afraid because I run, or is neither the cause of the other?

Perhaps these questions seem to be too theoretical, but they have a definite application to education. Some educators maintain that man's distinguishing characteristic is his rational faculty, and, therefore, all education should lead to the development of his power to reason. Others hold that he is entirely physical, that he is coexistent with nature and that mind is only another term for the functional aspect of the brain. The pupil is, therefore, to be trained by the careful and exact repetition of selected patterns of conduct. Some hold that man's nature is composed of mind, matter, and spirit and that his spiritual qualities are most important. These they maintain are developed by the exercise of faith.

Free Will

The whole matter of free will is also a concern of metaphysics. Most materialists and realists deny free will and accept the idea that man's actions are predetermined by natural laws over which he has no control. These thinkers are determinists and believe that man's conduct should be conditioned. Idealists generally hold that man has the power of choice and that his will must be trained to act according to the highest principles in making the right choice. Pragmatists believe that man has the power to delay his actions and, therefore, the consequences of his actions, and thus is enabled to select from many possibilities what seems to him to be the wisest choices. The whole matter of discipline and the motivation of learning centers around the point of view one takes of this issue.

The Individual and Society

Some philosophers think that man is a social being and attains his full stature only as he engages actively in the affairs of society. Others believe that man is essentially a lonely creature; that nobody can ever really know him and that he can never really know anybody or anything as it really is. Some believe that man becomes himself only through social, political, and religious institutions. Others, the existentialists for example, believe that institutions are taking the humanity out of human beings and that each person must strive to be himself and to find his own lonely way through existence. The Educational Policies Commission in 1938 stated one individualistic aim for education: self-realization, and three group aims: social, political, and vocational. Philosophy here asks what is the relationship between the public (group) and the private (individualistic) nature of man.

The Nature of God

Metaphysics is also concerned with the nature of God. Theorists about the nature of God fall into two groups. Those who deny the existence of God and believe that everything came into being by chance are called atheists. The philosophy of David Hume has been called atheistic, although he never subscribed to this point of view himself.[1] The communistic metaphysic is atheistic.

The other group which acknowledges the existence of a supreme being, force, or cause in the universe is again divided into several groups. Deists believe that God is the divine creator of the universe, but once having put it in order he has removed himself and has become disinterested in it. Thomas Jefferson has been referred to as a deist. Polytheists believe in the existence of many gods. The ancient Greeks and Romans were polytheists. William James has been termed a modern polytheist. Pantheists believe that God and his creatures are one, that all of creation is part of God and God is part of all creation. Baruch Spinoza is the classical example of pantheism in philosophy. Alfred North Whitehead taught a sort of pantheism known as panpsychism which stresses the universality of mind. Many oriental philosophies also teach a sort of pantheism. Orthodox Christians are theists because they believe in a personal God who not only created the universe but has a continuing personal interest in all that He has created. Theology is now con-

[1] The educational contributions of most of the men mentioned in this chapter are described in Part II. See Table of Contents.

sidered to be a separate discipline or study which concerns itself with an intensive study of theism in all its aspects.

Purpose

Questions about whether we live in a purposeful or purposeless universe are called teleological. Materialistic and atheistic philosophies maintain that the world came into being and is sustained by pure accident or chance. All religionists, idealists, and most realists believe that there has been purpose in the universe from the beginning, and that this purpose can be traced throughout history. Most experimentalists hold that the cosmos is without purpose, but that man may impose purpose upon it by purposeful activity.

The Problem of Existence

Ontology, from a Greek word which means "being," is the division of philosophy which deals with the meaning of existence. For example, St. Anselm, in his famous ontological argument for the existence of God, maintained that God is that, than which nothing greater can be imagined to exist, and that the objective existence of God is proved by the idea of God. In a non-theological sense, ontology is mainly concerned with the relationships, or categories in which reality exists. Aristotle in his *Metaphysics* described ten such categories. For example, he says things exist in quantity, in quality, in relation to other things, in time, in place, and so on. About two thousand years later, a great German philosopher, Immanuel Kant, described twelve modes of existence which he arranged in four groups of three each, namely: quality, quantity, relation, and modality (such as being possible, necessary, or contingent). Kant maintained that these categories needed no scientific or logical proof, but were the fundamental ways in which reality existed, and that they were, therefore, a priori, not needing the exercise of man's reason or observation. He believed, however, that man's comprehension of these categories begins with observation and ends with the exercise of pure reason.

Any discussion of "education for what is real" deals with metaphysics. For naturalists and realists it is the most important division of philosophy.

THE NATURE OF KNOWLEDGE

Epistemology, from a Greek word meaning "to know," is the area of philosophy which considers the nature of knowledge. The knowledge which the philosopher seeks is not merely a matter of opinion, or partial truths based upon observation, but is absolute certainty and beyond question. Some philosophers such as Kant and Herbert Spencer take an agnostic attitude toward the possibility of knowledge and maintain that it is impossible to know ultimate reality. Others like Hume and Michel Montaigne maintain a skeptical or questioning point of view. St. Anselm, Johann F. Herbart, and many others with different metaphysical backgrounds take an affirmative position that ultimate knowledge can be known. Pragmatists such as John Dewey and William James maintain that knowledge is fractional and functional and can be applied only to specific situations. This point of view follows naturally from their relativistic metaphysic that nothing remains the same long enough to be placed into a category.

Kinds of Knowledge

Philosophers maintain one of three points of view regarding the method by which knowledge is obtained. Above we mentioned Kant and his categories which he said were known a priori. Whatever is a priori possesses universal validity (is always true) and is known through pure reason. The axioms of geometry are claimed to be true a priori.

Another way to obtain knowledge is through observation. Such knowledge is called a posteriori (that which comes afterwards). This is the method of science. Technical advances in observation such as the microscope and the telescope are means of extending the power of sight. Other instruments make the power of the other senses more accurate, and statistical methods make the description and comparison of these observations more exact.

Pragmatists, experimentalists, believe that all knowledge is tentative and must be experienced to be useful. That is why they insist in education that curricular material must be learned by doing and should be of immediate interest to the learner.

Ways of Knowing

Empiricism, from two Greek words meaning "in" and "trial," is the method of scientific observation and of the laboratory. It is knowledge gained through the senses. Many materialists believe that this is the only method of gaining knowledge, while other philosophers, such as Kant, believe that one must begin with empirical observation, but then submit its findings to pure reason. The great popularity of the scientific method today has led many to believe that it is the only method by which knowledge can be obtained, but there are at least four other methods which also possess considerable validity.

Rationalism, the method of reason, is the technique of philosophy and will be discussed under the heading "Logic: The Methods of Philosophy."

Intuitionism is the view that Ultimate Truth is not reached by analysis, but by insight or immediate grasp of the content. Some psychologists have defined intuition as the activity of the mind at its supreme moment of concentration in which one is not aware of the infinitely complex organization and reorganization which has taken place to produce a given conclusion. Henri Bergson, whose book *Creative Evolution* achieved deserved popularity at the beginning of the present century, described intuition as human instinct becoming conscious of itself so that it can reflect upon itself and enlarge its knowledge and understanding.

Authoritarianism, holding a belief on the basis of authority, is a very common way of obtaining knowledge which is highly praised in some quarters and condemned in others. Some accepted sources of authority are the Church, the Bible, the law, journals of learned and scientific groups, and pronouncements of official commissions. Less acceptable is the authority of the gang, the demagogue, the newspaper, the popular magazine, and the advertiser. Before accepting authority as a purveyor of truth, it is well to examine the basis for the claim to possess truth and how often the claim has been violated.

Finally, we come to revelation, the belief that God is continually revealing himself and his truth to the world through his Church and his Word. The difference between this and the authoritarian view described above is in the evolutionary quality of the revelation. In other words the revelation is progressive, the individual filling in the gaps in empirical and intuitive knowledge by an act of faith. Making an *act of faith* is not only a religious necessity, but is a common practice in scientific procedure and in social, political, and economic practice.

For the idealist, epistemology is the crux of philosophy, for through a knowledge of the self in all its aspects one grasps a complete understanding of reality and values as well.

Epistemological considerations enter into all aspects of curriculum making. Those who are convinced that knowledge can be obtained only by the methods of science and empiricism will provide a curriculum which is heavily weighted with science and mathematics and will even try to apply the "scientific method" to the humanities. Those who believe that knowledge comes through the exercise of reason will stress logic, mathematics, and the cultural heritage, while those who maintain that knowledge is fractional and functional will stress the activity and life adjustment approach.

LOGIC: THE METHODS OF PHILOSOPHY

As the techniques of science are referred to as the scientific method, so the techniques or methods of philosophy are referred to as logic. Logic is a most important branch of philosophy because it reflects upon thinking itself, and is involved in every other branch. Logic deals only with the type of thinking called reasoning. It differs from psychology, which is a descriptive science because it describes the processes of thought. Logic, on the other hand, is normative and prescriptive because it sets forth the rules by which one thinks systematically and correctly. In reasoning, we must produce proofs which permit us to infer certain conclusions. Logic is the discipline which attempts to distinguish between good and bad inferences.

Logic has been traditionally divided into deductive and inductive logic. Deductive logic tries to establish conclusive inferences which are true beyond the shadow of a doubt and is, therefore, concerned with the rules which determine whether an argument is valid. It is the classical approach to thought and reasons from the general to the particular. A common form of deductive logic is the syllogism which can be roughly defined as an argument containing two statements or propositions, called premises, and a conclusion. One of the most famous examples of the syllogism is:

Major Premise: All men are mortal.

Minor Premise: Socrates is a man.

Conclusion: Therefore, Socrates is mortal.

Here we notice that we have three declarative sentences (statements of fact). The first sentence (major premise) refers to a class and a characteristic of that class. The second sentence (minor premise) asserts that a certain individual is a member of that class, and the third concludes that the individual possesses the characteristics of the class to which he is asserted to belong. If both premises are true, then the conclusion cannot be false. Another example might be:

All human beings are mortal.

All Englishmen are human beings.

Therefore all Englishmen are mortal.

But you may ask, is there a possibility that some human being is immortal, and that this human being, by chance, might be an Englishman? If, then, you wished to make a statement, your argument would have to be something like this:

No Englishman born before 1800 is known
to be still alive.

Englishmen are still dying.

Therefore, the probability is that all
Englishmen will die and, are, therefore, mortal.

This is called inductive reasoning. It starts by stating a number of particulars and arrives at a possible generalization. It is, therefore, concerned with probability rather than with certainty.

The inductive method is also the method of science. Investigators count the number of positive and negative results of an experiment or observation and then form a hypothetical conclusion which is then tested, and if no important deviations are noticed the hypothesis becomes conclusive evidence, or scientific truth.

Experimentalists believe that thought is both inductive and deductive. Dewey, in his complete act of thought, describes reflective thinking as having five sequential steps: (1) a felt difficulty or problem, (2) its location and definition, (3) suggestions for its possible solution, (4) development by reason of the bearings of the situation, and (5) evaluation and testing of the results.

Another method of reasoning has been developed by the German philosopher, Hegel. This method is called dialectic from Greek "dia," between, and "legein," discourse, literally a way of showing relationships. Hegel's dialectic begins with a statement which he calls a thesis. Next, the investigator must state the exact opposite which is called the antithesis. For example, if we assume the concept of spirit to be the thesis, its exact opposite or antithesis, so Hegel claims, is matter. Hegel next tries to resolve the thesis and antithesis into a synthesis or fusion of both, that is, a third condition containing elements of both thesis and antithesis in organic unity. In our illustration, Hegel deduces the systhesis to be mind. Paul Woodring in *A Fourth of a Nation*[2] describes essential education as the thesis, progressive education as the antithesis, and then tries to effect a synthesis which contains the best elements of both.

Hegel maintained that each synthesis in turn became another thesis and that these continuing resolutions described the inevitable evolution or unfoldment of history.

AXIOLOGY

The fourth and last division of philosophy which we shall discuss here is axiology, a study of values, from two Greek words, "axios," value or worth, and "logos," account or theory of. The term "axiology" was first applied in the twentieth century by Lapie and by Hartmann, and deals with such considerations as the nature and types of value and the criterion upon which value judgments are made.

[2] Paul Woodring, *A Fourth of a Nation* (New York: McGraw-Hill Book Company, 1957). See especially Chs. 3, 4, and 5.

Nature of Value

Some philosophers explain that a thing or experience has value if it fulfills a wish or desire. Others describe the nature of value as that which gives pleasure, or that which one is interested in, or again that for which one expresses a preference. Friedrich Nietzsche believed that what enhances life has value. Quite the opposite is the Stoic belief that values are developed from the exercise of the will and the determination to act justly in the face of an unfriendly nature. Kant's *categorical imperative* which demands that a person act only from the highest principles expresses much the same idea.

The pragmatists, Dewey in particular, stress the relationship between things as means to ends or consequences. Pragmatists would judge the value of an activity not by the intention of those who engage in it, but by the results accomplished, but since ends become means to future ends, both must be harmonious. This is directly opposed to the doctrine that the end justifies the means. Finally, there are those who believe that values are integral, active, objective parts of reality, existing in and of themselves. There are, of course, other views than those mentioned above.

Values are of two types: intrinsic and instrumental. Intrinsic values are ends which are prized for their own sake. Instrumental values are those which contribute to or are the cause of intrinsic values. Among commonly recognized values are the morally good, the love of truth, the beautiful, the holy. Other commonly recognized values are work, play, association, and bodily well-being.

Criterion of Value

An important axiological consideration is the standard for testing values. Hedonists and utilitarians, such as Jeremy Bentham, believe that the criterion for value is the amount of pleasure derived by the individual and society. Some idealists, Plato, for example, recognize a rational system of objective ideals, while others stress a rational system of values. On the other hand, the biological approach to values stresses survival and adjustment. This is the position of Herbert Spencer and John Dewey.

Realms of Values

Until the time of Kant (1724–1804), the various values were generally investigated as separate studies with different methods and standards. Ethics investigates the nature of good and evil; aesthetics the nature of beauty. Other areas in which value judgments must be made are religion, education, and the social and behavioral sciences. One of the problems to which the axiologist addresses himself is whether the approach to the study of values must be pluralistic, that is, having a different set of criteria for each value studied, or whether all values are related in one value system.

Values in Education

In education the question of values is of great importance. The aims of education are determined by the values which a society adopts. These aims in turn determine the method and the curriculum. Such questions as the following arise from a consideration of educational aims: Which subjects are most valuable, which least, and what is the order in between? Is value absolute so that we must strive for perfection in education and rank learners according to a fixed standard? Does a subject have the same value for all students? Should aims be immediate or remote? What is the relation between the interest and happiness of the learner and the subject learned? What is the relationship between intrinsic and instrumental values? Since intrinsic (or consummatory) values may also become instrumental (or contributory) values because they become means for future ends, should value be immediately apparent to the individual learner or should he be made to accept a deferred adult value which he neither understands nor desires, because it is supposed to be a part of his equipment for adult life? When, if ever, should a student study a subject for its own sake rather than for its immediate usefulness? What is the relationship between values which an individual accepts for himself and those demanded by society? These and other questions will be discussed in Part III.

SUMMARY

In this chapter we have discussed the four main divisions of philosophy, namely: metaphysics, epistemology, logic and axiology. *Metaphysics* deals with the nature of reality. It considers such problems as the nature and cause of the universe, the nature of man, the nature of God, the problems of purpose, free will, and the nature of existence. Metaphysics is of great concern to the philosophies of realism and naturalism. *Epistemology* is concerned with the nature of knowledge, the possibility of knowing, the kinds of knowledge, and the methods by which knowledge is obtained. Epistemology is the crux of the philosophy of idealism.

Logic is a normative discipline which prescribes the methods of exact thought. Most important among philosophical methods are deductive logic which reasons from the general to the particular and inductive logic which reasons from the particular to the general. The experimental method of John Dewey's complete act of thought which begins with a felt difficulty and ends with the evaluation of a tentative hypotheses and which involves both inductive and deductive logic was described as was Hegel's dialectic which is a method of resolving or synthesizing opposites. Logical positivists and rational realists lay much stress on logic.

Finally, *axiology* deals with the nature of values, whether they are absolute, relative, or contingent, whether they are determined by the satisfactions individuals receive, the demands of society, or are dependent upon a response to high principles, as in Kant's *categorical imperative*. Problems of value are of especial interest to pragmatists. Realms of value such as ethics, aesthetics, religion, education, and the social and behavioral sciences were discussed, and certain problems of values in education were enumerated.

BIBLIOGRAPHY

HISTORY AND THEORY

Alpern, Henry, *The March of Philosophy* (New York: The Dial Press, 1934).

Blau, Joseph L., *Men and Movements in American Philosophy* (New York: Prentice-Hall, Inc., 1952).

Copleston, Fredrick, *A History of Philosophy* (London: Burns, Oates and Washburne, 1946).

Curti, Merle, *The Growth of American Thought,* 2nd ed. (New York: Harper and Brothers, 1951).

Durant, William James, *The Story of Philosophy* (New York: Simon and Schuster, Inc., 1927).

Eby, Frederick, and Charles Arrowood, *The History and Philosophy of Education, Ancient and Medieval* (New York: Prentice-Hall, Inc., 1940),

———, *The Development of Modern Education* (New York: Prentice-Hall, Inc., 1947).

Erdmann, Johann Edward, *A History of Philosophy,* trans. Williston S. Haugh (3 vols.; New York: The Macmillan Company, 1890).

Gilson, Etienne Henry, *History of Christian Philosophy in the Middle Ages* (New York: Random House, Inc., 1955).

Hocking, William Ernest, *Types of Philosophy,* rev. ed. (New York: Charles Scribner's Sons, 1939).

Joad, C. E. M., *Guide to Philosophy* (New York: Dover Publications, Inc., 1936).

Lamprecht, Sterling Powers, *Our Philosophical Traditions* (New York: Appleton-Century-Crofts, Inc., 1955).

Martin, Seymour G., Gordon H. Clark, Francis P. Clarke, and Chester T. Ruddick, *A History of Philosophy,* (New York: F. S. Crofts & Co., 1941).

Miller, Hugh, *An Historical Introduction to Modern Philosophy* (New York: The Macmillan Company, 1947).

Montague, William Pepperell, *Great Visions of Philosophy* (La Salle, Ill.: Open Court Publishing Co., 1950).

Parrington, Vernon Louis, *Main Currents in American Thought* (New York: Harcourt, Brace and Company, 1930).

Peterfreund, Sheldon P., *An Introduction to American Philosophy* (New York: The Odyssey Press, 1959).

Russell, Bertrand, *A History of Western Philosophy* (New York: Simon and Schuster, Inc., 1945).

Titus, Harold H., *Living Issues in Philosophy* (New York: American Book Company, 1953).

Wheelwright, Philip, *The Way of Philosophy* (New York: The Odyssey Press, 1954).

Windelband, W., *A History of Philosophy,* trans. James H. Tufts (New York: The Macmillan Company, 1893).

DICTIONARIES

Good, Carter V. (ed.), *Dictionary of Education,* 2nd ed. (New York: McGraw-Hill Book Co., Inc., 1959).

Runes, Dagobert D. (ed.), *The Dictionary of Philosophy* (New York: The Philosophical Library, Inc., 1942).

Chapter II

Contemporary Philosophies of Education

CONTEMPORARY PHILOSOPHIES COMPARED

With the competition for the conquest of space goes the contest for the minds of men. The conflict of ideologies between the communist and the free world is now being waged in the classrooms of the world, for education is one of the most powerful weapons devised by men to confound their enemies and to perpetuate their way of life.

In the preceding chapter we have discussed the component parts of such ideologies and the methods by which they are derived. Our present task is to show how these concepts take actual form in some contemporary philosophies of American and Russian education.

The U.S.S.R. has set up an elaborate system of education on all age levels under party control to promulgate and to perpetuate the Marxist doctrine. In America our pluralistic political doctrine will not admit of complete centralization of control or of a single dogmatic type of education. Yet there are those who, believing that they have a clearer insight into the truth than the rest of us, and perhaps acting out of fear, would force us into their static pattern of democracy through authoritarian methods. Some would have us return to the supposed security of the medieval cloister or the Victorian era. Some believe that the advancement of men depends upon high ideals, on a knowledge of nature, on an increase in word power, on a return to faith or to reason. For the most part these philosophies of education are grounded in the American democratic tradition, and would subscribe to the same general aims.

Traditionally, philosophies of education have been grouped under three headings: idealism, realism, and pragmatism. Butler also lists naturalism in his treatment of the subject.[1]

Idealism holds that the most important element in the nature of reality is mind or spirit. This philosophy is sometimes described as mentalistic or transcendental. On the other hand, realism holds that the most important element in the nature of reality is matter. This philosophy is sometimes called materialism, positivism, or naturalism. Some realists hold to a double nature for reality, that is, that there are two distinct substances, mind and matter, while others hold a pluralistic view, that there are more than two substances (see Ch. I, p. 4). The view that there is but one substance to reality is called monistic. Both philosophies believe that knowledge is definite and fixed and that basic ethical standards are unchanging.

Naturalism claims that all the features of the universe can be explained from a study of nature and of human experience, as well as from the physical sciences. Mind and matter are both aspects of our experience.

Pragmatism, on the other hand, may be described as a method of solving intellectual problems, a theory of the kinds of knowledge man can acquire. Knowledge and standards are relative. Truth is discovered, made in the process of a social situation. Whatever achieves the best results for the greatest number in the present circumstance is most true or most valuable. Thus truth is developmental and changes with place, time, and conditions. Since pragmatic transactions occur between man and man or men and things the term "humanism" is sometimes applied to this philosophy.

Brameld lists four educational philosophies: essentialism, progressivism, perennialism, and reconstructionism.[2] Among the essentialists, he includes idealists, realists, and most naturalists. Such educators are concerned with transmitting the cultural heritage and conditioning the learner by varying methods to take his place

[1] J. Donald Butler, *Four Philosophies and Their Practice in Education and Religion* (New York: Harper and Brothers, 1951).

[2] Theodore Brameld, *Philosophies of Education in Cultural Perspective* (New York: Dryden Press, 1955).

in adult society. Reality, knowledge, and standards are fixed and eternal.

Progressivists are those educationalists who follow some form of pragmatism. Knowledge is constructed in the learning situation by solving current problems through reflective thinking. Truth is relative, and morals are standards set by social groups. The interest of the learner is paramount.

The perennialist would base educational procedures on the philosophy of Aristotle as interpreted by the scholastics, especially St. Thomas Aquinas. Truth is attained by reason or by supernatural revelation through the Catholic church.

Reconstructionism is a philosophy of education which would go a step beyond pragmatism and advocate the development of a program of social welfare to be implemented by organized action and socialistic governmental control.

Brubacher includes the essentialists and the perennialists in his conservative group and lists the various kinds of present day pragmatists and also the type of education through natural development which springs from the philosophy of Rousseau under the term "progressivism." Brubacher speaks about conservatism and progressivism,[3] while Broudy, Wynne, Thut and others use other classifications. In *Modern Philosophies and Education: The Fifty-fourth Yearbook of the National Society for the Study of Education,*[4] nine distinguished philosophers, each with an educational theorist as consultant and sometimes as interpreter, under the chairmanship of Professor Brubacher, then of Yale University, discussed nine of the major present day approaches to educational theory. The yearbook is probably the most representative and authoritative volume on the topic today. The types of philosophies described therein are realism, Thomism, idealism, experimentalism, Marxism, existentialism, linguistic (dramaticism), logical empiricism, and ontological (rhetoricism).

Realism, idealism, and experimentalism (pragmatism) have been described above. Marxism, frequently termed dialectical material-

[3] John Brubacher, *Modern Philosophies of Education* (New York: McGraw-Hill Book Company, 1951).

[4] *Modern Philosophies and Education: The Fifth-fourth Yearbook of the National Society for the Study of Education,* Part I, ed. Nelson B. Henry (Chicago: University of Chicago Press, 1955).

ism, is the philosophy of communism. Its method is based upon a way of solving problems dealing with abstract ideas developed by Hegel. His method is called dialectic (see Ch. I, p. 12), and his philosophy, absolute idealism. But instead of applying the dialectic to abstract ideas, Marx maintained that it is in nature alone that the process of overcoming contradictions takes place. Marx also maintains that social relations are conflicts of opposites controlled by the inevitable laws of nature. Education assists communism to resolve the class struggle by conditioning the learner to act as part of an inevitable social movement.

Existentialism, on the other hand, stresses the importance of the individual by maintaining that, for good or evil, each person is himself unique and irreplaceable. It is a revolt against institutionalism in all types of organizations, whether political, economic, social, or religious. Man is born into an indifferent world. He is completely free to choose his own world view, but there are no guides, of which he can be certain, to help him. Education must make man aware of this, must make him resolve to accept his responsibility for "finding a way home," and must help him return to some sort of personal security through his own efforts.

The linguistic approach to education maintains that man is a symbol-using animal. When men speak with men, as individuals or groups, they frequently misunderstand each other because of the different meanings and connotations they attach to word-symbols. Then, too, words are used in many ways, for example, to explain, to persuade, to deceive, to interrogate, to command. Education should make men aware of these problems and give them the requisite techniques for solving them.

Logical empiricism or logical positivism is based upon a theory of logic which maintains that the only statements useful to the philosopher are either mathematical or scientific. All other non-demonstrable statements, while valuable emotionally, are philosophically nonsensical. Value systems are more or less flexible. The student must be taught to observe nature scientifically and to think positively. Logical empiricism tries to follow a "golden mean" between conservatism and progressivism.

An ontological approach to the theory of education stresses the fact that during its long history mankind has developed patterns of thought and conduct based on erroneous conceptions of reality. Education should make men aware of this and, through imparting a sufficient factual background and a thorough training in logical thinking and objective analysis, should prepare the oncoming generations to overcome the past mistakes of society and to avoid making new ones.

MODERN PHILOSOPHIES AND EDUCATION

We shall now let the writers of *The Fifty-fourth Yearbook* speak for themselves, largely in their own words, by presenting a précis of their essays.

REALISM

In his essay, "Education and Human Society: A Realistic View," [5] John Wild of Harvard University maintains that

the universe is made up of real, substantial entities, existing in themselves and ordered to each other by extra mental relations; that these real entities and relations can be known in part by the human mind as they are in themselves, . . . [and that] such knowledge, especially that which treats of human nature, can provide us with immutable and trustworthy principles for the guidance of individual and social action. Education is for the transmission of culture. The school should be concerned with pure knowledge and detached from concrete life and practice. It should develop a broad and critical view of knowledge. Education aims to discern the truth about things as they really are and to extend and integrate such truth as is known; to gain such practical knowledge of life in general and of professional functions in particular as can be theoretically grounded and justified; and, finally, to transmit this in a coherent and convincing way both to young and to old throughout the human community. There is no natural opposition between the common good of the whole society and the good of the individual. Genuine authority must be grounded on independent being and then transmitted to the poor but ignorant minds who are prepared to receive it. . . . A human society is not a single great soul or substance containing many different parts like the cells of a giant organism. It is . . . a number of separate and autonomous individuals sharing invisible common purposes and the active attitudes and habits required to realize them in co-operation.

[5] *Ibid.*, pp. 17–56.

THOMISM

In "Thomistic Views on Education," [6] Jacques Maritain of Princeton University presents the Thomistic outlook which is in opposition to the philosophical systems to which progressive education most often appeals for support.

There is a difference in nature between the senses and the intellect. Knowledge is a value and an end in itself, and truth consists in conformity of mind with reality—with what is or exists independently of the mind. Natural intelligence must be perfected by the intellectual virtues. The primary aim of education is to form a man: an animal endowed with reason; a free individual in personal relation with God; voluntarily obeying the law of God; a sinful and wounded creature called to divine life. Liberal education is directed toward wisdom, centered in the humanities, aiming to develop in people the capacity to think correctly and to enjoy truth and beauty. Religious education is basically needed because if the existence of the Absolute Being is not believed in, no certitude in the unconditional and obligatory standards can be validly established and efficaciously adhered to.

IDEALISM

Theodore M. Greene of Yale University presents a liberal Christian idealist's approach to the philosophy of education in his essay "A Liberal Christian Idealist Philosophy of Education." [7]

Man can know, at least in part, his environment and thus adapt himself to it. Being, knowledge, and values must be studied in relation to each other. While accepting orthodox beliefs as true for himself, the objective idealist shuns all authoritarianism; he believes in the reality of objective values as pure essences, and that man is a purposive being. The school is the only institution in society whose primary function and responsibility are educational. The school is the "mind" of the body politic. It should never be merely an arm of the government. It should be committed to liberal education and stress the acquisition of knowledge and the development of the mind at all levels. It must cooperate with, but never replace, other social institutions. Liberal and vocational education are two essential and complementary aspects of the total preparation for life. Liberal education is essentially unified and organismic. It

[6] *Ibid.*, pp. 57–90.
[7] *Ibid.*, pp. 91–136.

is concerned with the development of four basic skills: logical-linguistic, factual, normative, and synoptic. The more liberal education is, the better, but those who cannot profit by it should have a curriculum adapted to them. The school will educate the individual for a life of social responsibility, it will introduce the child to existential living. It will teach the basic structures necessary for democracy, an attitude of honest criticism, and a passionate concern for social justice. It will introduce the student to the great alternative responses to religion, and a profound concern for whatever gives meaning to life.

EXPERIMENTALISM

In "An Experimentalist Approach to Education"[8] George R. Geiger of Antioch College sets forth the views of present-day pragmatists.

The knower as well as the perceived environment is part of knowledge. That something can be, when totally independent of any observer or frame of reference, is scientifically meaningless, for knowledge is transaction. As men chose, the process of evaluation becomes established. Education is the change experience makes in human beings; it is a moral affair; it is primarily a value enterprise. Education must be free to change. While traditional philosophies limit change to means only, experimentalism holds that ends in view, when reached, become means in a continuing serial process. Ends, like means, must be free to change. All men and women are educable. The school must promote a climate for growth. Men must employ their free time creatively. Liberal (i.e. liberating) education should make the individual free of the closed mind and free to change present society after having viewed it critically through historical perspective.

Liberal education is concerned with present problems. Vocational education should employ every opportunity to make men think, to make them sensitive to authentic and imperative problems, to enrich the "making of a living." The individual cannot be considered apart from society, nor society apart from the individual. The teacher must take the lead in supporting the most liberal interpretation of free thinking on social issues while avoiding being the dupe of subversive forces. The experimentalist believes that deep emotional commitments should be made to social welfare, creative intelligence and critical thinking, as well as to the supernatural and the remote.

[8] *Ibid.*, pp. 137–174.

EXISTENTIALISM

In "Significance of Existence and Recognition for Education,"[9] Ralph Harper of the Council for Religion in Independent Schools draws the outlines of an existentialist philosophy.

Our age is an age of private and public desolation, an age of longing for a presence that carries explanation and justice with it. At the bottom of existentialism is the principle of recognition which sees experience in terms of a wandering and a return, of homelessness and home-seeking. Man is born into an indifferent universe. For the homeless man, those things of worth are home, family, justice, law. Life is undercut by death; every good moves in a sea of annihilation. Man's dignity lies in a belief that no one is completely replaceable. Each individual should make this belief function in the world. The whole man is the object of education. Existence is personal, individual, irreplaceable; it is not life in a vacuum, but a life conditioned by times and places. Totalitarianism and middle class complacency are attempted ways out of spiritual homelessness. The free man is free to find the ends of human existence and to live in the way. Education makes the individual aware of the meaning of homelessness, of being-at-home, and of the ways of returning. Existential models in the past are found in stoicism, in tragedy, and in the Christian religion. Education is a formal process where there are the teacher, the pupil, and the curriculum. It is a natural process. The teacher leads while the pupil is moved, but teacher and pupil react reciprocally upon each other. Human freedom arises from and is directed toward an order of reality beyond any human circle. The world and truth are bright goals of free man. There is a world and there is a truth, but it is not possible to say that the world is this or that and truth is this or that. One cannot think of freedom without commitment, or moving without a goal. Man is not a cross-section of behavior patterns, he is somehow involved in reality itself. Existentialism helps us understand the relativity of words and isms in comparison to the great enterprise of living.

A LINGUISTIC APPROACH

Kenneth Burke of Bennington College discusses a "Linguistic Approach to Problems of Education."[10]

Man is a typically language-using or symbol-using animal. Education must restore the great emphasis once placed upon language. Man ap-

[9] *Ibid.*, pp. 215–258.
[10] *Ibid.*, pp. 259–303.

proaches the world symbol-wise, and symbol-foolish. Language-using is a mode of conduct. This position can be called "dramatistic" because it begins with a stress upon "action." The physical realm is properly treated in terms of motion. Action and motion must be interwoven insofar as a man's generic animality is experienced by him in terms of his specific symbolicity. Education is by and through language, beyond language.

Symbol-using is not to be confused with word-using. All the arts are symbol-using. The problem of human relations through language has four major aspects: logical or indicative, rhetorical or persuasive, poetic, and ethical or personal. The linguistic approach contends that the basic motives of human effort are concealed behind the clutter of the machinery, both technological and administrative, which civilization has amassed in the attempt to live well, that in a methodic study of symbolic action, men have their best chance of seeing beyond this clutter. Textual study begins with charting equations: What equals what, and what follows from what.

Education would be primarily admonitory, a sophisticated and methodized set of parables or fables. Only a truly "universal" attitude toward educational purposes can modify the intrinsic competitive emphasis of the individual, of groups, of nations. We should teach a fear of symbol-using and a methodic distrust of competitive ambitions. Educative training should be as negative as the Ten Commandments. It would center in the study of ambition as a disease. Education is not only preparing students for the market, but for a preparatory withdrawal to recover at crucial moments. Education would begin with narrow partisan indoctrination. The second step would acquaint the student with different points of view. Next would be a more "humanitarian" view of alien ways. A fourth step would give equal discussion to all points thought to be valid. There should be respect for the individual, subordination of the individual to the group, patriotism, and internationalism in happy balance. The study of religion fits perfectly with the approach to education in terms of symbolic action, but its approach is not doctrinal but formal. Education would take place in an atmosphere of mutual teacher-pupil respect.

LOGICAL EMPIRICISM

"Aims of Education for Our Age of Science: Reflections of a Logical Empiricist," [11] is the title of the essay of Herbert Feigl of the University of Minnesota.

[11] *Ibid.*, pp. 304–341.

Logical empiricism, sometimes called logical positivism or scientific humanism, is the twentieth century sequel to the age of enlightenment. The most striking differences between animals and man lie in the much greater role of instincts and simple learning processes in animals and the much more complex learning phenomena supplemented by a much higher level of ingenuity and symbolic behavior (language) in human beings. Human language differs from animal communication by its syntactical, semantical, and pragmatic rules, and has three functions: representation, expression, and appeal. Man also has a capacity for critical reflection. Patterns of expectation and of action develop through the responses of the organism to repeated stimuli (or stimuli-configurations) and through trial and error. Learning is most effective if we avoid the extremes of the complete rigidity of dogmatism and the utter fluidity of skepticism. Language is cognitive when it functions representatively, expressive when it reflects feelings and attitudes, and evocative when it is designed to influence the communicatee. A sentence is factually meaningful when it can be verified in whole or in part by means of observable data. The only meaningful way we can talk about reality is in terms of what is knowable, what can be confirmed by experience. The logical empiricist rejects the dualistic theory of the mind-body problem. To stress method at the expense of content or content at the expense of method is educationally foolish. Free will presupposes causal determination. As long as education promotes the formation of intelligence and character in a manner which allows for free learning, rational choice, and critical reflection, human beings so educated will have an excellent opportunity for being masters of their own activities and achievements. Education molds the original nature of man into a second nature. Education, with its atmosphere of moral approvals and disapprovals, develops in the individual the internal "still voice," the conscience, which, though corruptible, is nonetheless immensely powerful in its normal functions of a constraining and/or inciting force. Justice, kindness, and perfection are the results of adjustments of attitudes which are practically bound to emerge in the context of social interaction. Logical empiricist moral values are relativistic. Logical empiricism has no room for absolute values justified without reference to human needs, interests, and ideals. It refuses to anchor its beliefs in the unknown and unknowable. Democracy as a form of government and way of life is tremendously superior to all other forms. Man is a rational animal in the Aristotelian sense. The keynote of existence is scientific enlightenment. A large part of education should be devoted to the acquisition of the scientific attitude and an understanding of the problems and results of science, its history and philosophy. The best minds should be recognized early and given special opportunity to form an intellectual elite. Logical empiricism represents a golden mean between classical and progressive education.

AN ONTOLOGICAL APPROACH

James K. Feibleman of Tulane University develops "An Ontological Philosophy of Education."[12]

Education proper is the acquisition of existing knowledge on the principles of rhetoric. The practice of education is applied rhetoric. For most young persons, education does not start at the beginning but in the middle. Education often reassures the ignorant by intensifying the ignorance. The less we know, the more certainly we impart it to others. Most people, young as well as old, do not approach formal education with inviting ignorance, but with their ignorance and its limited virtues already lost to them. Due to the marvels of modern universal education, most people have been trained for a life to be led in this limbo. A very few struggle into a state we may call "ignorance regained." The first use of newly-acquired power is its misuse. The task of the theory of education is to substitute aids for obstacles, the questions for the answers, the methods of research for the absolute truth. The fear of false knowledge is the beginning of wisdom. The proper kind of education must consist in the eliciting of contradictions in the matter of unconsciously held beliefs, to demonstrate elements of untenability in the implicit, dominant ontology. Learning is the disciplined method of control whereby we utilize the knowledge of process of inquiry into being. It consists of three broad sub-divisions: preformal learning, informal learning, and formal learning. The methodology of teaching properly centers on the theory of the relation of theory to practice. The best type of education must teach theory as though it did not need applications, but also it must teach practice as though it did not need theory. We ought to abandon the old devotion to principles alone and substitute the technical practice separately, for only things which are properly distinguished can be properly related. We must begin with the problem as it faces us. Children are ethically neutral until taught otherwise. Establishing habit patterns with respect to principles as well as practices is more important for students than allowing them to express themselves. A teacher ought to be one who imparts tentative knowledge and especially acts as a leader in inquiry, a more or less blind, yet intuitive guide to the discovery of the truth.

[12] *Ibid.*, pp. 342–370.

The aims of education are to build right thoughts, right feelings, and right actions. Formal education ought to start with the fundamental tools of communication and soon advance to theoretical knowledge of some branch of philosophy and of mathematics, the working knowledge of one fine art, and the empirical knowledge of one laboratory science. A university ought to be a community of capable teachers who are trained enthusiasts, backed by productive scholars.

MARXISM

These are the current philosophies of American education. There remains still one essay in the *Fifty-Fourth Yearbook*, "On the Marxist Philosophy of Education,"[13] by Robert S. Cohen of Wesleyan University, Connecticut, which, while it is not an acknowledged philosophy of American education, completes the cycle of present day views of educational theories. We include a summary of it here because we believe it is necessary for American educators to have some acquaintance with Soviet educational principles in order to recognize the difference from their own systems and to strengthen their dedication to democratic education as America defines it.

The Soviet philosophy, then, is as follows:

The germs of the education of the future are to be found in the factory system. We cannot speak of "man," but only of "men," because they do not exist apart from society. There is a dominant and progressive causal process in change. The dominance of class struggle can be apprehended through a dynamic approach only. Logical necessity rests within the ideas and this internal relationship becomes, in Hegel's philosophy, the relation of opposites. Historical development is the result of conflicts among men, their social-economic status impelling them to have irreconcilable interests. The struggle of competitive social classes is the dynamic force leading to social change.

The knowing subject cannot be separated from the known object. Knowledge of society is a social product. Man makes his own history from his consciousness which is itself a social product. Man is oppressed by nature, and man is oppressed by other men via the relations of social classes. Overcome these and truth can be reached. A classless society will preserve the highest values of preceding times. Education will cure practical hypocrisy. Educate and inform the whole mass of

[13] *Ibid.*, pp. 175–214.

the people. A sound basis for education necessitates a sound relation to the labor process which is only possible in a reconstructed, genuinely equalitarian and cooperative society. The liberal educationist, in the name of individuality, confuses discipline with dogmatic authority and in the hypocritical setting of capitalism, confuses monopoly with free enterprise. Capitalist democracy cannot fulfill its promise of material and spiritual abundance. Genuine education can take place only in a society which is no longer rent by economic class divisions and cultural prejudices; therefore, a sound social relation to the labor process is necessary to a sound education. The two evils of pure verbalism and pure vocationalism will be avoided by stressing the role of the workshop, the laboratory and the relations of the school to the local community, factory, cooperative farm, and to provincial and national industrial, agricultural, and reforestation projects. All teaching should be organized about the recognition and practice of human labor and based on the purposive, creative, independent act of the pupil. The four goals of Soviet education are general, poly-technical, vocational, and aesthetic. It aims to develop in children the elemental virtues of the socially-conscious and independently-active citizen and to provide the gigantic quantities of qualified technical workers needed for industrial construction.

MODERN PHILOSOPHIES COMPARED

All the philosophers, with the exception of Geiger, indicate a belief that knowledge is definite and fixed. Geiger declares that knowledge is transaction. Harper says that, while there is knowledge, one can determine it only for oneself and not for another. Greene believes in knowledge as pure essence, Wild and Feigl, as universal reals and known entities. Maritain agrees but adds that these are perfected by divine revelation. Feibleman and Burke stress the importance of reason and linguistics. The Marxist dialectic roots truth in materialism and the class struggle.

Regarding school and society, Wild, Burke, and Feibleman would incline to separate formal education from practice. All recognize the necessary cooperation of the school with other social agencies, and that individual freedom requires commitment. Geiger would educate all men in and for society; the Soviets, for the state; Maritain, for the future life; Burke, for internationalism. All recognize the key position of the public school as society's principal educative agent. All the philosophers make explicit or imply that education of the "whole man" is the true function of education, but Greene and Maritain give the impression that the rational faculties are supremely a religious orientation. Wild, Maritain, and Feigl point out the necessity of training a leadership class.

In discussing aims of education, Wild believes that the school should transmit the culture of the race and principles for social guidance. Greene joins him in maintaining that the intellectually superior must transmit knowledge to the ignorant who should be prepared to receive it. Geiger and Harper believe that education should aim at change through experience: Geiger, in a social setting, Harper, through individual home-seeking. All the other philosophers believe in fixed aims of education determined by their theories of knowledge. Burke remarks that education should be chiefly admonitory, "as negative as the Ten Commandments." Feigl would have education follow Aristotle's golden mean and mold a new nature of man's original nature.

The content of the curriculum according to Wild should be pure knowledge. Maritain, Cohen, and Burke present what might be called a doctrinaire approach, the Soviet curriculum being centered in the class struggle, Maritain's in the Church, Burke's in linguistics. Feibleman stresses a theory of unlearning, believing that public and private prejudices and erroneous ideas must be unlearned before true education can begin. Wild and Greene insist that, while vocational education is necessary, it must be kept distinct from liberal education in the formal school. On the other hand, Geiger believes vocational education can also be liberalizing. Maritain, Burke, and Feibleman stress the importance of instruction in "right" reasoning, differently interpreted by each. Burke and Feigl argue for language training because man is a symbol-using animal.

With regard to teacher-pupil relations, Wild, Maritain, Greene, Cohen, Burke, and Feibleman insist on the teacher's dominant role. Harper and Feigl argue for mutual respect between teacher and pupil, and Geiger believes that both are learning simultaneously.

Maritain believes that religion, in a dogmatic sense, is basic for all education; he agrees with Greene that man is a divine creature. Greene and Harper maintain that religious beliefs are personal. Geiger, Harper, and Feigl state that moral values are relative but require individual dedication and commitment. Burke argues for studies about religion. The Marxist philosophy maintains that religion is the opiate of the people.

The philosophies of education just described are not mutually exclusive. Even those which are outwardly most antagonistic have points in common. Proponents of Marxism, experimentalism, and Thomism are most critical of each other. Yet all stress the education of the whole man, all insist upon the inculcation of moral and spiritual values, all maintain that individual freedom requires commitment, and all recognize the necessary cooperation between the school and society's other agencies. Thomist and Marxist education both agree upon the dominant role of the teacher. Both approach the process of education from a doctrinaire point of view—each from a different ideology. All three welcome the use of sensory techniques and devices in teaching.

Thus we see that neither the statement of aims, the degree of cooperation between school and community, nor the devices and techniques of instruction can show us fundamental differences in educational thinking. We must not be misled by appearances. The source of these differences lies much deeper. It is to be found in the theories of knowledge and the systems of values to which the several philosophies subscribe. When studying points of view about education, it is well to begin with such questions as, "What is the basis of knowledge, and upon what authority is knowledge accepted?" For example, the Thomist believes that the source of knowledge and authority is God through the Catholic church, the Marxist believes it lies in dialectic materialism, the experimentalist, that it lies in consensus arising from activity in a social setting, the rational humanist, in the exercise of reason, and the existentialist, through individual recognition.

Bases of authority might be arranged upon a continuity from the most remote, such as the supernatural or unchanging social or natural laws, through various kinds of permissiveness, to absolute personalism in which all authority rests in the will of the individual. On the one hand, there is complete authoritarianism and on the other, complete egalitarianism. Neither state actually exists in practice.

When we ask, "What is the basis of knowledge, or how is knowledge acquired," we can arrange philosophies of education on a continuity from belief and indoctrination through reasoning, scientific method, and observation, to "process," in which knowledge is made by the knower for one particular time, place, or circumstance.

Another and more specific way to judge an educational philosophy is to see how nearly it corresponds to certain alternate views with regard to education. Below are some statements about school and society, the curriculum, discipline, the teacher, and evaluation. Under each heading, the reader should first check the statement which more nearly corresponds to his point of view. When he has checked all nineteen items he should see how consistent his viewpoint has been, and how closely he has adhered to the conservative or the progressive view of education. (The conservative viewpoint is listed first.) Finally the reader should check his viewpoint against the philosophics discussed above in order to discover the degree of his agreement or disagreement with each. In every case he should examine his opinions to determine whether his data are objectively verifiable and whether his conclusions have been reached through generally accepted methods of logical thought.

ALTERNATE VIEWPOINTS IN EDUCATION

School and Society

1. Education in school should stimulate pupils to direct their efforts in greater degree towards:
   a. Self-preservation and advancement in a competitive world.
   b. Advancement of self and others through cooperative effort.
2. Education in school should:
   a. Confine its social teaching to transmitting the social heritage.
   b. Concern itself with the improvement of American society.
3. The general welfare of the American people is likely to be raised more by:
   a. Concentration of efforts on those most likely to succeed.
   b. Direct efforts to educate all.
4. Satisfactory leadership in a democracy is more likely to be secured by:
   a. Early selection and specific training of gifted pupils for leadership.

b. Emergence of leaders out of situations offering opportunity for leadership.

The Curriculum

1. The school curriculum should be based on the assumption that:
   a. Subject matter furnishes the starting point, the center, the end.
   b. The child is the starting point, the center, the end.
2. In determining curriculum content, greater emphasis should be placed on:
   a. Deferred or future needs and values.
   b. Present needs and values.
3. Learning is likely to be more permanent:
   a. When it results from performing a required task.
   b. When it is self-initiated and self-directed.
4. Learning is likely to be more permanent:
   a. When it is motivated by extrinsic rewards and compulsions.
   b. When it is motivated by intrinsic values.
5. Greater all-round development of pupils is likely to result from a policy which stresses:
   a. Following specific directions.
   b. Assuming responsibility.
6. Greater all-round development of pupils is likely to result from a policy which stresses:
   a. Being told by others.
   b. Finding things out for one's self.
7. The power to think is more likely to be developed by:
   a. Exercises to sharpen the wits and develop the mind.
   b. Attempt to solve problems in real life.

Discipline

1. The discipline likely to have greater value to a pupil is that which comes from:
   a. Control by authority.
   b. Self-control.
2. The discipline likely to have greater value to a pupil is that which comes from:

a. Hard work for the purpose of inuring the pupil to hard work.
b. Hard work as a means of attaining a desirable pupil purpose.

The Teacher

1. The teacher's role in a class group is better conceived as that of:
   a. One who controls the pupils and their activities.
   b. A counsellor of pupils and a participant in their activities.
2. When controls are exercised by the teacher, they should preferably be:
   a. Negative and restrictive.
   b. Positive and directive.
3. A teacher's greater concern should be with:
   a. The pupil's achievement in the subject or subjects studied.
   b. The all-round development of the pupil.

Evaluation

1. The better criterion for judging the results of schooling is:
   a. What pupils know in the sense of knowledge and information.
   b. What pupils do, how they live.
2. Standards for a pupil's achievement should be derived from:
   a. Comparing his achievements with the achievements of other pupils.
   b. Comparing his achievements with his past achievements and known capabilities.
3. The better criterion for judging the value of an educational experience to a pupil is:
   a. The contribution of the experience to the specific learning it was designed to bring about.
   b. The contribution of the experience to total learning, including elements for which it was not specifically designed.

SUMMARY

There has probably never been a time when public education was so widely discussed. While much of the criticism of the spectacular and noisy type is a matter of private opinion, as we have seen, many fine thinkers have given much serious thought to problems involving the relation of the school to society, the aims of American education, its content, its method, and its results. One of the best ways to bring these problems and their possible solutions into focus is to examine them in the light of the disciplines and techniques of the philosophy of education.

While many will speak glibly of their philosophy, careful questioning will prove it to be foggy, vague, and without form.

Philosophy, as we have already noted, literally means the love of wisdom. It seeks to give man an understanding of the meaning of life, of his place in the world around him, and of his relation to the universe. It seeks answers to such questions as what is reality, what is man, what is knowledge, and what things are of value. It fills life with meaning, purpose, direction. Philosophy is not an idle armchair exercise. It is an exacting, disciplined study with a body of subject matter and a method of its own. Its body of knowledge comes through a systematic study of the development of education through the ages including the many-faceted present. It attempts to give educationalists an insight into the present-day problems of education. It tries to define these problems and to arrive at basic principles which will guide in their solution. It seeks to give a basic orientation to other phases of the discipline of education such as administration, supervision, methods, guidance and evaluation. Specifically, philosophy of education assists the professional educator to achieve an integrated understanding of the whole field of education, to understand the position of the school among other community agencies which are also engaged in the educational function, to build an understanding of the historical development of certain educational concepts and practices, and to give a rational basis for educational planning and function.

Philosophy of education is therefore broad in scope. It not only wishes to be informed about education past and present, but it also wishes to compare, contrast, organize, and systematize this knowledge. It attempts to bring the outlines of the conflicting philosophies into focus. It attempts to show the relationship of education to other disciplines, especially the social and biological sciences.

Our exploratory study in this chapter has shown us the necessity of studying problems of education within a framework of the development of the ideas from which they have evolved. In Part II we shall develop such a frame of reference.

BIBLIOGRAPHY

Bayles, Ernest E., *Democratic Educational Theory* (New York: Harper and Brothers, 1960).

Brackenbury, Robert L., *Getting Down to Cases* (New York: G. P. Putnam's Sons, 1959).

Brameld, Theodore, *Cultural Foundations of Education* (New York: Harper and Brothers, 1957).

Broudy, Harry S., *Building a Philosophy of Education* (New York: Prentice-Hall, Inc., 1954).

Brubacher, John S., *Eclectic Philosophy of Education* (New York: Prentice-Hall, Inc., 1951).

———, *A History of the Problems of Education* (New York: McGraw-Hill Book Co., Inc., 1947).

———, *Modern Philosophies of Education* (New York: McGraw-Hill Book Co., Inc., 1950).

Butler, J. Donald, *Four Philosophies and Their Practice in Education and Religion* (New York: Harper and Brothers, 1958).

Childs, John L., *Education and Morals* (New York: Appleton-Century-Crofts, Inc., 1950).

Kilpatrick, William H., *Philosophy of Education* (New York: The Macmillan Company, 1951).

Kneller, George F., *Existentialism and Education* (New York: Philosophical Library, Inc., 1958).

McCluskey, S.J., Neil G., *Catholic Viewpoint on Education* (Garden City, N.Y.: Doubleday & Company, Inc., 1959).

Mason, Robert E., *Educational Ideals in American Society* (Boston: Allyn and Bacon, Inc., 1960).

Modern Philosophies and Education, The Fifty-fourth Yearbook of the National Society for the Study of Education, Part I, ed. Nelson B. Henry (Chicago: University of Chicago Press, 1955).

Park, Joe, *Selected Readings in the Philosophy of Education* (New York: The Macmillan Company, 1958).

Phenix, Philip H.: *Philosophy of Education* (New York: Henry Holt and Co., Inc., 1958).

Pounds, Ralph L. and James R. Bryner, *The School in American Society,* (New York: The Macmillan Company, 1959).

Redden, John Duand, and Francis A. Ryan, *A Catholic Philosophy of Education* (Milwaukee: The Bruce Publishing Co., 1948).

Rusk, Robert R., *The Philosophical Bases of Education* (Boston: Houghton Mifflin Company, 1956).

Sayers, Ephraim Vern, *A First Course in Philosophy of Education* (New York: Henry Holt and Co., Inc., 1952).
Scheffler, Israel, *Philosophy and Education* (Boston: Allyn and Bacon, Inc., 1958).
Thut, I. N., *The Story of Education* (New York: McGraw-Hill Book Co., Inc., 1957).
Ulich, Robert, *History of Educational Thought* (New York: American Book Company, 1945).
Wegener, Frank C., *The Organic Philosophy of Education* (Dubuque, Iowa: William C. Brown Company, 1957).

Part II

TWENTY-FIVE CENTURIES OF EDUCATIONAL THOUGHT

Chapter III

From Plato to St. Thomas Aquinas

PREVIEW

In our excursion into philosophy and philosophies we have been impressed with the diversity of philosophical speculation. We have seen that, among the traditional philosophies, realists and naturalists are most interested in metaphysics and the basic structure of reality, idealists are most concerned with problems of knowledge (epistemology) while pragmatists are interested in process, in the values inherent in situations (axiology). Each group of philosophers has developed its own logic or system of thought. It is little wonder, therefore, that starting from different premises and pursuing different methods, each philosopher and each *school* of philosophy arrives at a different set of conclusions. *The Fifty-fourth Yearbook* describes nine such points of view, and there are many others. The roots of all these philosophies may be traced to the writings of the ancient Greeks. For example, Greene's idealism follows some of the basic concepts of Plato. Maritain, Wild, and Feigl have theories rooted in Aristotle. Geiger's notion of change may be traced to the theories of Heraclitus.

Part II is divided into five chapters: "From Plato to St. Thomas Aquinas," or the ancient and medieval world; "The Renaissance, Reformation, and Counter Reformation"; "Rationalism and Enlightenment," beginning with Bacon and ending with Rousseau; "Humanitarianism, Idealism, and Realism," especially as these philosophies developed in England, Switzerland, and Germany; and finally, "Post-Hegelianism and the Century of Darwin," dealing with English and American thought from Spencer and Emerson to the present time.

In preparation for a study of ancient and medieval thought, it will be helpful to remember that by the time of Plato the Greek colonies had spread to the coast of Asia Minor and westward along the Mediterranean coast, especially the southwestern shore of Italy. Greek thought flourished here for over a century before Plato. Pythagoras of Samos (an island off the coast of Asia Minor), Parmenides of Elea (a Greek colony in southwestern Italy below Naples), and Euclid of Megara (a Doric town not many miles northwest of Athens) all taught a mystical philosophy, while Thales of Miletus, Heraclitus of Ephesus (both towns in Asia Minor) together with their disciples taught an atomistic, materialistic metaphysic. Athens stood at the crossroads, receiving goods and ideas from both East and West. It was in this fertile climate of ideas that Plato and the other Greek philosophers whom we shall consider attempted to form a synthesis that would illuminate the true essence of reality.

It has been said that Roman arms conquered Greece, but that Greek thought conquered the Western world. This saying will become clearer as we pursue our study, especially as we see Greek thought come into conflict with the Christian ethic; as we see the attempts of St. Augustine and others to effect a reconciliation between the two, ending in the supreme synthesis of Aristotle and St. Paul in St. Thomas Aquinas.

THE PRE-SOCRATIC PHILOSOPHERS

All Western philosophy, declared Whitehead, is a footnote on Plato. To a large extent, this is true, for, aside from a few fragments, much of what we know of Plato's predecessors and contemporaries, we know from Plato's discussion of them in his dialogues, and much of subsequent thought has been written to support or to refute his works and those of his disciples.

It is true that Plato's reporting is not without bias. On the one hand, he strongly disapproved of the sophists and the atomists, and on the other he idealized his teacher, Socrates, who, under the influence of his pen, became a Grecian cultural hero.

THE ATOMISTS

Among Plato's contemporaries, Democritus (460–370 B.C.) had brought atomism to its highest formulation. At Miletus, in the seventh century, and probably before, certain Greek thinkers tried to find a single or universal substance to which all the varying aspects of nature could be traced—something permanent, persisting through change. Thales (624–550 B.C.), Anaximander (611–547 B.C.), and Anaximines (588–525 B.C.) believed this substance to be water, infinity or boundlessness, and air respectively. Heraclitus of Ephesus (535–475 B.C.) advanced the theory that fire was the universal substance and a perfect example of the principle of the eternal change which constitutes reality. Permanence, said Heraclitus, is illusion, and men must be brought to understand this and that their senses deceive them. Nothing abides; the only certainty in the world is change itself. No man can step into the same river twice. Indeed, according to Cratylus, his disciple, no man can step into the same river once; for not only the river, but we ourselves change also. Parmenides of Elia (fl. 495 B.C.), on the other hand, opposed Heracletianism and declared that substantial change is impossible. These views of a changing or of a changeless universe form the great philosophical paradox of the classical Greek period. Leucippus (fl. 440 B.C.), a student of Parmenides, tried to reconcile these two points of view and founded the theory of atomism. Democritus (460–370 B.C.), the greatest representative of the school, resolved the paradox by stating the basic principle that there is an infinite number of homogeneous elements—atoms—moving in an infinite void. The world is permanent because of the physical characteristics of the atoms; the world is changing because of their motion in space. Sensation, therefore, is concerned with changeable phenomena and cannot yield true knowledge, which can only be attained by reflection. Democritus applied his theory to the practical concerns of life and developed a system of ethics in which happiness was the highest good and a theology in which the gods existed as examples for the inspiration of man, and to perform whatever functions they performed. This movement was directly opposed to the idealism of Plato.

THE SOPHISTS

Plato disliked the sophists, not only on rational grounds, but because, unlike him, they took pay for their teaching. Believing that he had a particularly clear insight into the eternal, he strongly disapproved of their practical teaching and relativistic views.

Sophism was a development of the Greek enlightenment which was characterized by a spirit of independent reflection and criticism. The sophists substituted the right of private judgment for the authority of existing institutions which they considered to be contracts between those in power to dominate the weak. Greek thought had reached an impasse in the Heraclitian-Parmenidesian paradox. The sophists turned from what they considered to be vain metaphysical speculation to practical affairs which they thought gave a better foundation for the duties of the citizen of the rising Greek democracies. They were rhetoricians who taught the fine art of how men may become citizens to their own advantage.

Protagoras (481–411 B.C.), about whom Plato wrote a dialogue, maintained that man is the measure of all things. He based his ethics on a relativistic epistemology and taught that truth and goodness are products of individual situations, and that there are two sides to every question. He dismissed theological problems on the excuse that they were obscure and life too short. Gorgias (fl. 480 B.C.), his contemporary, achieved a complete skepticism when he held that nothing could be known; if it could be known, it could not be told; if it could be told, it could not be understood. Out of the sophist movement grew the philosophy of skepticism against which Socrates set himself solidly.

Nothing he wrote, if he ever did, has come down to us. His method, known since his time as the Socratic method, was one of drawing out the truth from the student by judicious questioning, on the theory that knowledge is recollection. The method has been suspect in many quarters because it is believed that it does not seek to discover truth, but to justify the answers already in the mind of the questioner.

There is scarcely any philosophy which does not claim direct descent from Socrates. Even the skepticism which he so strongly opposed claims to have derived its inspiration from his questioning approach to truth. He taught that skills and values are parts of a larger whole which he calls virtue.

PLATO

The most famous of the philosophers of the classical Greek period was Plato (427–347 B.C.). To attempt to formulate his philosophy into a rigid system is a fruitless task, for both he and the principal protagonist of his dialogues, Socrates, were willing to consider all sides of a complex situation in a search for the eternal truth they considered to exist behind the phenomena of life. Their search was not for information or isolated bits of knowledge, but for profoundness of insight.

Plato conceived the thousands of fleeting phenomena of experience to be parts of a meaningful and ordered world. These ordering forces are reflected in the mind of man in a way which transcends his day by day observations and renders his mind capable of realizing meanings and interrelationships between himself and the psychic forces of the universe. This unity of ideas, this "logos," cannot be described so concretely as this pen or that chair, but for Plato it possesses a far greater reality than things we can see, or taste, or handle. Thus, for Plato, the greatest activity of man is the search for this eternal truth, not only to discover what really is, but what ought to be. It was in order to set up goals for social and moral conduct that he wrote *The Laws* and *The Republic,* two utopias which hold great interest for the educator.

Plato believed that the true aim of human existence was the attainment of the beautiful and virtuous man, the *aner kalos k' agathos,* and that the true conduct of life rested on the four moral concepts: worth, wisdom, service, and political leadership. Thus, in his search for perfection, man was not to seek wisdom and knowledge alone, but was to transform them into reality in a social setting. The utopias were not only to be studied, but to be put into action. Man alone is given the blessing of perfecting himself through increasing insight into the essence of the world. Thus man alone can project himself beyond his own ego into the realm of the logos, and it is the duty of the elders to fit the oncoming generation to fulfill the eternal mission of man.

"Education," wrote Plato, "is the process of drawing and guiding children towards that principle which is pronounced right by law and confirmed as truly right by the experience of the oldest and most just."[1]

The Greek democracies of Plato's day differed in certain important respects from ours. There was a sharp distinction between the Greek citizens and the slaves who outnumbered them about five to one. The Greeks themselves distinguished between those who were citizens of a city-state and those who lived outside of the city-state.[2] Finally, within the city-state itself, the relatively small group of citizens was again divided into classes. Plato was either oblivious of these differences or took them for granted. He even admitted a double standard of morality. For example, rulers were permitted to lie in the interest of the state, but a workman was to be punished with the severest penalty for telling a falsehood.[3] The following quotation from *The Republic* illustrates these points.

We shall tell our people, in mythical language; You are doubtless all brethren, or as many as inhabit the city, but the God who created you mixed gold in the composition of such of you are as qualified to rule, which gives them the highest value; while, in the auxiliaries, he made silver an ingredient, assigning iron and copper to the cultivators of the soil and the other workmen. Therefore, inasmuch as you are all related to one another, although your children will generally resemble their parents, yet sometimes a golden parent will produce a silver child, and a silver parent a golden child, and so on, each producing any. The rulers therefore have received this in charge first and above all from the gods, to observe nothing more closely, in their character of vigilant guardians, than the children that are born, to see which of these metals enters into the composition of their souls; and if a child be born in their class with an alloy of copper or iron, they are to have no manner of pity upon it, but giving it the value that belongs to its nature, they are to thrust it away into the class of artisans or agriculturalists; and if again among these a child be born with any admixture of gold or silver, when they have assayed it, they are to raise it either to the class of guardians, or to that of auxiliaries: because there is an oracle which

[1] Plato, *The Laws*, Bk. II, Sec. 659D, trans. R. C. Bury. Loeb Classical Library (Cambridge, Mass.: Harvard University Press, 1926).

[2] It is estimated that in the city of Athens one-fifth of the small group of free men were citizens of other states, and, therefore, were not included in the small group of Athenians of which Plato writes.

[3] Plato, *The Republic*, Bk. III, Sec. 389, trans. J. L. Davies and D. J. Vaughan (New York: The Macmillan Company, 1927).

declares that the city shall then perish when it is guarded by iron or copper.[4]

Thus, Plato recommended a state-controlled system of education with censorship of art, literature,[5] and music [6] so that society would reflect the true, the beautiful, and the good. He also recommended a type of communal life for the philosopher-kings so that they would not be influenced by possessions or family relationships in making judgments for the public welfare.[7] These ideas greatly affected the organization of the medieval church and form the basis for some present-day practices.

Generally speaking, Plato's educational ideas implied that the child belonged to the state, which would supervise his entire development. The earliest years were to be spent in developing physical health and in inculcating accepted ideas of religion and patriotism. More formal education began at six and continued to eighteen when a series of examinations separated the iron and copper workmen from the gold and silver upper classes. For boys between eighteen and twenty, the courses would be military. The soldier class could be eliminated at the end of this course. For the philosopher-rulers, education would continue until thirty when an examination would eliminate the less brilliant who would be assigned administrative posts in the government. The next five years would be spent by the most brilliant in a study of pure abstractions with the goal of catching a vision of the "Idea of the Good." From thirty-five to fifty, these philosopher-kings would rule the state, after which they would retire to contemplate the highest happiness.[8]

Another important allegory of Plato's beside the myth of the metals is that of the cave. Plato imagines a number of persons chained in a cave with their backs to the entrance. A fire burns behind them, casting shadows of the objects passers-by carry on their heads. The inhabitants of the cave do not know reality, but only its shadow. One of the prisoners is released and taken to the surface. When he becomes accustomed to the light, he is able to

[4] *Ibid.*, Bk. III, Sec. 415.
[5] *Ibid.*, Bk. III, Secs. 392, 394–396.
[6] *Ibid.*, Bk. III, Sec. 399.
[7] *Ibid.*, Bk. III, Secs. 416–417; Bk. V, Sec. 449.
[8] *Ibid.*, Bk. VII, Sec. 540.

see the reality he had experienced only in shadows before. After a time, he returns to the cave, resumes his former duties and occupations, but now he can interpret the shadows for his fellow prisoners in terms of the reality he has come to know. So it is with the philosopher-kings in Plato's aristocratic state, and so it is with the intellectual elite in any society whose education is based upon this concept of Plato.

Some philosophers, however, point out that Plato uses the "state" as a symbol for mankind, and that *The Republic* is itself an allegory of the education of man. Lamprecht points out that Plato considered the three social classes to represent the three divisions of the human soul.[9] The desires or passions represent the lowest class, the dynamic, energetic force corresponds to the soldier class, and the intelligence or reason is symbolized by the philosopher-kings. Only as man is ruled by his intellect will he attain a state of perfection. Plato pursues this triadic grouping further when he maintains that justice is composed of three elements: temperance, courage, and wisdom.[10] He further states that a good education should comprise music, gymnastics, and dialectic.[11]

Music for Plato was an intellectual discipline which included literature and history. Gymnastics was not only for physical development, but for morals as well. It disciplined the will and developed manliness and courage. Dialectic was a determined effort to systematize knowledge and to bring its various elements into logical relations with each other. It was a discipline reserved for those who were to be trained as magistrates.

Knowledge for Plato was a recollection, for men's souls existed as pure forms before they descended to earth to be imprisoned in the body. The highest vocation of man, therefore, was to seek to understand, to reconstruct, to recollect these pure forms. While the artisan or soldier thinks of circles, the geometrician contemplates the nature of the perfect circle. The person of lofty thoughts attaches little importance to the petty details of life.[12]

For Plato, knowledge of things as they really exist constituted a comprehension of form which suggested a philosophical monism.[13]

[9] Sterling P. Lamprecht, *Our Philosophical Tradition* (New York: Appleton-Century-Crofts, Inc., 1955), pp. 37–43.

[10] *The Republic,* Bk. IV, Secs. 428, 429, 430.

[11] *Ibid.,* Bk. II, Secs. 376–383; Bk. III, Secs. 383–414.

[12] *Ibid.,* Bk. VI, Sec. 486.

[13] *Ibid.,* Bk. VI, Sec. 484.

Ideas are independent entities and exist before and are independent of their discovery by the human mind. This popular concept of Plato's epistemology has been questioned in recent years.[14] Be that as it may, however, reality for Plato existed in the realm of ideas in pure form. Thus, while Plato did not specifically deny the existence of things outside the realm of ideas and was free to admit the difficulties of coming to a complete understanding of knowledge, his theory of ideas has been a starting point for much of the idealism of the present day. This theory was developed, perhaps transformed, into a system of idealistic monism by Plotinus (A.D. 205–270), who taught at Rome and is credited with establishing the Neoplatonic tradition.

The genius of Plato was so great that it has been very difficult for lesser minds to comprehend it entirely, which probably accounts for many of the misconceptions with regard to some of his theories. His emphasis on the unreality of the physical world had a tremendous influence in fashioning the thought of the early middle ages, and his interest in ideas has caused many a schoolman even to the present day to develop an abstract and theoretical educational program, forgetting all the while that Plato insisted that these abstract ideas should be translated into social action. His class education has found a parallel in many existing forms of European educational systems with their rigid systems of examinations and the emphasis on pure philosophy and science on the university level. On the other hand, Plato's emphasis on individualism has had a great effect on the Renaissance mind. Humanism and Protestantism derive much from Plato.

Through the Academy which he founded in Athens, his influence spread through the ancient world. It was carried to Rome by Cicero (106–43 B.C.), and through Plotinus's restatement known as Neoplatonism, it influenced St. Augustine (A.D. 354–430) and the medieval schoolmen.

ARISTOTLE

Aristotle (384–322 B.C.) was born in the Greek colony of Stagira in Macedon. At eighteen, he became the pupil of Plato in the Academy at Athens where he remained almost twenty years. He left Athens to become tutor to Alexander the Great, but returned

[14] See Lamprecht, *op. cit.*, p. 48.

in 335 to found the Lyceum which he conducted for twelve years. In 323, anti-Macedenonian feeling caused him to flee to Calchis where he died a year later.

His work represents the greatest achievement of the human mind in the Western world and has materially influenced the ideas of men over two millennia. For his chief instrument of thought, Aristotle developed a science of Logic, based upon the syllogism which he elaborated in considerable detail (see Ch. I, pp. 10–11). This "deductive method" he considered to be the true method of science, although he recognized induction as the process for establishing first premises.

Aristotle maintained that reality ultimately consisted of many concrete individual things. These, he thought, were real in a primary sense. In a derivative sense, he considered that the qualities of these things, their forms, and the relations among them were also real. All substances, then, consist of matter and form. Matter is not some formless stuff as the atomists maintained, but is a way that real things differ from imaginary things and is a locus of potentialities which become actual through the activity of form. Movement and change are fundamental to all matter, and it is through them that substances fulfill the complete reality or entelechy which their nature ideally indicates. To exist at all involves being good for some specific end or ends which are consciously conceived by man and are latent in things. Thus, man could not consciously exploit nature if nature were not of itself teleologically prior to and apart from these ends. Man could not use wood for fuel if it were not a quality of wood to burn.

Aristotle believed that every movement of change must have a cause. To account for the first cause, he developed the concept of the Unmoved Mover—an eternal, indivisible, immutable reality existing at the circumference of the world.[15] The perfection of his being makes him not only the supreme object of knowledge, but also the ultimate object of all desire.

For Aristotle, every substance is a union of matter and form. All knowledge comes from previous knowledge just as that which exists comes from previous being. The form of a substance is

[15] Aristotle, *Physics*, Bk. VIII, especially Chs. 4–6. References to Aristotle's works have been taken from *The Basic Works of Aristotle*, ed. Richard McKeon (New York: Random House, 1941).

what makes it intelligible and therefore able to be known. When a man knows a substance which confronts him, it is the form of the substance that is in his mind. The entire substance does not enter into the man's mind, but the form does. Conversely, a man has no right to assume that a substance exists because he has the idea or form in his mind, but he must substantiate the idea with sensory evidence.

Our thinking about the world is controlled by the nature of the world itself which exhibits certain universal traits and relationships. These Aristotle listed as ten fundamental categories, namely: substance, quality, quantity, relation, place, time, action, possession, position, and condition.[16]

For Aristotle the highest good, "summum bonum," is the contemplation of truth. He uses the word "eudaemonia"[17] (happiness) for the moral ends men ought to pursue. The soul is not a substance but an action. A particular man is a substance, but his soul is what he does. Virtue is, therefore, a condition; particular instances of virtue are actions. The virtue of justice is a condition—the condition of having a well-established habit.

Basing his whole system of ethics upon this point, Aristotle maintained that ethics and politics are mutually dependent. Ethics examines how men may live best, but as man is by nature a political animal, it is in society that he finds his noblest fulfillment. States are formed to enable men to live: they are perpetuated to make them live well. An important function of the state is to educate its citizens.[18] Basic to education in a cultural and political sense is the development of right habits, which Aristotle considers man's second nature. Human nature consists of two aspects: the irrational and the rational. Concerning the irrational, there is that over which a person has no control and any natural excellence is a matter of good fortune or luck. But that part which can be controlled by reason is moral virtue. The possession of well-established habits is what we mean by character; and character is good or bad according to the nature of the habits.[19] Character is, thus, the outcome of a long and consistent period of moral training.

[16] Aristotle, Organon, *Categoriae,* Chs. 1–9.
[17] Aristotle, *Nicomachean Ethics,* Bk. I, Chs. 1–5.
[18] Aristotle, *Politics,* Bk. VIII, Ch. I.
[19] *Ibid.*, Bk. VII, Ch. 13; Book VIII, Ch. 3

Other functions of the state are to stabilize socially profitable policies in laws, and to allow some citizens to live the contemplative life. The laws when good should be supreme [20] but the right to criticize the judicial and legislative powers of the state should be reserved to both rulers and citizens. "The nature of the state is to be a plurality." [21] Aristotle believed that the best men should be placed in the highest positions and that a balance of authority among groups should be maintained. The unity of the state should not be sought by coercion, but by fostering common purposes among the interacting and cooperating groups.

Life for Aristotle is the process of nutrition and growth. Therefore his psychology can scarcely be separated from his biology because the soul is the principle of life, the primary actualization of a natural body, the form of a natural body potential possessed by life. There are two types of souls: the nutritive and propagational, and the sensitive, which includes imagination, reason, thought, knowledge and opinion.[22] Imagination he defined as a combination of knowledge and opinion, and "reason" as the faculty of apprehending the universals and first principles involved in all knowledge.

All plants and animals have nutritive souls, all animals have sensitive souls, the higher animals have imagination by which their apparent rational behavior is explained, but men alone, unless there be beings superior to men, have reason or intellect. Since the mind is to know, it cannot have a form of its own. It is actually nothing before it thinks, but by thinking it becomes like its object. Or in other words, life (or soul) is the form of the living body as cutting is the form or soul of the axe and as sight is the form or soul of the eye.[23]

The educator leads his pupil to discover where and of what kind his creative powers are and helps him to become a living form. This forming energy, entelechy, enables a person to grow organically toward the realization of his inherent form.

Education begins with health and a sound physique. Therefore,

[20] *Ibid.*, Bk. III, Ch. II.
[21] *Ibid.*, Bk. II, Ch. II.
[22] Aristotle, *De Anima*, Bk. II, Ch. 4.
[23] *Ibid.*, Bks. II and III.

right diet and exercise are essential as are heredity and good race, for they are basic to a sound body. The pupil must submit to all suggestions, exercises, and disciplines of the master, for these are necessary to the development of his moral and intellectual character. The master must also lead a disciplined life, for Aristotle maintains that the teacher learns what he teaches.[24]

Happiness (eudaemonia) comes only from a well-balanced, productive life. The teacher directs the unreflective energy of the young child so that the constructive powers are developed and the destructive are negated. The regulation of the passions is a matter of habituation or conditioning.

Methods of teaching properly begin with what is most knowable to man and develop toward what is most knowable in itself, from empirical observation to a contemplation of form.

Education ends in reason, but the reason of the adult determines the method and material for the training of youth. Education teaches one to avoid excesses and to adhere to the golden mean. Wisdom is a combination of intuitive and scientific knowledge used as a guide to the solution of the practical problems of life.

Aristotle was inclined to consider himself a Platonist. Both men agreed that all nature could be explained teleologically. However, Aristotle did not believe, as Plato seemed to, that there was one supreme principle from which all knowledge of nature could be brought into one complete system. The differences here as elsewhere may be rather one of degree. Plato enumerates five fundamental relationships or categories based upon his theory of ideas, namely: being, same, other, rest, and motion; Aristotle developed ten based upon empirical observation, namely: substance, quality, quantity, relation, space, time, activity, possession, position, and passivity or condition.

Plato was a mathematician, absorbed in ideas. His philosophy deals with universals and envisions ideal ends. Beginning with man, he viewed the world as a setting for man's search for the ideal. He recognized the science of his day only as it fitted in with his scheme of knowledge. He conceived truth as a recollection and, as it were, brought truth down from heaven.

Aristotle was a zoologist. He was fascinated by things, inter-

[24] *Politics*, Bk. VII, Chs. 13–17; Bk. VIII, Chs. 1–7.

ested in particulars, and absorbed in present actualities. Beginning with nature he viewed man as a specialized case, at once typical and distinctive of nature's general ways. He advanced the cause of science by his detailed observation, studies, realistic analyses, and writings. He conceived truth as a construct from first steps and observation, and by his system of philosophy lifted things up to ultimate truth.

The German poet Heinrich Heine considered Plato and Aristotle as representative of two different kinds of human nature, the former contemplative and mystical, and the latter practical and systematic. He assigns the individualistic, visionary, creative spirit to Platonism and the dogmatic, institutional spirit to Aristotelianism.[25] While the distinctions between the two philosophers are not so sharp and plain as Heine would have it, yet, in the main, the development of Western thought clearly shows an admixture of their two points of view. "Like a splendid sonnet sequence in literature, the moral and metaphysical movement of Greek life at its height passes from the quest of Socrates through the faith of Plato to the systematization of Aristotle." [26]

Aristotle's influence is clearly seen in the contention of medieval nominalists that there is nothing in the intellect which was not first in sense and in the contention of modern empiricists that all ideas are copies of antecedent impressions. His theory of individuation, that expressible qualities rested upon an inexpressible substratum, was further developed by John Locke. Aristotle's theories influenced the critical idealism of Kant and much of Renaissance and modern humanism. Some types of modern materialism attribute to Aristotle the theory that matter is the one underlying permanent substance and that all else is by-product. In general, the acceptance of Aristotelian thought by the Christian world can be attributed to St. Thomas Aquinas whose monumental commentaries on "The Philosopher" have helped to form the thought of medieval and modern scholasticism and the philosophy and theology of the Roman Catholic church.

[25] See Robert Ulich, *History of Educational Thought* (New York: American Book Company, 1945), pp. 25–26.

[26] T. V. Smith, *From Thales to Plato* (Chicago: University of Chicago Press, 1956), p. 70.

EPICURUS

The Epicurean school dated back to Aristippus (435–355 B.C.), a disciple of Socrates who set up a school to teach one aspect of his master's philosophy. He taught that the end of life is pleasure, however induced, and that, since violence brings pain, the wise man lives so as to secure the maximum of pleasure through gentle living. This philosophy is often called hedonism.

His successor in this tradition was Epicurus (341–270 B.C.) who established his school, the Gardens, at Athens in 306 B.C. Drawing his metaphysics from Democritus, he pictured a world in which pure chance reduced the function of intelligence. The real world, he taught, is a materialistic one made of eternal and indivisible atoms which differ in weight, shape, and size. Pleasure and pain, he wrote, are the criteria by which we judge between right and wrong. What causes pain is bad; what causes pleasure is good, and mental pleasures are superior to the physical. Men, he demanded, should live quiet lives, avoid the tensions of the world by returning to the Gardens to live with kindred spirits, protected from the hurts of the world in a little oasis within a vast desert of misery. They should eat simple foods, pursue quiet pleasures, observe a balance in work and play, and be moderate in all things.

This philosophy of withdrawal and abstinence together with the skepticism of Pyrrho of Elis (365–275 B.C.) was but the logical conclusion of the general recession from the confidence of Plato and Aristotle in the rationality of the natural world and in the power of mind to understand and control it.

LUCRETIUS

Lucretius (96–55 B.C.), the author of the great poem *De Rerum Natura, On the Nature of Things,* was the major voice in the Roman world for the atomism of Democritus and the hedonism of Epicurus. His was a religious age. Lucretius believed that if the fear of death could be eliminated superstition would disappear and religion could become practical and make a real contribution to life. Atomism, according to Lucretius, denied immortality; therefore nothing could happen to us after death. Since there is nothing to fear, man may appropriate the earth and the gods to positive ends. We should live, declared Lucretius, dispassionately, detachedly, observantly, and serenely, looking at all things with a mind at peace.

ZENO OF CITIUM

Stoicism, the fourth of the major Athenian schools, was founded by Zeno of Citium (340–265 B.C.) and was perpetuated by Cleanthes (300–220 B.C.) and Chrysippus (280–208 B.C.).

It is connected with a philosophical movement dating back to Socrates and purports to represent his cynical spirit. Other early representatives of the school are Antisthenes (fl. 406 B.C.) and Diogenes of Sinope (412–322 B.C.) of tub and lantern fame. These men exemplified the doctrine "the best life is the one that can get along with the least." It is not only a philosophy but also a religion built upon the ruins of an ancient polytheism. The soul, said the Stoics, is made up of fiery atoms in a materialistic universe. Knowledge of this world and morals are based on a faith in the unity of divine Providence throughout all nature. Thus man should accept the world because he is a part of it, and be resigned and happy regardless of how little he has, for he knows all is for the best. Since man and nature are continuous, mankind all over the world is one. This doctrine led to the cosmopolitanism of the later Roman empire and has been permanently influential in the West. The wise man, maintains the Stoic, will achieve the best life, which is in harmony with nature, and which is devoted to virtue for virtue's sake.

Polybius (204–122 B.C.), a Greek hostage, and Cicero (106–43 B.C.) carried the doctrine to Rome with little modification. It is largely through the influence of the latter that Greek culture was transplanted to Rome and made intelligible to the Roman mind. Cicero wrote extensively on political philosophy to which he applied the doctrine of Stoicism. His conception of the nature of law permeated medieval political theory by way of the Church fathers, and his fine style became the model for the schools after the Renaissance.

Seneca (4 B.C.–A.D. 65) taught that the Stoic philosophy was a way of life and an unfailing source of consolation. Epictetus (A.D. 60–117), a crippled slave who afterwards became free, expounded the Stoic doctrine in his discourses in which he urged that man should accept magnanimously whatever befalls him, assured of the rationality of the universe, and that all things work together for good.

The emperor Marcus Aurelius (A.D. 121–180) is possibly the best known of the Roman Stoics, especially because of his *Meditations.* His writings are genuinely religious in tone and preach the omnipotent providence of divine reason to which evil itself must minister. He believed that genuine happiness results from self-renunciation and cooperation with the divine purpose.

QUINTILIAN

Quintilian (A.D. 35–95), the Roman rhetorician, has been called the Schoolmaster of the West. He followed in the tradition of the Stoics and the sophists and wrote the *Institutes of Oratory* for the practical training of orators. This work has been a standard text book for teachers and orators since the Renaissance. He believed in accepting a situation as one found it, and that moral standards and responsibilities do not spring from meditation about them, but from action. He wrote regarding the training of teachers of oratory and believed that the ideal teacher should have the following nine qualifications.

1. He should assume a parental attitude toward his pupil.
2. He should be free from vice and refuse to tolerate it in others.
3. He should be strict but not austere.
4. He should be genial but not familiar.
5. He should speak of what is honorable, for the more he admonishes the less he will have to punish.
6. He should control his temper.
7. He should be free from affectation.
8. He should be possessed of great industry.
9. His demands on his class should be continuous, but not extravagant.[27]

[27] Marcus Fabius Quintilian, *Institutio Oratoria,* Vol. I, Bk. II, Ch. II, trans. H. E. Butler, Loeb Classical Library (London: William Heinemann Ltd., 1921).

Stoicism, skepticism and Epicurianism, as has been seen, were based upon a pre-Socratic metaphysic. With the decline of the Roman empire and the spread of Christianity, their influence waned in the West. Since the Renaissance and Sir Francis Bacon, interest in these philosophies has increased. They are basic to much modern educational thought which goes under various names, such as naturalism, experimentalism, and logical empiricism.

PLOTINUS

Plotinus (A.D. 205–270), first at Alexandria and later at Rome, effected an adjustment to the altered conditions of life of his times based upon the classical Greek philosophers, chiefly Plato. Starting from the super-rational which he called God, he proceeded to build a scale of reality through mind and soul to matter. All things come from God; matter, which is farthest from God, is the source of evil, but it is not wholly so, because it is derived from God. It is the better part of wisdom to treat the body and whatever partakes of matter with contempt and to concentrate on the things of the spirit which are nearer the Source of Being. Philosophy, said Plotinus, is a way of salvation whereby men can climb step by step the steep road that leads from the evil world to the realm of absolute good. Plotinus also developed a theory of psychology dealing with sensation, imagination, memory, and thought. The good life consists of reflection, good works, and finally, the mystical experience which is rarely given to men. His doctrine, edited by Porphyry (A.D. 233–304), was for many years a strong rival of Christianity until it was transformed into a Christian ethic by the genius of St. Augustine.

The Athenian schools: the Academy of Plato, the Lyceum of Aristotle, the Gardens of Epicurus and the Stoa or Porch of Zeno, the Stoic, had a long existence and influence. In the course of time, they intermingled. Skepticism, while not a school, had a wide acceptance and considerable influence on the organized schools. The Academy passed through three stages: the Older, the Middle, and the New, until the sixth century of the Christian era. The Lyceum continued to the third. Both schools became increasingly eclectic and vaguely Neoplatonic. The Epicurian dispersed into brotherhoods at the beginning of our era. Its influence was spread in Rome by the writings of Lucretius. The influence of the Stoic school continued long after the Stoa at Athens had disappeared, and under the influence of Cicero, Seneca, Epictetus, and Marcus Aurelius, became the official philosophy of life of the empire.

ST. AUGUSTINE

In St. Augustine (A.D. 354–430), considered by many to be the greatest of the Church fathers, the Platonic tradition and Christianity blended constructively. For him, knowledge of the self is immediate and indubitable. As in Plotinus, ideas are real entities and present themselves through revelation. "Divine illumination takes the place in Augustine's thought of reminiscence in the Platonic philosophy." [28]

"Plato," writes Lamprecht, "is the locus classicus in history for a vision of the spiritual values which define the ideal fulfillment of man's natural resources and powers, Plotinus is the locus classicus in history for the argument that in spite of the seeming multiplicity of finite existences everything has its respective status in one all inclusive and spiritual world, St. Augustine is the locus classicus in history for the faith that above and beyond all changes in the lives of men lie the wisdom and the goodness of one spiritual power." [29]

Through St. Augustine, Neoplatonism passed into the life of the Church and of the Western world. Amended by St. Thomas and restated by Luther and Calvin, its influence is felt to the present day. He held with Plato a belief in a super-sensible world. For him, there was a temporal city and also a City of God. Each of these had its visible and invisible forms. Although the physical city of Rome might be destroyed, the culture and traditions which are the real Rome still survive. On the other hand, the Church militant is the visible form of the City of God and is supreme in all spiritual matters. Many thinkers, especially after the Reformation, have quoted this doctrine of St. Augustine as authority for the separation of church and state, but it is doubtful if St. Augustine meant it to be so. In any case, he considered education to be wholly a function of the Church.

[28] Frederick Copleston, S.J., *A History of Philosophy* (London: Burns Ltd., 1950), II, 64.

[29] Lamprecht, *op. cit.*, p. 146.

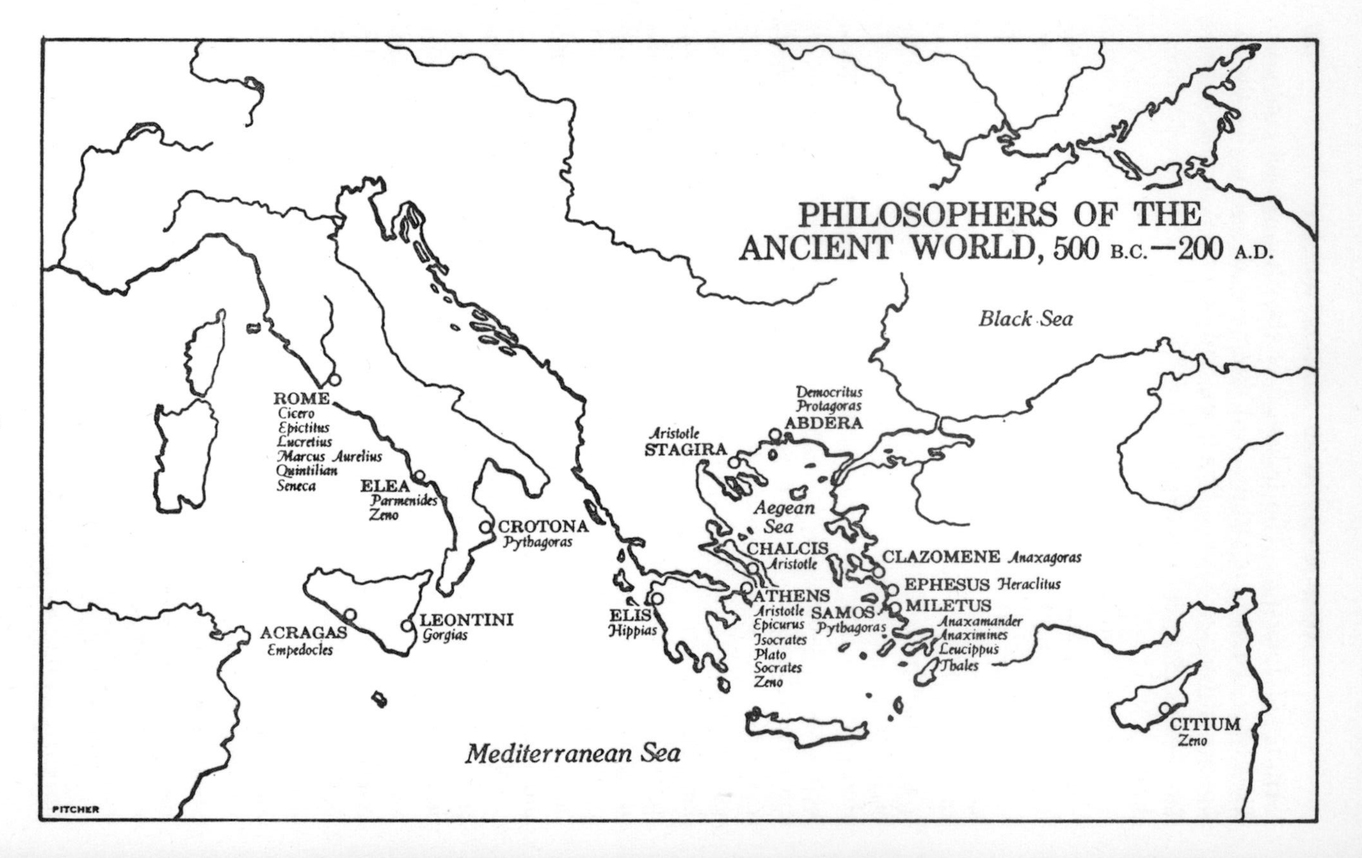
PHILOSOPHERS OF THE
ANCIENT WORLD, 500 B.C.—200 A.D.
Black Sea
ROME
Cicero
Epictitus
Lucretius
Marcus Aurelius
Quintilian
Seneca
ELEA
Parmenides
Zeno
CROTONA
Pythagoras
ACRAGAS
Empedocles
LEONTINI
Gorgias
ELIS
Hippias
Democritus
Protagoras
ABDERA
Aristotle
STAGIRA
Aegean
Sea
CHALCIS
Aristotle
ATHENS
Aristotle
Epicurus
Isocrates
Plato
Socrates
Zeno
SAMOS
Pythagoras
CLAZOMENE Anaxagoras
EPHESUS Heraclitus
MILETUS
Anaxamander
Anaximines
Leucippus
Thales
CITIUM
Zeno
Mediterranean Sea
PITCHER

He believed in the depravity of man. "God created man upright. He is the author of all natures insofar as they are, but certainly not of the blemishes in them. But man, having become deliberately depraved and justly condemned begat depraved and condemned children." [30]

Since children are thus depraved, the pathway to true knowledge is hard. They must be disciplined for there is no learning without punishment. The birch, the strap, the cane are necessary to subdue the child. Only by such means is it possible to overcome ignorance and bridle evil desires—these evils with which we come into the world.[31]

St. Augustine recommended that the learning of ancient Rome be mastered for its use in living the Christian life. History, natural philosophy, logic, grammar, rhetoric, arithmetic, even philosophy, were recommended, because these studies, if carefully pursued, will show the difference between knowledge and superstition. "For it is one thing to say: If you bruise down this herb and drink it, it will remove the pain from your stomach; and another to say; If you hang this herb around your neck it will remove the pain from your stomach. In the former case the wholesome mixture is approved of, in the latter the superstitious charm is condemned." [32] Study of all these subjects must be carefully guarded and subject always to the authority of the Scripture and of the Church, because sense and reason without faith lead to error.

While he supported the current belief that the aim of all education was to prepare man for the life after death through an understanding and practice of the Christian virtues, chiefly faith,

[30] St. Augustine, *The City of God,* ed. Vernon J. Burke (Garden City, N.Y.: Doubleday and Company, Inc., 1958), Bk. XII, Ch. 14.

[31] *Ibid.*, Bk. XXIII, Ch. 12, *passim.*

[32] St. Augustine, *Of Christian Doctrine,* trans. Sister Thérèse Sullivan (Washington, D.C.: The Catholic University of America, 1930), Bk. II, Ch. 26.

Figure 1. Athens was both the cultural and commercial center of the Greek world. The mysticism and idealism of the West, influenced by the mathematics of Alexandria, crossed currents with the materialism and naturalism of the East and formed a synthesis in Socrates, Plato, Aristotle, and Epicurus. The sophists were more cosmopolitan in their background and practical in their philosophy. The philosophies of Rome were derivative for the most part.

Twenty-five Centuries of Educational Thought

CHART 1: THE ANCIENT GREEKS TO ST. JEROME

B.C. 600 500 400 300 200 100 0 100 200 300 400 500 A.D.

THALES 624-550	Water is the basic stuff of reality
ANAXIMANDER 611-547	Naturalist; anticipated modern theory of energy
ANAXIMENES 588-525	Naturalist; air the basic substance of reality
PYTHAGORAS 572-497	Astronomy; right angle triangle
HERACLITUS 535-475	Law, the rational principle, pervades the universe; change the fundamental principle
PARMENIDES fl. 495	Basic doctrine of idealism
ANAXAGORAS 500-428	Pluralism of realities
EMPEDOCLES c. 495-435	Four irreducible substances: earth, air, fire, water
ZENO OF ELEA 490-430	Plurality and change impossible
PROTAGORAS 481-411	Man is the measure of all things; relativism
DEMOCRITUS 460-370	Atomist; explained world in mechanical terms
PLATO 427-347	Theory of Ideas
ARISTOTLE 384-322	Rationalism
PYRRHO 361-270	Skepticism
EPICURUS 341-270	Happiness is the goal of life
ZENO OF CITIUM 335-265	Stoicism
CICERO 106-43	Transmitted Greek culture to Rome
ST. PAUL ?-64	Salvation through Jesus
QUINTILIAN 35-95	"Institutes of Oratory"
EPICTITUS 60-117	Stoicism; human will is one thing under man's control
FLAVIUS JUSTINIUS (Martyr) 105-165	God's rational power given to all
MARCUS AURELIUS 121-180	Stoic emperor; "Meditations"
GALEN 130-200	Aristotelian; medical science
CLEMENT OF ALEXANDRIA ?-216	Knowledge without faith does not exist
TERTULLIAN 160-230	Studied Plato; put faith above reason
PLOTINUS 205-270	Neoplatonist
ARIUS 280-336	Monotheism; the Son subordinate to the Father
ST. ATHANASIUS 298-373	Trinitarian
ST. AMBROSE 340-397	Opposed Arius; converted Augustine
ST. JEROME 344-420	Retranslated Bible into Latin—The Vulgate

hope, charity, and humility, he maintained that the truly educated man was one who was capable of forming a consistent unity out of all arts and knowledge and who could experience the essential unity between reason and faith. Only after merging himself with the great laws of the universe can man dare to behold the face of God. The rule of St. Augustine and his reliance on faith and revelation profoundly influenced the educational pattern of the middle ages.

The Augustinian tradition in philosophy and education was carried on by such men as Alcuin (735–804), who taught at the palace school of Charlemagne, St. Anselm (1033–1109), famous for his ontological argument for the existence of God—that the Being than whom none greater can be thought of must exist, and William of Conches (fl. 1122), who taught Platonic realism at Paris.

At the same time, the philosophy of Aristotle began to be reintroduced into the West by way of the Arabian culture. Al Farabi (870–950) introduced Aristotle to the Arabs. Rocellinus (1050–1120), called the new founder of the Lyceum, interpreted Aristotle and was the teacher of Abelard. His theory of knowledge was one of sense-empiricism. He was a nominalist, believing that universals are merely words, and was the traditional opponent of St. Anselm, the Platonic realist. Averroes (1126–1198) is said to have been the greatest medieval commentator on Aristotle. Roger Bacon (1214–1294), at Oxford and Paris, valued Aristotle highly, condemned the deductive method, and advocated observation and experimentation in science. William Moerbeke (1215–1286) translated Aristotle into Latin.

Chart 1. Note that in the three centuries between 600 and 300 B.C. the basis of Western philosophy was laid in Greece. There is a fallow period so far as creative thought is concerned for more than a hundred years before Cicero brought Greek thought to Rome, followed by almost a century of silence until St. Paul wrote his epistles to give substance to Christian theology. From the first to the fourth centuries of our era, we can trace the rivalry between pagan and Christian thought and the doctrinal disputes among the Church fathers, especially regarding the Trinity. St. Jerome's translation of the Scriptures produced a document upon which the commentaries of the scholastics could be based for over a thousand years.

CHART 2: ST. AUGUSTINE TO ST. THOMAS AQUINAS

300 400 500 600 700 800 900 1000 1100 1200 1300

ST. AUGUSTINE 354-430	Reconciled pagan learning with Christianity
NESTORIUS fl. 428	Two natures in Christ
PROCLUS 411-485	Last important Neoplatonic philosopher in Athens
ST. GREGORY THE GREAT 540-604	Increased authority of the Holy See
ALCUIN 735-804	Influenced by St. Augustine; taught at Charlemagne's palace Academy
AL-KINDI 800-870	First great Arab philosopher
JOHN SCOTUS ERIGENA 810-877	Neoplatonist
AL-FARABI 870-950	Introduced Aristotle to Arabs
AVICENNA 980-1037	Moderate realism; studied Aristotle, Neoplatonism, Medici
BERENGER 999-1088	Influenced by St. Augustine
ST. ANSELM 1033-1109	Platonic realist; followed St. Augustine
THEODORE OF CHARTRES fl. 1121-1150	Neoplatonist
WILLIAM OF CONCHES fl. 1122	Taught Platonic realism at Paris
JOHN OF SALISBURY ?-1180	Combined Augustinian and Aristotelian philosophy
RICHARD OF ST. VICTOR fl. 1162-1173	Neoplatonist; all truth not confirmed by Scripture is suspect
AVERROES 1126-1198	Greatest commentator on Aristotle
ROBERT OF LINCOLN 1175-1253	Nationalist, Neoplatonist; opposed papal appointments
ALEXANDER OF HALES c. 1180-1245	Attempted reconciliation of Augustine, Arabs, Aristotle
ALBERT THE GREAT 1193-1280	Influenced by Alexander of Hales
ROGER BACON 1214-1294	Aristotelian
WILLIAM OF MOERBEKE 1215-1286	Translated Aristotle into Latin
ST. THOMAS AQUINAS 1225-1274	Aristotelian; The Angelic Doctor

ST. THOMAS AQUINAS

Many medieval scholars attempted to reconcile the teachings of Plato and Aristotle, among them being Avicenna (980–1037), Abelard (1079–1142), John of Salisbury (?–1180), and St. Bonaventura (1221–1274). But it was the monumental work of St. Thomas Aquinas (1225–1274) that successfully dislodged Neoplatonism and brought the philosophy of Aristotle and the doctrines of the Church into harmony with each other.

St. Thomas Aquinas, the Angelic Doctor, reconciled Aristotelian reasoning with Christian concepts by showing the relationship between reason and faith through a logical synthesis of seemingly opposite views. The essential point of his theory of knowledge is that there is one level concerned with the facts of nature with which reason is competent to deal and another concerned with what is beyond nature and is revealed by faith. Faith begins when reason has reached its limit. Reason is largely inductive and begins with sensory data, passing through ever larger generalizations, through science to philosophy. Theology also has two divisions: the natural, understood by reason and the supernatural, revealed by faith. Universals exist *before* things in the mind of God, *in* things

---

Chart 2. Note on this chart the development of scholasticism, the realist-nominalist controversy, and the beginnings of nationalism. Here again we see time gaps beween Proclus, the last of the pagans, and St. Gregory, the strengthener of the papacy. Noteworthy is the gap of six centuries between Galen the Roman and al Farabi the Arab, both followers of Aristotle who was lost to the Western world during the intervening period. It was not until after the Muslim conquest of Spain in 711 that Aristotle re-entered Western thought by way of the north coast of Africa and Spain. The conflict between Platonism and Aristotelianism took almost half a millennium to be resolved. The great impetus to the study of "The Philosopher" came after the crusades in the twelfth century. The synthesis of St. Augustine and Aristotle was effected by St. Thomas almost two centuries before the fall of Constantinople in 1453. Finally, the growth of nationalism and the desire for local autonomy among churchmen should be noted in Robert of Lincoln who objected to papal appointments without local consent about 300 years before Luther posted his ninety-five theses.

in the natural world and *after* things in the mind of man.[33] Man himself is composed of soul and body, the one immortal and the other mortal, yet in this life essentially they are one as form and matter are in any material object.

St. Thomas wrote only one short disputation, "Concerning the Teacher," but, in a sense, all his works may be considered as dealing with the philosophy of education, for he wrote a complete philosophy of life which certainly has implications for education. He maintained that the teacher is a vessel or agent who, with the help of God, can be said to teach just as a physician, with the help of nature, can be said to heal, and that teaching is a function of the contemplative rather than the active life. He believed that will and intellect elevate man above the brute and must be trained through discipline. He held that learning about the physical world comes through the senses and advocated sense training and the direct experimental approach. He placed the intellect and theoretical knowledge above practical knowledge. The purpose of education, he indicated, is to develop the total personality through drawing out the dormant capabilities and bringing them into complete harmony with each other. The final purpose of education is sanctity. Man is incomplete until the physical, social, and intellectual aspects of his nature have been crowned by faith and he submits joyfully to Divine Will as expressed through the Church. The philosophy of St. Thomas is the basis for present day Catholic education.

SUMMARY

In the preceding chapter we have seen the beginning of Western philosophy in the Greek islands and coastal towns of the Mediterranean. We have seen the mature development of these ideas in Hellenistic Athens. We have been impressed with the importance which these philosophers placed upon the proper education of youth for citizenship and with the insights which some of them, especially Aristotle, had into the workings of the human mind. We saw how the culture of Athens was carried by Alexander and later by the Roman legions to all coasts of the Mediterranean Sea

[33] Albert E. Avery, *Handbook in the History of Philosophy* (New York: Barnes and Noble, Inc., 1955), p. 94.

and to England. We noted the rise of Stoicism as a philosophy in imperial Rome before the advent of Christianity. Beginning with what seemed to be two irreconcilable viewpoints, the "sacred" learning of the Church fathers and the "profane" writings of the ancients, St. Augustine and others achieved a reconciliation based on Plato. We followed the conflict between Plato's theory of the reality of abstract ideas and the nominalist theory based upon Aristotle's "forms" inherent in things. We acknowledged our debt to Arab culture for re-introducing Aristotle into the West, and saw the final triumph of Aristotle through the writings of St. Thomas Aquinas. Despite the insistence of Aristotle on a sound mind in a sound body, education in the later Roman empire and in the early Christian era had separated the two. Roman education tended to be practical and concerned with making the best of temporal existence. Early Christian education taught men to despise the body and the temporal world and to fix their gaze on the life of the world to come. The later middle ages saw the development of scholasticism, a philosophy for a Christian community, concerned with making commentaries (summae) on single or collected texts. Problems were largely theological, methods were deductive, dialectic, and disputatious, and faith and revelation controlled reason. In St. Thomas scholasticism reached its zenith.

BIBLIOGRAPHY

Aristotle, *Aristotle on Education,* being extracted from the *Ethics* and *Publius,* trans. and ed. John Burnet (Cambridge: Cambridge University Press, 1905).

———, *The Nicomachean Ethics,* trans. H. Rackham, rev. ed. (Cambridge, Mass.: Harvard University Press, 1947).

Augustine, Aurelius, Saint, Bishop of Hippo, *The City of God,* trans. and ed. Marcus Dods (New York: Hafner Publishing Co., 1948).

Augustinus, Aurelius, Saint, Bishop of Hippo, *Confessions,* trans. F. J. Sheed (New York: Sheed & Ward, 1943).

Burnet, John, *Early Greek Philosophy,* 4th ed. (London: Adam & Charles Block, 1945).

Cicero, Marcus Tullius, *Cicero in His Letters,* 4th ed., ed. Robert Yelverton Tyrell (2 vols.; London: Macmillan & Co., Ltd., 1915).

Cicero, Marcus Tullius, *De Oratoni,* trans. E. W. Sutton (2 vols.; Cambridge, Mass.: Harvard University Press, 1942).

De Witt, Norman Wentworth, *Epicurus and His Philosophy* (Minneapolis: University of Minnesota Press, 1954).

Faucett, Lawrence, *The Thinking Shop of Socrates* (Tokyo: Shinozaki Shorin, 1957).

Lodge, Rupert Clendon, *Plato's Theory of Education* (London: Kegan Paul, Trench, Trubner & Co., Ltd., 1947).

Nettleship, Richard Lewis, *The Theory of Education in Plato's Republic* (Oxford: The Clarendon Press, 1935).

McCabe, Joseph, *St. Augustine and His Age* (London: Duckworth, 1902).

Plato, *The Dialogues of Plato,* trans. Benjamin Jowett (New York: Random House, 1937).

Quintilianus, Marcus Fabius, *Institutes Oratorio,* with an English summary and concordance (Nashville, Tenn.: Printed for George Peabody College for Teachers, 1951).

Richmond, William Kenneth, *Socrates and the Western World* (New York: Citadel Press, 1955).

Smith, T. V., *From Thales to Plato* (Chicago: University of Chicago Press, 1956).

Chapter IV

Renaissance, Reformation, and Counter Reformation

PREVIEW

The fall of Constantinople and the discovery of the works of Greek and Roman authors gave the final stimulus to the rebirth of learning which had been going on for several centuries. The movement began in Italy, but later spread to the Low Countries, France, Germany, and England.

When the conquests of Islam made the established overland trade routes to India difficult, commerce turned to the German free cities with outlets to the North Sea (see Figure 2, p. 74). The rich natural resources of central Europe stimulated manufacturing. The rising merchant middle class of the Hanseatic towns, the flourishing guilds, and the distance from the seat of Church and State encouraged the growth of nationalism in both political and ecclesiastical affairs. As the Renaissance spread slowly from Italy it blended into the nationalistic, middle-class, guild, and commercial civilization of the Germanic north and was transformed into what is generally known as the Reformation or the Protestant revolt. Although the period is dominated by such men as Luther and Calvin, western Europe had been preparing for the Reformation for 300 years.

Philosophically, both movements were stimulated by Plato's theory of ideas and the individualism of the ancient Greeks. Humanism in its heyday drew heavily upon the Stoicism of Cicero and the sophist approach of Protagoras and Quintilian. The Reformation was for the most part a throwback to the anti-intellectualism of the early Church. In a short time the two movements joined in northern Europe and individual issues became confused. Both humanists and reformers considered education as one of their most powerful tools. This we have found not to be a new phenomenon. Both Plato and Aristotle acknowledged it. Medieval cathedral, monastic, and town schools flourished, and universities were established throughout the Western world. We shall find in our subsequent study that education is universally used for initiating the young into the group and for perpetuating group ideals.

Humanism was class-conscious, and soon settled into a fixed system of formal discipline. The reformers distrusted the minds of the masses almost as much as their predecessors. But the seeds of revolt had been sown and began to flourish with the rise of the scientific movement after Galileo and Copernicus. This we shall discuss in Chapter V.

THE RENAISSANCE EDUCATORS

The Renaissance was a slow spiritual awakening which can be traced back to the twelfth century. With "Back to Plato" as its battle cry, it inspired high hopes for the liberation of man. It encouraged humanistic teachers to revolt against monkish schoolmasters and dislodged the sacred authority of "The Philosopher," Aristotle. It began with a new vitality and a new spirit of self-assertion and self-realization. It aimed at freeing the human spirit and developing the all-round cultivated world citizen who should be litterateur, artist, diplomat, soldier, esthete, courtier, and polite conversationalist. The movement is generally conceded to have begun in Italy, spread to France, and then moved to Germany and northern Europe where it became connected with the Reformation. Of the seventy-nine European universities founded before 1500, forty-five were in existence before the fourteenth century. The greatest growth in universities in the fifteenth century was in France and Germany where nine and eleven institutions were founded respectively (see Figure 3, p. 85). For the most part these universities followed the scholastic tradition.

In England, under the influence of Sir Francis Bacon (1561–1626), the Renaissance gave an incentive to rationalism (discussed in Chapter V) and the rise of the scientific movement. Of these three movements—Renaissance, Reformation, and rationalism—the Renaissance is educationally least important.

VITTORINO DA FELTRE

Vittorino da Feltre (1378–1446) established a school at Mantua which exemplified the best of the educational thought of the period. He insisted on a harmonious development of the mind and body, on classical studies in both Latin and Greek, on free self-expression, on character training, and on the inculcation of Christian piety. These subjects, together with fine arts and history, constituted the new curriculum. Attention to personal hygiene, manners, and dress was continued as in the schools for noblemen of the later middle ages.

Unfortunately, Vittorino da Feltre left no writings, but treatises on education were not lacking. As early as 1400, Pietro Vergerio wrote a treatise on *Good Morals and School Studies* but probably most important of these early works was Maffeo Vegio's *On the Liberal and Moral Training of Children* which appeared about 1450. For the most part, however, the curriculum was still based upon the seven liberal arts and required a tremendous amount of memorization.[1] Quintilian's *Institutes of Oratory,* rediscovered by Andrea Poggio in the Cloister of Saint Gall, became the textbook of the schools, and its author became the model of the Renaissance schoolmaster. Cicero was a favorite author, and his style supplanted that of the contemporary Latin not only in writing but also in speaking. A number of humanists even insisted that parents speak only classical Latin with their children.

Some humanists were ridiculously self-conscious and vainglorious. They often lacked the quiet solemnity and pious dignity of the great scholastics. Some were bookish and ascetic. The Italian poet Petrarch (1304–1374) exemplified many of these traits. They loved

[1] The seven liberal arts are divided into two groups. The lower group, the trivium, includes the three language arts: grammar, rhetoric, and dialectic. The upper group, the quadrivium, is made up of the four mathematical arts: geometry, arithmetic, music, and astronomy.

words so well that means became ends, and they became slaves to Cicero as the scholastics had been to Aristotle. Those humanists who remained in the Church, including many of the higher clergy, valued religion chiefly as a means of preserving the existing social order. When humanism was linked to the Reformation, it became the servant of supernaturalism and new theological orthodoxies. What had begun as a movement to set men free became but a new type of oppression.

On the positive side, we may say that humanism created a new concept of art and the art of living. By teaching the art of systematic observation and experimentation it modified the relation of man to nature. The finest representative of the "universal man" is Leonardo da Vinci (1452–1519). There is possibly no phase of life, art, or learning which has not been influenced by the life of this great genius who maintained that certainty comes only from mathematical formulation.

NICCOLÒ MACHIAVELLI

Da Vinci's contemporary, Machiavelli (1467–1527), is most famous for his educational treatise, *The Prince.* Being disillusioned by the corruption of the churchmen of his day, he made the *state* the *center* of human life. He was a thoroughgoing materialist, and advocated absolute monarchy. Another contemporary, Castiglione (1478–1529), wrote a companion piece in the *Book of the Courtier* in which he stressed the education of the nobility. Michel Montaigne (1533–1592) is perhaps the most famous of the French humanists. Like his Italian contemporaries, he was interested in the education of the gentleman. In his *Essays,* he stated that the aim of education was to teach the young the art of living through observation and travel, rather than through memorization. "I would have his manners, behavior, and bearing cultivated at the same time with his mind. It is not the mind, it is not the body we are training; it is the man, and we must not divide him into two parts." [2]

The Renaissance was not a popular movement. It was completely

[2] Michel Montaigne: *The Education of Children,* trans. L. E. Rector, International Education Series No. 69 (New York: D. Appleton and Company, 1899), p. 61.

class-conscious and confined to the aristocracy. Renaissance schools and educational writings were directed toward the education of the nobility or as in Milton, the wealthy gentry, an attitude deriving from Socrates and Plato. This same class-consciousness, the confusion of ends and means, and the love of words for their own sake are characteristic of present day humanistic education.

DESIDERIUS ERASMUS

Desiderius Erasmus of Rotterdam (1466–1536) was the most outstanding humanist of the Low Countries. He became an Augustinian monk with reluctance because he was more inclined to literary studies than to the affairs of the Church. However, he fulfilled his obligations to the Church with great distinction and was frequently the arbiter in ecclesiastical matters. He was interested in reform within the Church, and, therefore, broke with Luther and the more radical group when it became apparent that a schism would develop because of their teaching. One of his most popular works was a biting satire on all classes of men, *Encomium Moriae* (In Praise of Folly), written with a play on the name of his friend, Sir Thomas More (1478–1535), who was an outstanding representative of Renaissance humanism in England, a lecturer on Augustinianism, and author of *Utopia*, which described an ideal commonwealth. In More's utopia the individual would be subordinate to the community which would own all natural resources, provide free education and "universal employment" for all. Many of these ideas had been expressed by Erasmus in his *Enchiridion* or *Manual of the Christian Knight* (1503). In this work Erasmus advocated a limited absolute monarchy as the best form of government. He believed that the ruler should live with a sense of honor and with self-discipline. The ruler, he thought, should control all the country's natural resources, should prevent crime by economic and political measures, and abolish wars against the spirit of Christ.

In *Upon the Method of Right Instruction* (1511), Erasmus held that proper methods will increase learning, that a nation should supply trained teachers for all grades, and that the teacher should know the nature of the child and the psychology of learning. He believed that nature, training, and practice determined individual progress. "For it is not by learning rules that we acquire the power of speaking a language, but by daily intercourse with those accustomed to express themselves with expertness and refinement, and by the copious reading of the best authors." He was a great rationalist, and despised all types of physical exercise and the empirical method of science.

Although he spoke of abolishing all classes, his attitude toward

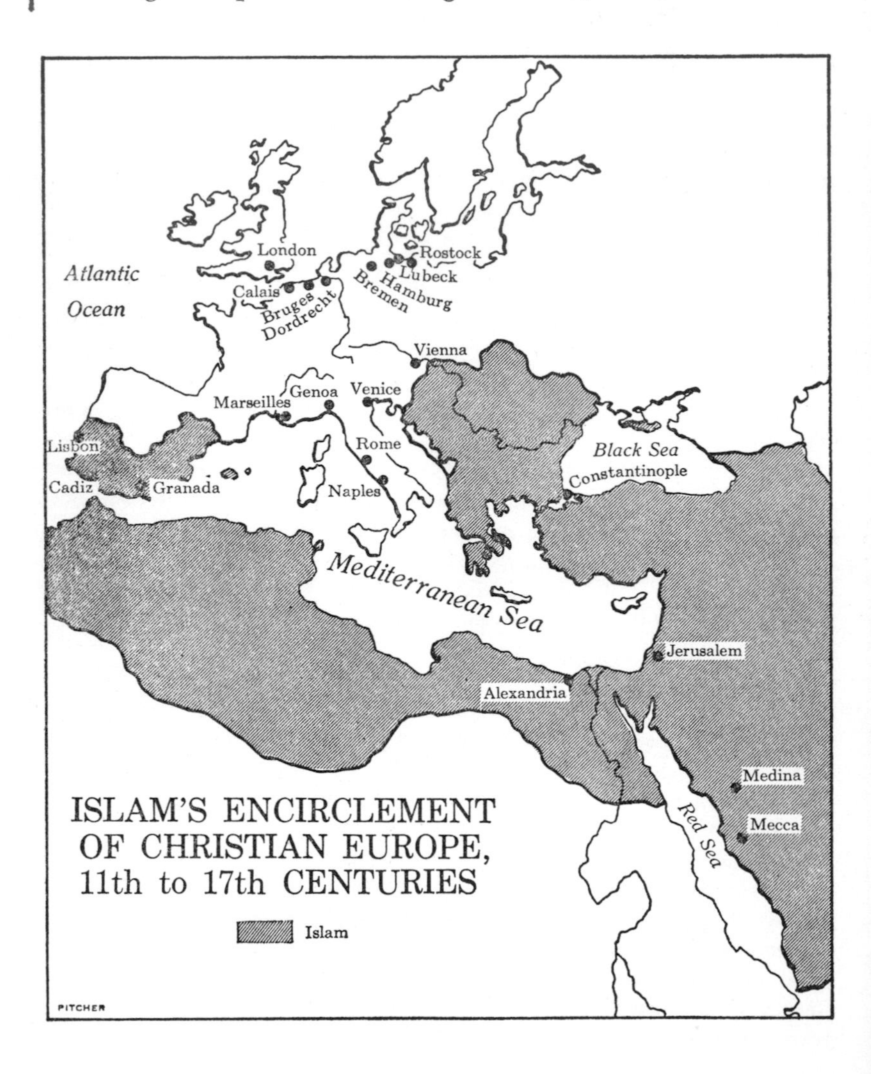

ISLAM'S ENCIRCLEMENT OF CHRISTIAN EUROPE, 11th to 17th CENTURIES

the common people was paternalistic. His was an education for an aristocracy of brains and birth.

THE REFORMATION

Just as Italy had been prepared over several centuries for the cultural flowering of the Renaissance, so the European mind was made ready for the tremendous events which marked the Reforma-

---

Figure 2. This map shows the farthest reaches of Islam beginning with the conquests of North Africa and Spain in the eleventh century and culminating with the siege of Vienna in 1683.

As the house of Castile began its conquests in Spain, the might of Islam increased in the East. On May 29, 1453, the Crescent of the Moslems entered Constantinople and the Byzantine empire was irrevocably lost. The Balkans came under the political and religious domination of the "sons of the prophet," who were checked only at the gates of Vienna.

The Mediterranean became an inland lake, and commercial interests shifted from such important ports as Venice, Genoa, and Marseilles to the more accessible outlets on the Atlantic Coast and the Hansa cities along the North Sea.

Cultural, religious, and nationalistic interests followed trade. This period saw the rise of the guild, the development of a prosperous merchant middle class, and the assertion of feelings of nationalism which demanded freedom and local autonomy in religion, business, and politics.

The Renaissance in Italy was indeed not only a cultural movement, but had its commercial implications as well as is reflected in the insistence of the humanistic educators on training world citizens rather than subjects of local lords. This movement along the Mediterranean, however, was kept in check by the area's proximity to the power of the Roman Pontiff and the Emperor of the Holy Roman Empire. But as the Renaissance dispersed through the mountains and the lush river valleys of central and northern Europe, as it stretched out in the age of discovery, beginning with the early voyages of the Portuguese, Spanish, Dutch, and British navigators, it became closely attached to the aspiring commercial middle classes, to the free cities of northern Europe, and to growing feeling of national unity and independence. Men such as Melanchthon played the double role of humanist and reformer. The Renaissance entered into an uneasy marriage with the reform church movement in Germany, Scandinavia, Great Britain, and the Low Countries, and the grand medieval unity of Christendom had come to an end.

tion and Counter Reformation of the sixteenth century. Meister Eckhart (1260–1327), a Dominican monk, early in the fourteenth century began the philosophical German language through his preaching in the vernacular. Marsilius of Padua (1270–1342) laid the foundation for the Protestant revolt by asserting that, although God is the ultimate source of all power, it comes immediately from the people; therefore, law is the expression of the will of the people and not of the prince. William of Ockham (1280–1346), chiefly remembered because of Ockham's razor (that in understanding things one must not use more concepts than are necessary), maintained that belief in God and morality were matters of faith, and wrote much in opposition to the temporal power of the pope. John Wycliffe (1320–1384) translated large sections of the Bible into English and argued in favor of nationalism in the control of religion. Among his followers, the most famous was John Huss (1370–1415), rector of the University of Prague, who was burned for heresy. Many felt that the old order with its entrenched institutions was passing, and that a new era was being born.

MARTIN LUTHER

It was into this age of striving toward nationalism, of growing individualism in thought and belief, of the rise of the middle class to wealth and power, especially in England, the Low Countries, and northern Germany, of the development and expansion of commerce through the opening of new markets, following the discovery of America and the rounding of the Cape of Good Hope that Martin Luther (1483–1546) was born.

It might be said that he contributed nothing new, but by the force of his character and by seizing upon the circumstances of the times, he brought ideas about understanding through faith, individualism of men and of nations, and the need for mass education in the vernacular into a system, and succeeded in implementing it.

Although Luther wanted to deliver the world from medieval institutionalism, he approached the educational situation as a religious reformer rather than as a humanist or a practical schoolmaster, for "as [Charles] Beard has well said Luther was Hebraic rather than Hellenic in spirit." [3] His contributions to education

[3] Frederick Eby, *Early Protestant Educators* (New York: McGraw-Hill Book Company, 1931), p. 43.

have been praised by some [4] and just as strongly criticized by others.[5] He denounced the medieval universities as "dens of corruption." [6] Yet he urged the study of the ancient languages [7] and urged Elector Frederick to establish several universities within his principality for the training of preachers, pastors, secretaries, and councilors,[8] adding that "if studying is to be good you must have not empty cloisters and deserted monasteries, and endowed churches, but a city in which many people come together and practice on one another and stir each other up and drive each other on." [9]

Luther's individualism did not rest in the feeling of rational self-autonomy, as the ancients believed, but in the Augustinian concept of the joyful experience of personal or individual salvation through faith in God's eternal grace. He hated Aristotle who he thought had injected the venom of personal pride into the body of the Church. He was conservative in his theology and would have sided with the twelfth-century theologians against St. Thomas Aquinas.

Unlike the humanists, Luther was much concerned with the education of the common man. In 1524 he issued a stirring appeal to the mayors and aldermen of the cities of Germany to revive their municipal schools.[10] Neither his theology nor his educational and social programs were entirely new, but the force of his personality and his great energy brought many of them to fruition. His belief

[4] See F. V. N. Painter, *Luther on Education* (St. Louis, Mo.: Concordia Publishing House, 1928); C. M. Bruce, *Luther as an Educator* (Minneapolis Augusburg Publishing House, 1928); T. M. Lindsay, *Luther and the German Reformation* (New York: Charles Scribner's Sons, 1900); and Robert Ulich, *History of Educational Thought* (New York: American Book Company, 1945), pp. 114–129.

[5] Johannes Janssen, *History of the German People at the Close of the Middle Ages,* I, III, and XIII (London: K. Paul, Trench, Trubner and Company, 1905); John I. von Dollinger, *Die Reformation* (Regensburg: Manz, 1851), L, 422; and F. Paulsen, *German Education Past and Present* (London: Unwin, 1908), pp. 76–77.

[6] Johannes Janssen, *op. cit.,* III, 335. Quoted in Frederick Eby and Charles Flinn Arrowood, *The Development of Modern Education* (New York: Prentice-Hall, Inc., 1934), p. 96.

[7] "Letter to Eeban Hess" in Frederick Eby, *op. cit.,* p. 44.

[8] *Ibid.,* pp. 98–99.

[9] *Ibid.,* p. 99.

[10] Painter, *op. cit.,* "Letter to the Mayors and Aldermen," pp. 169–209 and "Sermon on the Duty of Sending Children to School," pp. 218–271.

in the supreme authority of the scriptures led him to compile a complete translation of the Bible from already existing texts and to put it into the hands of the common man. However, he wished to guard its interpretation and accordingly wrote the smaller and the larger catechisms which were to be used for religious instruction. He maintained that "the catechism is the right Bible for the Laitie." [11]

According to Luther the aim of education is to lead the young toward that degree of piety and understanding as will render a Christian community possible. In addition to his recommendation for the establishment of town and village schools he also urged stipends for the support of a few bright scholars. Luther is the first modern reformer to advocate compulsory school attendance. In his "Sermon on the Duty of Sending Children to School" (1530) he wrote, "If the government can compel such citizens as are fit for military service to bear spear and rifle, to mount ramparts, and perform other martial duties in time of war, how much more has it a right to compel the people to send their children to school, because in this case we are warring with the Devil." [12]

Luther also urged and participated in one of the earliest school surveys.[13] He was strongly opposed to parents who were indifferent about sending their children to school,[14] and though he pointed out the evils of lax discipline,[15] he was opposed to harsh methods.[16] His educational program included schooling for girls as well as boys. In 1520 he wrote "Would to God each town had also a girls' school in which girls might be taught the Gospel for an hour a day either in German or in Latin." [17]

He maintained that the Christian endowed with faith in the grace of God does "all things gaily and freely," and as this becomes easier in a healthy mind and body, education has to take care not

[11] Quoted in Eby, *op. cit.*, p. 97, from Capt. Henrie Bell, "Dr. Martin Luther's Divine Discourse at His Table."

[12] *Ibid.*, pp. 149–150.

[13] See Eby and Arrowood, *op. cit.*, p. 87.

[14] Eby, *op. cit.*, pp. 22–27. Original in George Walch, *Luther's Samtlich Schriften*, III, 1817–1825.

[15] *Ibid.*

[16] Quoted in Henry Barnard, *German Teachers and Educators* (Hartford, Conn.: Brown and Gross, 1878), p. 152. "Commentary on the Epistle to the Galatians," in *Dr. Martin Luther's Werke*, Weimar edition, XL, 529.

[17] Eby, *op. cit.*, p. 41.

only of the religious and intellectual but of the total physical and emotional development of the child.[18] He was also interested in the continuing education of adults and recommended the establishment of libraries for the reading of good books.

Luther's ideal of a perfect state was a benevolent and patriarchal absolutism under enlightened princes. He supported the doctrine *cujus regio ejus religio* (whose territory, whose religion) and enjoined all his followers to give their princes faithful obedience. All rulers were to acknowledge their responsibility to the Spiritual Kingdom of God which was higher than all earthly kingdoms, and in this kingdom all individuals whether high or low were citizens of equal merit. These ideas of individual merit and Christian liberty have persisted in idealistic philosophy to the present day. By placing both school and church under the direct authority of the state he laid the foundation for popular state-controlled education throughout Germany.

Other educators of the Lutheran group include Philipp Melanchthon (1497–1560) and Johann Sturm (1507–1589). Melanchthon's work in the establishment of Latin schools, the conduct of school surveys, and the writing of textbooks earned for him the title of "Praeceptor Germaniae." Johann Sturm is known as the Father of the Gymnasium because of his work in reorganizing the medieval town Latin school into a nine-year secondary school or gymnasium at Strassburg in 1537 with its curriculum of religion, Latin, Greek, and logic. Both men despised the common vernacular school and established programs of education for the socially and intellectually elite, thus making a definite cleavage between the education of the common man and that of those destined for the universities. The influence of these two humanistic educators is felt in the organization and curriculum of the classical secondary school in Europe to the present day.

Other more radical types of religious reform and political organization were being developed. Ulrich Zwingli (1484–1531) was a friend of Erasmus and an outstanding humanist. With Luther he accepted the Augustinian doctrine of original sin, but differed from him with regard to the nature of the sacraments. It was hoped that the views of the two reformers could be reconciled, but after negotiations were broken off between them, Zwingli gave

[18] Ulich, *op. cit.*, p. 123.

his support to Calvin and subsequently died at Kappel in the Swiss religious wars which his doctrines had incited.

JOHN CALVIN

John Calvin (1509–1564) stands slightly to the left of Luther's theology. He abolished all practices and doctrines which did not have direct biblical support. He gave much authority to the laity and established a Consistorium of lay elders and deacons in Geneva who were charged with inspecting not only the churches, but homes and municipal and business institutions as well. Writing from Geneva in 1610, Lutheran Pastor Andrea remarks: "Not only is there in existence an absolutely free commonwealth, but . . . a censorship of morals . . . with investigations . . . each week into the morals and even into the slightest transgressions of the citizens. . . . As a result, all cursing, gambling, luxury, quarreling, hatred, conceit, deceit, extravagance and the like, to say nothing of greater sins, are prevented." [19]

While Luther recommended a state church where the civil authorities were dominant, Calvin's system called for an organization where the regulation of both civil and religious affairs was dominated by the clergy. "Civil government," he wrote, "is designed as long as we live in this world, to cherish and support the eternal worship of God." [20] His recommendations had a great influence in the establishment of church-state educational programs in Geneva, Holland, Scotland, and New England. Calvin established his Academy at Geneva in 1559 with its classical Gymnasium and theological school. All details of life and instruction were carefully planned and regulated and all teachers were bound by oath to adhere to the profession of faith of the reformed church. The Academy was considered a model educational institution and was widely copied. It influenced the Universities of Leyden and Edinburgh, Emmanuel College of Cambridge University, and Harvard College.[21]

[19] Felix Emil Held, *Johann Valentin Andrea's Christianopolis* (Urbana: University of Illinois, 1914), p. 27. Quoted in Eby and Arrowood, *op. cit.*, p. 129.

[20] Eby, *op. cit.*, p. 127.

[21] *Ibid.*, pp. 252–253.

Calvin believed in the total depravity of man and in predestination: ". . . infants themselves as they bring their condemnation into the world with them, are rendered obnoxious to punishment by their own sinfulness, not by the sinfulness of another . . . their whole nature is . . . odious and abominable to God. This depravity never ceases in us. Our nature is not only destitute of all good, but is so fertile to evil that it cannot remain inactive."[22]

Since man cannot set himself free from this original sin, every man's salvation or damnation is therefore predestined, according to the Augustinian theology from which Calvinism is derived. The emphasis, then, is on the negative aspect of morality which consists of abstinence from evil acts and indulgence of bodily passions through the exercise of man's free will. As Wheelwright remarks: "Those Christian creeds which declare that God is omniscient (in the precise sense of the word) and also that man has free will (also in the precise sense) are trying to digest a hard logical contradiction."[23]

The movement stemming from the theology of John Calvin did much to establish state supported systems of education in order to provide instruction in reading the Bible and other types of sacred literature. In the Netherlands, the church synods gave Calvinist civil magistrates the authority to establish and maintain orthodox Calvinist religious vernacular schools free to the poor. The curriculum included the vernacular, the Heidelberg Catechism, prayers, and lessons in patriotism. Early attempts at a similar educational program were made by John Knox in Scotland, but a free system of parish education was not established until the eighteenth century. In colonial New England, the theocratic governments established systems of free schools as early as 1642 so that "all children might learn to read and understand the principles of religion and the capital lawes of this country."[24]

It is usually conceded that both Calvin and Luther derived their idealism especially with regard to the freedom and integrity of the individual from Plato through St. Augustine. This respect for the individual, although not always honored in the observance, is a

[22] John Calvin, *Institutes of the Christian Religion*, ed. John Allen (Philadelphia: Presbyterian Board of Publications, n.d.), I, 229–231.

[23] Philip Wheelwright, *The Way of Philosophy* (New York: The Odyssey Press, Inc., 1954), p. 305.

[24] Quoted in Eby and Arrowood, *op. cit.*, p. 169.

basic principle of present day idealism. "The weight of Protestant ethics has been upon the religious significance of the present life, . . . the bearing of religious faith upon the reorganization of economic and political practices, and the right of the Christian man to possess abundantly the natural goods of God's world." [25]

THE COUNTER REFORMATION

ST. IGNATIUS OF LOYOLA

St. Ignatius of Loyola (1491–1556), a Spanish soldier of noble lineage, was seriously wounded in battle while in his early thirties. During his long recovery he decided to abandon the profession of arms and to devote himself to a life of religion, and after long hard study was ordained to the priesthood. He and six companions founded the Society of Jesus (Jesuits) in 1534, and the order was approved by the Pope in 1540. The *Constitution* which set forth the guiding principles and organization of the "Society" was issued practically in its final form in the year of Loyola's death. The fourth part of this document, the "Ratio Studiorum," deals with education. The aim of Jesuit education is to train loyal members of the Roman Catholic church. St. Ignatius's military training is reflected in the title, "General," given to the head of the order in its aggressive rather than contemplative nature, in his insistence on absolute obedience and discipline, and in giving awards and prizes.

The "Ratio" can hardly be called a philosophy, but is rather a method of implementing a philosophy which the student accepts without question. Method consists in two types of class exercises; prelection and repetition. In the former the teacher gave a clear and detailed exposition of the material to be learned, after which the student committed it to memory or was otherwise drilled and questioned until he made it his own. Sometimes the prelection was merely a lecture followed by a summary.

Loyola said,

> Man . . . was created to be happy by giving service and praise or glory to God. . . . All other creatures are created as means to aid man in attaining his end. . . . If faced with a choice between two creatures

[25] Sterling P. Lamprecht, *Our Philosophical Traditions* (New York: Appleton-Century-Crofts, Inc.,), p. 215.

or courses of action, he should choose the one which is more conducive to his end. . . . In imparting such education and motivation, a director or teacher should endeavor to procure not passive absorption of his own statements or opinions, but intensive self-activity by which the learner acquires intimate understanding, personal conviction, and relish of the truth.[26]

Jesuit education was concerned with strengthening the Roman Catholic position and the authority of the Pope against the adherents of the Protestant revolt. It was directed toward the sons of the wealthy and of the aristocracy and was concerned with secondary and higher education almost exclusively. It developed no new intellectual insights, but was designed to secure unwavering loyalty to the accepted doctrine of the Church. Jesuit educational method and organization has been of great influence not only in predominantly Catholic countries, but throughout the world. The missionary zeal of the order is great.

OTHER CATHOLIC EDUCATORS

Catholic education for the lower classes had been carried on for many years by parish priests, and was often of poor quality. In order to strengthen the Catholic position and to combat Protestantism, about thirty teaching orders were established between 1525 and 1700. St. Jean Baptiste de la Salle (1651–1753) founded the order of Christian Brothers in France in 1682 to provide elementary education for poor children. Other orders like the Ursuline Nuns (1535) and the Sisters of Charity (1634) were concerned with educating girls to take their places in fashionable society and to direct the affairs of their households. This type of convent school was widely adopted for the education of girls even in Protestant countries, and greatly influenced the private girls' schools in America.

SUMMARY

The Renaissance and Counter Reformation developed education for the aristocracy. Protestant education appealed most strongly to the rising commercial middle class. The Renaissance broke the

[26] Quoted in George E. Ganss, S.J., *Saint Ignatius' Idea of a Jesuit University* (Milwaukee: The Marquette University Press, 1954), pp. 19–20.

hold of scholasticism on the European mind, but crystallized all too soon into a dry humanism which had little connection with the political, economic, and social changes taking place in western Europe. The Reformation, which began with an appeal to individual freedom, bound itself all too soon to an infallible Book. The Counter Reformation was in the main an attempt to hold the line and relied upon an infallible Church, especially after the Council of Trent (1534–1563). It remained for the next age to declare the doctrine of an infallible Reason.

BIBLIOGRAPHY

Bruce, G. M., *Luther as an Educator* (Minneapolis: Augsburg Publishing House, 1928).

Calvin, John, *Institutes of the Christian Religion*, trans. Henry Beveridge (London: J. Clarke, 1953).

Eby, Frederick, *Early Protestant Educators* (New York: McGraw-Hill Book Co., Inc., 1931).

Erasmus, Desiderius, *The Praise of Folly*, trans. Leonard F. Dean (Chicago: Packard and Co., 1946).

Ganss, S.J., George E., *Saint Ignatius' Idea of a Jesuit University* (Milwaukee: The Marquette University Press, 1954).

Hughes, Thomas, *Loyola and the Educational System of the Jesuits* (New York: Charles Scribner's Sons, 1892).

Huizinga, Johan, *Erasmus and the Age of Reformation*, with a selection from the letters of Erasmus (New York: Harper and Brothers, 1951).

Machiavelli, Niccolò, *The Prince and The Discourses* (New York: The Modern Library, 1940).

Montaigne, Michel Elquiem de, *The Complete Works: Essays, Travel Journal, Letters*, trans. Donald M. Frome (Stanford, Calif.: Stanford University Press, 1957).

Painter, F. V. N., *Luther on Education* (St. Louis, Mo.: Concordia Publishing House, 1928).

Paulsen, F., *German Education Past and Present* (London: T. F. Unwin, 1908).

Woodward, William Harrison, *Vittorino Da Feltre and Other Humanist Educators* (Cambridge: Cambridge University Press, 1921).

CHART 3: RENAISSANCE, REFORMATION, AND COUNTER REFORMATION

1200 1300 1400 1500 1600 1700

MEISTER ECKHART 1260-1327	Combined Aristotelianism and mysticism; preached and wrote in German
MARSILIUS OF PADUA 1270-1342	God the ultimate source of power; law expresses will of people; basis of Reformation
WILLIAM OF OCKHAM 1280-1342	Ockham's Razor (Law of Parsimony); belief in God and immortality are matters of faith
JOHN WYCLIFFE 1320-1384	English translator of the Bible; supported nationalist control of religion
VITTORINO DA FELTRE 1378-1446	Humanist; founded school for boys in Mantua
JOHN HUSS c. 1370-1415	Rector of University of Prague; follower of Wycliffe
MARSILIO FICINO 1433-1499	Florentine humanist; translated Plato
LEONARDO DA VINCI 1452-1519	Certitude comes only from mathematical formulation
DESIDERIUS ERASMUS 1466-1536	Greatest humanist of northern Europe
NICCOLO MACHIAVELLI 1467-1527	"The Prince"
SIR THOMAS MORE 1478-1535	Humanist, lawyer; lectured on Augustine; wrote "Utopia"
MARTIN LUTHER 1483-1546	Reformer; translated Bible into German; advocated free schools
HULDREICH ZWINGLI 1484-1531	Humanist reformer; associated with Calvinism
ST. IGNATIUS LOYOLA 1491-1556	Counter Reformation; founded Jesuits
JOHN CALVIN 1509-1564	Reformer; advocated theocratic state
ST. JEAN BAPTISTE DE LA SALLE 1651-1719	Founder of Christian Brothers; education of the poor

Contrary to the period discussed in Chapter III, important men and significant movements overlap each other historically. The years of Reformation and Counter Reformation saw many great contemporaries. There is an unbroken flow in the development towards Protestantism and nationalism. Two centuries before Luther, men like Eckhart and Wycliffe advocated the use of the vernacular in the reading and interpretation of the Scriptures. At the same time a spirit of nationalism and of independence of foreign domination in Church and State was growing.

The Renaissance preceded the Protestant revolt by more than a century. Leonardo da Vinci, acknowledged to be the greatest man of the Renaissance, died a few years after Luther had posted his ninety-five theses. The foundations of the earliest universities are lost in legend and tradition. Beginning in Italy, centers of culture and learning spread to France, Spain, and England. The Mediterranean lands and England knew more than thirty universities before the first foundation in central and northern Europe.

The Reformation stimulated the founding of Protestant universities in northern Europe. Within a hundred years as many new seats of learning were founded there as had been established in the four preceding centuries. The Reformation stimulated the growth of the common reading and writing schools with their emphasis on religion and Bible reading in the Protestant countries. It was not until a century after the death of Luther and Calvin that St. Jean Baptiste de la Salle founded his Brothers of the Christian Schools whose aims were in many respects similar to the schoolmasters of the public schools already established in Germany, the Low Countries, and America.

Figure 3. European universities in the order of their founding. Historians believe that the earliest universities of western Europe grew out of congregations of great teachers and devoted disciples banded together by common interests. To place universities founded before the thirteenth century is difficult because of the obscurity of their origins. The following list follows tradition. It does not claim accuracy.

Bologna	chartered 1158	Salerno	founded early 12th cent., recognized 1230
Oxford	chartered 1167		
Paris	chartered 1180		
Reggio	chartered 1188	Montpellier	founded 12th

	cent., chartered 13th cent.
Vicenza	1204
Cambridge	1209
Palencia	1212–1214
Arezzo	1215
Padua	1222
Naples	1224
Vercelli	1228
Toulouse	1230
Salamanca	1230
Orleans	1231
Curia Romana	1244
Siena	1246
Piacenza	1248
Seville	1254
Lisbon-Coimbra	1290
Lerida	1300
Avignon	1303
Rome Studium Urbis	1303
Perugia	1308
Treviso	1318
Cahors	1332
Grenoble	1339
Pisa	1343
Prague	1347
Florence	1349
Perpignan	1349
Huesca	1359
Pavia	1361
Cracow	1364–1397
Orange	1365
Vienna	1365
Erfurt	1379–1392
Fünfkirken	1367
Heidelberg	1385
Cologne	1388
Buda	1389
Ferrara	1391
Würzburg	1402
Turin	1405
Aix	1409
Leipzig	1409
St. Andrews	1413
Rostock	1419
Dôle	1422
Louvain	1425
Greifswald	1428
Poitiers	1431
Bordeaux	1441
Catania	1444
Barcelona	1450
Glasgow	1451
Trèves	1454–1473
Freiburg-im-Breisgau	1455
Valence	1459
Bâle (Basel)	1459
Ingolstadt	1459
Nantes	1460
Bourges	1464
Poszony (Pressburg)	1465–1467
Saragossa	1474
Mainz	1476
Tubingen	1476
Upsala	1477
Copenhagen	1478
Palma (Majorca)	1483
Besançon	1485
Aberdeen	1494
Alcalà	1499
Valencia	1500
Halle	1502
Wittenberg	1502
Marburg	1527
Königsberg	1544
Leyden	1575
Helmstadt	1576
Altdorf	1578
Franken	1585
Jena	1588

Chapter V

Rationalism and the Enlightenment

PREVIEW

In Chapter V we shall see a decided naturalistic influence in psychology and education. Copernicus gave the initial impulse to the scientific movement through his startling demonstration that neither man nor the world he lives on is the center of the universe and that heaven does not occupy a fixed place a short distance above the clouds. Bacon's insistence on breaking with tradition and a re-examination of reality by use of an inductive method based upon empirical observation led the way to Hume's materialistic psychology, which insists that perception is a transaction between sense organs and external objects. Comenius, although a mystic and a classicist, likewise insisted upon sense realism as a basis for educational method.

Descartes believed he had solved the old realist-nominalist controversy described in Chapter IV by accepting two basic substances for reality, mind and matter, and thus imposed a dualism on western thought which we shall find to have wide repercussions. Descartes believed that reason was a gift from God and could be relied upon for absolute truth, but that it must be disciplined by the laws of mathematics. Spinoza accepted Descarte's mathematics but not his dualism. On the other hand, Locke accepted his dualism. He conceived of the mind as a blank tablet which received all its impressions from the external world. Followers of Locke's psychology could no longer accept Plato's doctrine of innate ideas.

Leibnitz, we shall see, tried to combine the atomism of Democritus (see Chapter III) with the metaphysics of Plotinus (see Chapter IV) in his theory of clear and unclear self-activated monads, and thus laid the basis for pure idealism. On the other hand Berkeley believed that all perception began with observation, but that there was no knowledge without a knower. His saying, "to be is to be perceived," is foundational for objective idealism.

Upon investigating the theories of his predecessors, Hume maintained that matter beyond sensory observation is not verifiable, and that reality is a series of sense impressions the causes and results of which cannot be proved. Finally, we shall see that Rousseau believed that man should get back to nature by close association with it in childhood, but that at adolescence he should realize his dependence and the dependence of all mankind upon the state for whatever civilization man has thus far achieved.

THE COPERNICAN REVOLUTION

Greater than the Renaissance and the Reformation was the revolution caused by the publication in 1543 of *De Revolutionibus Orbium* by Nicholas Copernicus (1473–1543). Although in presenting his work to Pope Paul III, Copernicus declared that it was merely a convenient hypothesis for the easy solution of certain astronomical problems, he was aware of the consequences to which his audacious theory would lead. The theory was condemned by the orthodox, Catholic and Protestant, clerical and lay, and the work was placed on the Index Expurgatorius. Luther called him "an ass who wants to pervert the whole art of Astronomy and deny what is said in the Book of Joshua." Although a general acceptance of the validity of the theory came slowly it may be considered as the beginning of the development of modern science, for it not only removed the earth from the center of the universe, but man and heaven as well. The era beginning with Francis Bacon (1561–1626) and ending with David Hume (1711–1776) might well be characterized as the period in which many of the philosophies which have affected the theory and practice of education began to take definite form. Beginning with the comparative orthodoxy of Bacon, it ended with the complete atheism of Hume. Thinkers and observers of the period took advantage of the conflict in religious and moral beliefs to investigate the foundations on which these beliefs had been predicated. The terminology and method of scholasticism, which derived ultimately from Aristotle, were discarded in favor of empiricism and the vocabulary of mathematics. From the time of Isaac Newton (1642–1727), natural philosophy began to separate from the main stream of philosophy and to form a definite method and discipline of its own. Out of this separation developed the physical, biological, and social sciences with their emphasis on exact observation and quantitative measurement.

SIR FRANCIS BACON

Sir Francis Bacon (1561–1626) has variously been termed the last philosopher of the Renaissance and the father of modern science. He was a subtile and many-sided thinker. Standing as he did at the end of the English Renaissance, his birth, position, wealth, influence, and immense mental activity made him a unique instrument for directing English thought along the road of empiricism and inductive reasoning. His works were more exuberant than logical, and he was a spokesman for, rather than a prophet of, the new learning. His was the role of a publicist rather than of a scientist. He attacked Aristotelian logic because it ignored the problem of how the general statements were reached, because the generalizations were hasty, and because it was merely a method of recording and organizing knowledge which had already been obtained rather than an instrument for securing new knowledge. In its place he suggested systematic experimentation and induction. He recognized that the validity of scientific conclusions rests on taking into account negative as well as positive instances, and that the power of a scientific theory depends upon the broadness of its application. He believed that only in theology it is necessary to appeal to authority and began a movement toward a critical study of the human mind. He maintained that there were four obstacles to the advancement of the human mind.[1] These he called "idols," the first of which is Idols of the Tribe: These idols are the limitations placed upon the capacities of men because they

[1] Francis Bacon, *Novum Organum*, Bk. I, "*Aphorisms*," pp. 41–44.

are human beings. Man imposes his own nature upon whatever comes into the range of his senses. One's perception is often faulty, and there is an impulse to accept too simple an explanation.

Second are Idols of the Cave or Den. Men mold their views of the world to fit their own mental patterns and private prejudices or the patterns of one's social group.

Third are Idols of the Market Place which arise from the necessity of using language for communication. Aside from a deliberate attempt to decieve others and to falsify the truth, too often an attempted meeting of minds fails because different speakers may be using the same words with different meanings so that in effect they are speaking different languages.

Lastly, there are the Idols of the Theater. Man adopts systems of dogma in philosophy, in social, political, and economic affairs, even in science, which preclude new thoughts. Men are obsessed by the power of great names.

These idols, Bacon writes, should be discarded for the new faith in observation and the scientific method which he develops in his two great works, *The Advancement of Learning* (1605) *and Novum Organum* (1620).

Aside from such statements as "some books are to be tasted, others swallowed, and some few to be chewed and digested," his specific suggestions with regard to education were inconsequential and marked no considerable advance over the Jesuitical method, but the force of his writing has had both a direct and an indirect effect on all educational theorists who followed him.

THOMAS HOBBES

Thomas Hobbes (1588–1679), the English philosopher, was a materialist and secularist. He was also accused of being an atheist because of his materialism, but this he never admitted. Many consider him to be the father of modern psychology and the first great English writer on the science of government. In his early manhood he spent many years with Bacon, translating his works into Latin, and in his middle years was considerably influenced by the work of Descartes whom he read with excitement. Noteworthy among his many works was *Leviathan*, published in 1651. Living at the time of much confusion in religion and uncertainty in government,

Hobbes longed for the security of a stable government far removed from the state of nature which he held to be synonymous with anarchy. In the state of nature he believed every man to be an enemy of every other man, where every man seeks his own profit and advantage. Lamprecht writes: "No orthodox Christian theologian with doctrines of original sin and total depravity ever pictured the condition of the damned more forcefully than Hobbes pictured the state of nature. No orthodox Christian theologian ever sought to save man from his unredeemed state more earnestly than Hobbes sought to rescue man from the state of nature."[2] In the field of politics, he defended absolutism on the theory that in the dim past the people had agreed to surrender their rights to a single person in order to escape from continual warfare with each other, and that these rights, once given up, could never be reclaimed. Therefore, right and morality are created by the state, and religion and education should be controlled by it. Since freedom of conscience, he believed, had produced anarchy, men must submit to the rule of the state so that peace and order could be maintained.

Together with Descartes and Locke, Hobbes advanced the science of psychology. His epistemology was tough and materialistic. Beginning with a simple causal notion of perception as transaction between sense organs and external objects which set up a train of motions in the brain, he develops the theory that these motions give rise to "imagination" which he defines as the experience of having mental images. Memory, he continues, in a way of talking about imagination when we wish to emphasize the past origin of images. This theory bears a close resemblance to that of present day logical positivists. His consideration was largely physiological. Although he was alive to the necessity of precise mathematical statements, he did not realize the philosophical questions which arise about perception, e.g., how do we know what external objects are really like? Locke and Berkeley were later to recognize these problems and to elaborate the theory which Hobbes stated. Spinoza, too, was also influenced by Hobbes's insisting on a geometrical statement of epistemological problems when he came to write the *Ethics*.

[2] Sterling P. Lamprecht, *Our Philosophical Traditions* (New York: Appleton-Century-Crofts, Inc., 1955), p. 278.

JOHN AMOS COMENIUS

John Amos Comenius (1592–1670), called the first sense realist, was a bishop of the Moravian church. His life was fraught with persecution and disappointment, especially with regard to his "Pansophia," a plan for a college and research center of universal knowledge. His thought was influenced by Calvinism as well as by the writings of Bacon and Locke. Laurie rates him as the most eminent figure in the history of European education.[3] He combined the mysticism of the Moravians with empiricism, believing that life was a continuous state of development toward the divine. Man, he declared, is a rational creature, the lord of all creatures, the image and joy of his creator. He held that the human race could be improved since the seeds of knowledge, virtue, and piety are found in everybody. Unlike Milton and Locke, he was greatly concerned with the education and welfare of the common man. "We wish all men to be trained in all the virtues, especially in modesty, sociability, and politeness, and it is therefore undesirable to create class distinctions at such an early age, or to give some children the opportunity of considering their own lot with satisfaction and that of others with scorn."[4] He carried his pansophic idea into the realm of politics and advocated a league of nations with universal schools, books, and language.

He aimed to make method so definite that the length of time could be predicted accurately. His educational psychology was set forth in the *Great Didactic*, published first in Czech and later in Latin at Amsterdam in 1657. Briefly, his principles of method are as follows: Education should begin early before the mind is corrupted. The mind should be duly prepared to receive instruction. Education should proceed from the general to the particular and from the easy to the difficult. Progress should be slow in every case, and the pupil should not be overburdened with too many subjects, nor should the intellect be forced to anything to which its natural bent does not incline it in accordance with its age and

[3] S. S. Laurie, *Educational Opinion from the Renaissance* (London: Cambridge University Press, 1903), p. 157.

[4] Quoted in Frederick Eby and Charles F. Arrowood, *The Development of Modern Education* (New York: Prentice-Hall, Inc., 1947), p. 258.

with the right method. "Let our maxim be to follow the lead of nature in all things to observe how the faculties develop one after the other, and to base our method on this principle of succession." [5] Everything should be taught through one and the same method, that is, through the medium of the senses, and its use is continually to be kept in mind.

About the classical education of his day he writes: "Most men possess no information but the quotations, sentences, and opinions they have collected by rummaging about in various authors, and thus piece their knowledge together like a patchwork quilt." [6]

But for Comenius's pupils, "They will learn not from school but from life." [7] "Nothing should be learned solely for its value at school, but for its use in life." [8]

In his other great work, *Orbis Sensualium Pictus* (1658), he applied his theory to the teaching of Latin vocabulary by first presenting a picture of the object followed by a Latin statement with translation. For example, following a picture of a wolf is the sentence "Lupus ululat" with its translation, "The *wolf* howleth," the letter "l" and the sounds "lu" and "ulu." [9] It remained, however, for Pestalozzi (1746–1827) to realize that objects must precede pictures in learning.

In organizing formal education Comenius planned schooling up to the age of twenty-four. He divided this period into four segments of six years each: First, during infancy, birth to six years, the school should be the "mother's knee"; second, for childhood, ages seven to twelve, the vernacular school; third, for boyhood, ages thirteen to eighteen, the Latin school or gymnasium; and fourth, for youth, ages nineteen to twenty-four, the university and travel. Education on the European continent follows this plan closely.

The influence of Comenius was widespread. Basedow (1723–1790) followed his lead in the use of pictures, Rousseau (1712–1778) stressed the education of the young in the things of nature, and Froebel (1782–1852) developed the concept of early childhood education and its implementation.

[5] *Ibid.*, p. 267.
[6] *Ibid.*, p. 261.
[7] *Ibid.*, p. 259.
[8] *Ibid.*, p. 273.
[9] *Ibid.*, p. 281.

RENÉ DESCARTES

René Descartes (1596–1650), born of a noble French family, received a Jesuitical education. Viewing the world of thought, especially in view of the writings of Galileo, he set himself the task of freeing philosophy from its burdensome traditions and of constructing a new system which would bring philosophy, science, and religion into complete harmony. To arrive at complete certainty, Descartes believed that one must begin with complete doubt. These doubts he considered to be two in number: first, whether sense experiences were a valid basis for opinions of the external world, and second, whether the mind can reach beyond the experiences which come to it through the senses to arrive at a genuine knowledge of the world outside oneself. In his moment of extreme doubt he concluded that, even if what he perceived were mere illusion, he must exist in order to be thus deluded. So he cries triumphantly: "Je pense, donc je suis," "Cogito, ergo sum": I think, therefore I am; I doubt, therefore I am. Having established his own existence, he proceeded to the second step in his epistemological problem: "what right has he to use his reason with regard to other existences?" He found this guarantee in the existence of a perfect Being or God. Having established, then, the existence of the self and the existence of God, Descartes proceeded by the method of mathematics to rear the structure of his system. Ideas, he declared, are of three kinds: (1) adventitious, those produced by things outside the self; (2) factitious, those formed by the imagination; and (3) innate ideas, those determined by reason or intuition. The idea of God is such an intuitive or innate idea. This notion of innate ideas differs considerably from the Platonic theory of innate ideas because Descartes did not consider them necessarily to have been present at birth, or to have pre-existed, or to be part of a universal mind.

Descartes believed in the ability of the intellect to ascertain truth. He concluded that the world was God's world and that man's intellect was a gift of God. Such a divine gift could, therefore, be trusted when used correctly as an instrument for reaching infallible knowledge and truth.

Believing that human reason is the final authority in all matters of knowledge, Descartes may be called a rationalist in his epistemology. On the other hand he may be called a dualist with regard to his ontology and axiology. Cartesian dualism is the belief that reality exists in two irreducible substances: soul which is thinking, unextended substance and body, unthinking, extended substance. Man partakes of both natures. Descartes solved the problem of the interaction of soul and body by establishing a point of contact in the pineal gland. Thus physical stimuli could cause sensations to arise in the soul, and conversely, acts of the will arising from the soul could be transmitted to the rest of the body.

This Cartesian dualism—mind and matter with regard to existence, and reason and faith with regard to values—has been widely accepted as a rather convenient compromise between science and religion and between the upper and lower classes in society. The theory was particularly acceptable to Locke and through him became part of the American intellectual heritage through the influence of Jefferson. Among popular dualisms in current American thought that need investigation are: liberal–vocational, humanistic–materialistic, spiritual–physical, individual–social, heredity–environment, and practical–theoretical.

Possibly no seventeenth-century philosopher has influenced the thought of the western world or the direction of education more than Descartes. His insistence upon mathematics as a tool for thinking formed a basis for much of the method of philosophy today. By publishing his works in French he pointed the direction to the use of the vernacular in scientific and philosophical writing. With regard to thinking he set forth three rules:

1. Never accept anything that can be doubted.
2. Analyze every problem into its component parts.
3. Begin with the simple and proceed to the complex.

JOHN MILTON

John Milton (1608–1674), along with Samuel Hartlib, John Drury, and Sir William Petty, formed a quartet of Commonwealth educators. They invited Comenius to England to discuss his pansophic ideas with a view to establishing such a research center under the auspices of Parliament, but the plan never materialized. Milton was also interested in the development of the classical gymnasium in The Netherlands and criticized the English public schools in the light of this development. He was a classicist and one of the most erudite men of his day, and recommended the abolition of the English public schools in favor of classical academies where students were to learn to solve present problems by steeping themselves in the writings of men who had died almost twenty centuries before. This notion seems to be a perennial favorite with classicists. It will probably be no more successful today than it was in the time of Cromwell.

At the solicitation of his friend, Samuel Hartlib, Milton wrote the *Tractate on Education* (1644). In it he expressed his puritanical and archaic ideas about the reform of education, in which connection it is interesting to note that the word "reform" is more often connected with movements backward than forward. He spoke with contempt of Comenius, sense realism, and universal education. His was an education for the gentry. "I call, therefore, a complete and generous education, that which fits a man to perform justly, skillfully, and magnanimously all the offices, both private and public, of peace and war." [10]

He had little understanding of childhood and advocated that children should learn to despise and scorn their childish and ill-taught qualities. "The end of learning is to repair the ruin of our first parents by regaining to know God aright, and out of that knowledge to love him, to imitate him, to be like him as we may the nearest by possessing our souls of true virtue, which being united to the heavenly grace of faith makes up the highest perfection." [11]

As a concession to the activities of the English gentlemen of public affairs, he advocated riding, fencing, wrestling, sailing, music, and travel in England followed by the Grand Tour. "But if they desire to see other countries at three or four and twenty years of age, not to learn principles, but to enlarge experience and make wise observations, they will by that time be such as shall deserve the regard and honor of all men where they pass, and the society

[10] John Milton, *Of Education* (London: John Dring, 1673), p. 102.
[11] *Ibid.*, pp. 97–98.

and friendship of those in all places who are best and most eminent. And perhaps then other nations will be glad to visit us for their breeding or else to imitate us in their own country." [12]

BARUCH SPINOZA

Baruch (Benedict) Spinoza (1632–1677) has been called "the most noble and lovable of the great philosophers." [13] He was born in Amsterdam in 1632 of a propserous Jewish commercial family that had fled from Portugal in the sixteenth century. He was excluded from the Jewish community in 1656 as a free thinker. As his ideas were not acceptable to either Christian or Jew, he spent the greater part of his life in comparative seclusion in Amsterdam, The Hague, and their environs, grinding lenses and writing his great works, most of which were published after his death. He received many a distinguished visitor and kept up a voluminous correspondence with most of the great minds of his day.

His thought was influenced by Jewish moral and intellectual tradition, especially the works of Hasdai Crescas (1340–1410) of Barcelona who opposed the influence of Aristotle. Like Bruno (1548–1600) he embraced a pantheistic doctrine in which God and Nature are one. The form of his greatest work, *The Ethics,* published posthumously in 1677, follows the injunction of Hobbes that statements of epistemological problems should be in geometric form. He read Descartes with great interest and wrote a treatise on the *Principles of Descartes' Philosophy* which he published in 1670. Although his monistic theories differed from Cartesian dualism, he adhered strictly to Descartes' canons of clarity and deductive rigor.

Beginning with Descartes' definition that substance is that which requires nothing but itself to exist, he proceeded to show that body, extended substance, and mind, thinking substance, are but modes of substance and that, therefore, there can be but one Substance having two aspects, mind and body, which Spinoza called "God." There is no body without mind, nor mind without body.

[12] Edward E. Morris, *Tractate of Education by John Milton* (New York: Macmillan and Co., 1895), p. 25.

[13] Bertrand Russell, *A History of Western Philosophy* (New York: Simon and Schuster, Inc., 1945), p. 569.

God, nature, and the universe are all one. Although minds and bodies are independent of each other, whenever something happens in one, it also happens in the other. This doctrine is called psychophysical parallelism. Man is a form of God, of the universal substance of reality, more complex than other objects of nature, and conscious of his own acts.

During his lifetime Spinoza felt the sting and persecution of warring religious sects. He, therefore, like Hobbes, wished to strengthen the power of the secular arm which would be indifferent to matters of religious doctrines and would guarantee freedom of thought. "A subject," he writes, "obeys the orders of the sovereign power, given for the common interest, wherein he is included."[14]

"If men's minds were as easily controlled as their tongues, every king would sit safely on his throne, and government by compulsion would cease. . . . However, no man's mind can possibly lie wholly at the disposition of another. . . . For this reason," he continues, in the spirit of Locke, "government which attempts to control minds is accounted tyrannical . . . and a usurpation of the right of subjects to seek to prescribe what shall be accepted as true . . . or what opinions should actuate men in their worship of God. All these questions fall within a man's natural right, which he cannot abdicate even with his own consent."[15]

"Education," he concludes, "must be understood and estimated through the study of human nature. . . . As a process which affects every member of society and which makes every man responsible not only for his own development, but for that of his neighbor, education is the prerogative of government."[16]

The function of government, he believed, was not to found and maintain schools but to allow all to teach publicly at their own cost and risk.[17]

According to Spinoza, "the end for which man is to be educated is that he may exercise his power to the utmost."[18]

[14] Baruch Spinoza, *Tractatus Theologico-Politicus,* Ch. XV. Quoted in William L. Rabenort, *Spinoza as Educator* (New York: Teacher's College, Columbia University, 1911), p. 81.

[15] *Ibid.,* Ch. XX. Quoted in Joseph Ratner, *The Philosophy of Spinoza* (New York: The Modern Library, 1927), p. 333.

[16] *Ibid.,* Ch. XVIII. Quoted in Rabenort, *op. cit.,* p. 84.

[17] See Dagobert Runes (ed.), *Spinoza Dictionary* (New York: Philosophical Library), p. 15.

[18] Rabenort, *op. cit.,* p. 76.

The end of education determines the method which in turn determines the subject matter. These aims he considered to be first, the knowledge of nature both as extension and thought, and second, social participation by a regulation of the passions to secure a happy life. "It is as an element of the social environment that the teacher finds justification." [19]

"The teacher is that person to whom is delegated by reason of special fitness for the task, that function of society which consists in aiding men to exercise their power rationally. In a sense the teacher is the curiculum. Because he understands the learner and their common environment, he is able to interpret and direct interaction." [20]

Experience and reason as the two forms of consciousness are the basis for Spinoza's classification of the educational process. He believed that the natural abilities of men are too dull to grasp total reality at once, but they approach it by constant consulting, listening, and debating. As the criteria for method lie in human nature which is applicable to teacher and pupil alike, Spinoza declared "that the teacher has the right to choose his own method. His are the ideas to be set forth and his the manner of their exposition." [21]

Spinoza was above all a moral philosopher. He believed that God decrees that the good prosper while the wicked come to naught. Therefore, there should be no sentimental attitude toward misconduct, but it should be treated as a physician treats a pathological condition: cured if possible; removed if necessary. Since no man will live long enough to understand the reason behind every virtuous act, Spinoza recommends the regulation of conduct by rote.

Although now considered to be one of the greatest of all philosophers, his work remained neglected until the close of the eighteenth century when it was rediscovered by Goethe, Shelley, Coleridge, and other romantic writers. Johann G. Herder (1744–1803) was particularly influenced by him. In the nineteenth century he was greatly admired, if not always understood, by rationalists, materialists, and mystical pantheists. F. A. Lange (1828–1875), the neo-Kantian, labeled Spinoza's views correct, as did the idealist Leon

[19] *Ibid.*, p. 73.
[20] *Ibid.*
[21] *Ibid.*, p. 68.

Brunschvicg (1869–1944). He was a precursor of the Higher Criticism of the Bible and advocated liberalism and toleration. He is most often considered a "realist" because of his insistence that the study of nature consists of the examination of the history of nature and the deduction of definition of natural phenomena according to certain fixed axioms.

JOHN LOCKE

John Locke (1632–1704) was born of Puritan ancestry in the same year as Spinoza. From fourteen to twenty, he was enrolled in Westminister School under the direction of Dr. Busby, the notorious flogger, where he studied Latin and Greek exclusively. From this experience he developed a revulsion to boys and schools which he carried throughout life. He obtained a studentship at Christ Church College, Oxford, where he remained for over thirty years. He became confidential secretary to the Earl of Shaftesbury and the tutor to his heir and grandson. He spent four years in France and then went to Holland where he wrote his principal philosophical and educational treatises. Returning to England with William of Orange, he held important government posts and received many honors.

Locke's thought was greatly influenced by Rabelais (1483–1553) and by Bacon's empiricism. Like Bacon and Hobbes his interests were practical and social. His theory of the "tabula rasa" had been anticipated by Comenius, but it is doubtful whether Locke had ever read his great work on method. He followed Descartes in the belief that man is both a sensory and a rational creature, and his educational writings show the influence of Montaigne and the practice of the best English families.

Following the sensory origin of knowledge advocated by Bacon, he destroyed forever, in its older form, the theory of innate ideas as held by Descartes and the Cambridge Platonists. He argued that innate ideas may not conflict with each other and should also be found in idiots, infants, and all primitive peoples. They should be in the minds of all peoples at all times and in all places and immediately perceived as necessary, self-evident propositions. As a physician and anthropologist he could find no evidence that this was true. The study of history from Greek and Roman antiquity and the works of the greatest philosophers show great variations, so that he concludes that not a single idea known to the human mind can be said to be universal and therefore innate. By doing this he gave the science of education a new beginning.

He suggested a new explanation for the growth of knowledge, insisting that all knowledge comes from experience—reflection and observation being the chief instruments. He was inclined to nominalism since he held that general ideas, being framed by us, are nominal rather than real.

The mind in its original state he likened to a sheet of white paper, a "tabula rasa," a wax tablet upon which impressions are made through the senses, thus forming mental images. The "tabula rasa" theory discredited the rationalistic claims that all knowledge can be deduced from "first principles."

He justified the acceptance of Christianity as reasonable and useful in practical living, and is sometimes classified as a deist.

Locke concluded that we have an intuitive knowledge of ourselves, a demonstrative knowledge of the existence of God, and a sensitive knowledge of the material world.

His *Treatise on Government* (1690) advocated the rights of the individual and the need to limit the powers of the throne. He influenced the writings on constitutional government. He argued against the divine right of kings and declared that in a state of nature all men are free, independent, and equal, thus setting forth a naturalistic basis for the personal and civil rights of the individual. In a letter on toleration, he insisted upon the rights of conscience, saying: "Absolute liberty, just and true liberty, equal and impartial liberty, is the thing we stand in need of."[22]

Locke's principles of psychology and education are to be found in the *Essay Concerning Human Understanding* (1687), in *Some Thoughts Concerning Education* (1693), and a number of posthumous essays. He declared the doctrine of human depravity to be false since there were no "innate ideas." If such ideas existed the child would be a miniature adult, but since they do not, he differs radically from his elders. Locke's position thus opened the way to a more realistic study of human development. He had, however, little notion of the function of heredity. Believing that all

[22] John Locke, "Letter on Toleration," quoted in Frederick Eby and Charles F. Arrowood, *The Development of Modern Education*, p. 366.

children are equal at birth, he maintained that whether they are good or bad, useful or worthless, depended on education.

Education, for Locke, was primarily a moral discipline based upon the habit of self-control rather than on a process of intellectual instruction. His observations regarding perception, reasoning, doubting, and other mental processes were keen. All intellectual capacities he thought are the result of habit. It appears that he did not believe in general powers of the mind, although Graves credits him with having first stated the doctrine of formal discipline.[23]

"We are born with faculties and powers capable almost of anything, such at least as would carry us farther than can easily be imagined: but it is only the exercise of those powers, which gives us ability and skill in anything and leads us toward perfection. . . . As it is in the body so it is in the mind: practice makes it what it is; and most even of those excellencies, which are looked on as natural endowments, will be found, when examined into more narrowly, to be the product of exercise and to be raised to that pitch only by repeated actions."[24]

"Strength of memory," he wrote, "is owing to a happy constitution, and not to any habitual improvement got by exercise."[25] He would train the powers of attention by having the learner "buckle" to the things to be learned, but he insisted that the teacher should have great skill in getting and maintaining attention through an appeal to the child's sense of usefulness and power. "The Great Skill of a Teacher is to get and keep the Attention of his Scholar; whilst he has that, he is sure to advance as fast as the Learner's Abilities will carry him."[26]

He was among the first to recognize the factor of readiness. "The fittest Time for Children to learn any Thing is when their Minds are in Tune and well dispos'd to it."[27] Human actions, he believed, are motivated by inner needs such as hunger, cold and sleep, by

[23] Frank Pierpont Graves, *History of Education during the Middle Ages and the Transition to Modern Times* (New York: The Macmillan Company, 1920), p. 309.

[24] John Locke, *Conduct of the Understanding*, Secs. 4 and 6, quoted in Eby and Arrowood, *op. cit.*, p. 419.

[25] *Ibid.*, p. 410.

[26] *Ibid.*, p. 411.

[27] *Ibid.*, p. 414.

desires to avoid pain or to experience pleasure, and by acquired habits such as the "itch" for power, and many others brought about by custom, example, and education.

Locke could not conceive of a society without an upper and lower class. His discussion of equality seems to have been confined to the upper classes. He was solicitious of improving the condition of paupers as were the other philanthropists of his day. As King's Commissioner for the Board of Trade he drew up a plan for poor relief whereby children of the indigent were to be taken from their parents and to be kept in working schools from three to fourteen years of age after which they were to be apprenticed. They were to be fed on bread and gruel and taught religion, respect for their betters, habits of industry, and the simpler handicrafts. This formula of simple piety, handicrafts, and respect for superiors is repeated over and over in western Europe today and has a considerable following in America.

His principal concern was with the education of the future gentlemen, for he maintained that if they are once set right they will quickly bring the rest in order. With Milton he opposed and ridiculed the practices of the eighteenth-century grammar schools, and branded them as producers of vice, trickery, violence, and self-conceit. He recommended private tutoring as the best kind of pre-university education.

His curriculum included everything which would make a youth a gentleman of virtue, wisdom, breeding, and learning, for he maintained a virtuous man is worth more than a great scholar. With Rabelais and Montaigne he insisted that all learning should be made not only pleasant, but easy. The guiding principle for curriculum building was usefulness, but usefulness to the future citizen and not to the child. He proposed the elimination of Greek for the general student and would retain only such study of Latin as would give the student the ability to read a Roman author. He stressed the study of English and foreign languages, especially French. There was no place for poetry or music in his plan. He criticized the stress on linguistic education in his day, pointing out that children possess ability to learn words but frequently do not attach the right meanings to them. Rhetoric, he declared, was a powerful instrument of error and deceit.

He recommended the study of mathematics to improve children's ability to reason and to train in methods of consecutive and exact thought, for he insisted the method of mathematics when once learned, could be transferred to the learning of other subjects.

He urged the inclusion of physical education as basic to the development of a sound mind in a sound body. Boys were to swim and to exercise in the open air, and to engage in manual arts, gardening, and painting for health and recreation. Other subjects included geography, geometry, chronology, natural philosophy, ethics, and psychology. Travel in England and on the continent completed formal education.

Locke's views were so comprehensive that materialists and idealists, sensationalists, empiricists, and rationalists, formal disciplinarians and utilitarians found support in them. His influence in England can be readily seen in the writings of Hume and Berkeley. In France he influenced the Enlightenment, and in America, Franklin and Jefferson owe much to his writings. Basedow, Pestalozzi, and Herbart carried his ideas into education. He was not without his critics, among them being Leibnitz who wrote a rebuttal to "The Essay" but did not publish it because it was finished just at the time of Locke's death. It was published after the death of Leibnitz in 1865.

Locke transformed the ideas of men by declaring that many errors are due to mistaking words for things, that minds can be described as accurately as plants and animals, that the findings of philosophers should keep close to common sense, and that problems in philosophy are due more often to confusion among philosophers than to difficulties inherent in these problems.

GOTTFRIED WILHELM LEIBNITZ

Gottfried Wilhelm Leibnitz (1646–1716) was born at Leipzig, the son of a university professor at the time that Germany was recovering from the Thirty Years War. He was not only considered one of the greatest mathematicians and philosophers of his day, but was also trusted with numerous diplomatic missions to London and Paris. He served the Elector of Mainz, the Duke of Brunswick, was librarian at Hanover, and founded the Prussian Academy of Science in Berlin in 1700. He has been called the most universal genius of the modern world and has been compared to Newton (1642–

1727) with whom he made extensive contributions to mathematics including the theory and notation of the calculus. His *Monadology* (1714) supplied the roots of symbolic logic. He constructed an idealistic metaphysic balancing the empiricism of Berkeley and the rationalism of Descartes.

The entire universe, he maintained, is built on units of force called monads (force atoms) which are eternal and unchangeable or indestructible. Monads have different degrees of clearness, the clearest being God and the least clear being inorganic matter. Living beings contain queen monads or souls. Each monad contains the entire universe within itself. All that it becomes was contained in it from the beginning. Monads are, therefore, "windowless." They do not influence each other but appear to do so. All monads are continually active and dynamic with God the supreme Monad. Man is a construct of monads, having a central monad or soul. Every monad acts in harmony with every other monad because God has so constructed the universe. Man, like all nature, is subject to law, order, and uniformity. Leibnitz reduced matter to force. He explained that this was the best of all possible worlds, though not perfect since God had limited himself in creating it. These limits result in suffering and sin, but "evil" serves to make "good" good. This idea has been satirized by Voltaire (1696–1778) in *Candide.*

With regard to free will, he maintained that man is never entirely free to decide one action from another from a wide range of possibilities, but must strive to be guided by a clear ideal. He decides on the desire which is strongest and acts accordingly. Man's acts are determined by his own inner nature, and he is therefore free.

In this way Leibnitz believed he had saved Christianity and had developed a concept of God which would avoid the criticisms heaped upon the philosophy of Spinoza, and would be acceptable to scientists and all religionists alike. A comparison of some of the basic notions of the two philosophers will illuminate this point.

LEIBNITZ	SPINOZA
There must be numberless substances (monads) all different.	There can be only one substance.
God is the creator of his substances.	God is identical with the one substance.

LEIBNITZ (*cont.*)	SPINOZA (*cont.*)
God is a free agent who chooses among possibilities to bring about the best possible world.	God cannot possess an individual will.
Man enjoys free will of the traditional pattern.	There is no such free will. Virtuous man struggles to make himself free by gaining an understanding of the nature and origins of the passions from which he suffers.
The explanation of anything involves mentioning its cause. There is a succession of causes leading back to a necessary Being which is the First Cause.	The explanation of anything involves mentioning its cause. The "cause of itself" is that whose essence involves existence. That which is its own cause involves reference only to itself. God, Substance, and Cause of Itself are identical.

Leibnitz's theory of the self-contained monad which could not be influenced from outside countered the psychology of John Locke. Kant accepted his view of experience but criticized his over-reliance on human reason. His theories, however, formed the springboard for the absolute idealism of Fichte and Hegel which later formed the pattern for the Prussian system of education and influenced the American public schools through Mann and Harris.

GEORGE BERKELEY

George Berkeley (1685–1753) was born in the county of Kilkenny, Ireland. He entered Trinity College, Dublin, in 1700 and remained till 1720 as student, master, and fellow. In 1728 he immigrated to Rhode Island with what he considered to be a promise of support to accomplish his dream of converting the American Indians to Christianity and establishing a university in Bermuda. When the support was not forthcoming he gave his library and real estate to the college of New Haven, now Yale University, and returned to England, becoming bishop of Cloyne, Ireland, in 1734.

Berkeley read Descartes, Spinoza, and Locke. Among his earlier works perhaps the most important is *An Essay Toward a Theory of Vision* (1709). He extended and modified Locke's theory that all ideas come through sense experiences by maintaining that we cannot know anything beyond that which is in the mind. Things immediately perceived are real things, they are ideas which exist only in the mind; therefore "to be is to be perceived." Reality is of two kinds: *spirits* which are active or causally productive, indivisible and incorruptible; and *ideas* which are passive and inert, fleeting and perishable. The mind of God sustains the many ideas which constitute the frame of the world. There is a *rerum natura* in the mind of God involving ideas of hardness, force, heat, and the like. God is the Supreme Spirit and source of everything that is in the universe. What is perceived in the mind of God exists even if no human knower perceives it.

By such reasoning he believed he had solved the problem of Descartes (mind and matter are two secondary substances coming from the primary substance, God) and of Spinoza (mind and matter are two aspects of the same substance, God). He also considered that he had dealt a death blow to atheism by asserting that matter is an idea in the mind of God.

His theory of knowledge has been called realism and sometimes nominalism, but his metaphysic labels him an idealist. The idealism of Berkeley differs from that of the classical Greeks who considered ideas to exist apart from minds. Berkeley is considered to be an objective idealist.

His contributions lay in his recognition of the diverse use of language: expository, descriptive, hortatory, etc., his substantial refutation of the Cartesian dualistic metaphysics, and the cue he gave to phenomenalism when he maintained that to say something now perceived exists is to say that if an observer were properly situated he would perceive it. The philosophy of J. S. Mill and Bertrand Russell reflect the influence of Berkeley's thought.

DAVID HUME

David Hume (1711–1776) was born in Edinburgh of a family in comfortable circumstances. After unsuccessful attempts at the law and in business he decided to become a scholar. During three years sojourn in France he outlined his major philosophical works and published his *Treatise of Human Knowledge* about a year after his return to Great Britain. The work was stillborn. He spent the remaining years of his life in writing, as a tutor, and in diplomatic and military missions. His *History of England* won him immediate success and established him as a historian. At his death he was much beloved for his kindness and was recognized as one of the foremost men of genius of his time.

Founding his thinking on the sense-empiricism of Locke, he agreed with Berkeley that the immediate facts of experience are sense impressions and that matter beyond sense impressions is not verifiable. There is in Hume's view, no certain knowledge of either material or spiritual substance. There is no material world and no mind, just a succession of impressions, a stream of ideas, one following the other. We cannot prove the cause of these ideas. The idea of necessity and cause which men hold are the result of the observation of the uniformity of nature. As a phenomenalist he could, therefore, record only the succession of phenomena.

Hume carried his skepticism into the realm of religion and ethics. He taught that belief in God, who is to be considered as the active principle of the universe, comes not from reason, but from a desire for happiness and a fear of death. Ethical principles are founded upon what is agreeable or disagreeable, and the dictates of the moral law are the dictates of social utility.

When philosophy began to abandon revelation as the source of all knowledge it set up the human mind in its place. Locke insisted that the powers of the human mind itself should be studied. Berkeley and Hume began with Locke and carried the theory to its ultimate conclusion. Berkeley abandoned the idea of matter but distinguished between the mind itself and what was in the mind. Hume denied mind as an independent entity and left man standing alone. Subsequent philosophy has largely been devoted to supporting or to disproving his theories. Kant and Mill were directly influenced by his thought and utilitarians, positivists, and phenomenalists owe much to his writings.

BENJAMIN FRANKLIN

Born in Boston, Benjamin Franklin (1706–1790) soon removed to Philadelphia where he quickly established his reputation as a printer, writer, scientist, and statesman. He had little formal education and cannot be considered a philosopher in the traditional sense of the word. His chief contribution to education and to politics was his application of the theories of others to cultural institutions. Being largely self-taught he advocated utilitarian and practical education over the traditional humanistic curriculum, and followed the ideas of Bacon, Defoe, and Comenius. He advocated the teaching of the vernacular and together with William Smith and Henry Melchior Muhlenberg proposed the establishment of charity schools to teach English to the German population of Pennsylvania as a means of unifying the colony.

Daniel Defoe's (1659–1731) *Essay on Projects* had considerable influence on his formulation of the Proposals for the Academy of Philadelphia (1743). He wrote: "The Good Education of youth has been esteemed by wise men in all ages, as the surest foundation of the happiness both of private families and of commonwealths. Almost all governments have therefore made it a principal object of their attention, to establish and endow with proper revenues, such seminaries of learning, as might supply the succeeding age with men qualified to serve the public with honor to themselves, and to their country." [28]

The wide scope of his proposed curriculum is well set forth in his *Constitution of the Public Academy in the City of Philadelphia.*

As nothing can more effectually contribute to the cultivation and improvement of a country, the wisdom, riches and strength, virtue and piety, the welfare and happiness of a people than a proper education of youth by forming their manners, imbuing their tender minds with principles of rectitude and morality, instructing them in the dead and living languages, particularly in their mother tongue and all branches of liberal arts and sciences; for attaining these great and important advantages so far as the present state of our infant country will admit, and laying a foundation for posterity to erect a seminary of learning more extensive and suitable to their future circumstances; an Academy for teaching the Latin and the Greek languages, the English tongue grammatically, and as a language, the most useful foreign languages, French, German, and Spanish; as matters of erudition naturally flowing from the languages, history, geography, chronology, logic and rhetoric, writing, arithmetic, the several branches of the mathematics, natural and

[28] Quoted in Frederick C. Gruber (ed.), *The Good Education of Youth,* (Philadelphia: University of Pennsylvania Press, 1957), p. 5.

mechanical philosophy, drawing in perspective, and every other part of useful learning and knowledge shall be set up, maintained and have continuance within the City of Philadelphia.[29]

Because of Franklin's insistence on the non-interference of dogmatic religion in education, the College of Philadelphia, now the University of Pennsylvania, is the only colonial college to have been established without denominational affiliations. He was one of the strongest advocates of Locke's theory of the social contract which is reflected in the Declaration of Independence and in the Constitution of the United States.

JEAN JACQUES ROUSSEAU

Jean Jacques Rousseau (1712–1778) was born in Geneva of a poor but highly respected Calvinist family. As his mother died when he was a week old, he was brought up by his father, an eccentric watchmaker with a passion for reading which Rousseau soon acquired. At ten his father deserted him, and he was sent to boarding school for three years to receive the only systematic education he ever had. Being unsuccessful as an apprentice he became a vagabond wandering through France and Italy where he was converted to Catholicism which he later deserted for deism. He came to Paris where he earned a meager living as a copyist, musician, and writer, and in spite of his eccentricities was accepted into the circle of the leaders of the Enlightenment. Although his reading was desultory it included the works of the principal philosophers from Plato to his own time. The works of Montaigne, Locke, Voltaire, and Defoe probably made the greatest impression upon him.

In 1762 he published two of his greatest works in which he wrestled with two seemingly irreconcilable problems. "Man is born free, but everwhere he is in chains" is the opening cry of the *Social Contract*. "All is good as it comes from the hand of God" declares the *Emile*. The problem might be joined thus: What is man's relation and responsibility to the state, and how can a child born into such a state be reared as to be uncorrupted by the vices of civilization?

Briefly, men become social beings only by associating with each

[29] *Ibid.*, pp. 5–6.

other. This association especially in its social and political aspects is called the "state." In the course of time the state became corrupted and could no longer save itself. Society can only renew itself through the proper education of boys according to nature. Only thus can man develop fully and harmoniously. Up to the age of fourteen the child should be allowed free play and to have experience with nature without adult interference, except that the teacher should set up desirable situations to encourage the pupil to right action. At the age of fourteen there will come a great spiritual and moral awakening, and the youth will feel love and justice for himself. Girls should be trained to be docile, to serve men, and to make them happy.

Rousseau differed from Locke in many fundamental ways. With regard to the state, Locke offered a practical common-sense solution to justify the political, economic, and religious organization of his day. God created man, and not only gave him the whole world for his use but also endowed him with certain rights such as life, liberty, and property which could not be taken away from him. Men formed governments by social contract to guarantee (secure) these divine rights which belong to all gentlemen, not only to kings. When governments no longer foster these natural rights, it is man's duty to rebel and to set up such governments as do. Locke's theory is thoroughly individualistic, Protestant, and capitalistic. Private rights are morally grounded in the will of God, and are superior to law and order.

On the other hand, Rousseau contrasts the civil state with the state of nature. In the state of nature there is no justice because there are no laws; there is no equality because each differs in his ability to grab and to retain; there is no freedom, only license, because each man strives to satisfy his own desires. There is no morality among men without government.

The state is primary. It creates conventions, civilization, culture, even reason. Social conventions decide between right and wrong, between good and bad behavior. Only by becoming a citizen can one become a man. The individual cannot be superior to the state of which he is a citizen. The only freedom which exists is *in* and *by* the state. The schools express the will and the wisdom of the community. The teacher is its agent and attempts to bring the individual into conformity with a pattern.

With regard to education, Locke's principal concern was with the English gentleman. Believing that the mind at birth was like a wax tablet, he considered the teacher's function to be to write desirable impressions of the outside world upon it. The purpose of education was practical in this sense and was designed to achieve the happiness of the individual through experience with nature and society by means of private tutors and travel.

Rousseau stated but did not solve the relationship between freedom on the one hand and imposed authority and required obedience on the other. He showed the necessity for attention to individual differences on the ground that unless we know what he is now, we cannot make a pupil what he ought to be. He recommended the elimination of terms of external coercion such as duty, obedience, and obligation from the vocabulary and advocated that from earliest infancy a child should learn to accept responsibility and be motivated by an internal sense of duty. His method was naturalistic, but his curriculum was traditional. The purpose of the school is to help the child make these necessary adjustments. On the whole, Rousseau believed, society's influence is evil. Therefore, he prescribed that the child be educated apart from society: from birth to four years his activities should be largely physical to develop the body; the period from five to twelve should be spent in acquiring knowledge of the world through sensory impressions; from thirteen to fifteen is the period to begin intellectual training through books and the time to learn a trade. This ends the period of his natural education apart from society. During the last period of formal education, from fifteen to twenty, the youth should come into contact with his fellow men where he would learn the great moral and spiritual principles of sympathy, goodness, and service. As can be readily seen, Rousseau revolted against his precarious education by constructing a romantic picture of what it might have been under ideal circumstances.

Rousseau was one of the greatest creative geniuses of modern times. His thoughts were often paradoxical and extreme. Taken together they made little "common sense"; they were absurd, but never ridiculous. He fought for unity as well as diversity among men; for individual freedom as well as for the authority of an absolute general will. His influence on modern thought has been considerable. Kant, who was so methodical that the people of

Twenty-five Centuries of Educational Thought CHART 4: RATIONALISM AND THE ENLIGHTENMENT

1500 1600 1700 1800	
SIR FRANCIS BACON 1561-1626	Inductive method; Father of Modern Science
GALILEO GALILEI 1564-1642	Scientific interpretation of universe
CORNELIUS JANSEN 1585-1638	Augustinian; Jansenists; severity of discipline
THOMAS HOBBES 1588-1679	"Leviathan"; men surrender liberty to State; naturalism
JOHANN AMOS COMENIUS 1592-1670	First sense realist; "Orbis Pictus"
RENE DESCARTES 1596-1650	Mind-body dualism; "Cogito ergo sum"
GEORGE FOX 1624-1691	Founded Society of Friends; rated all institutions low
BARUCH SPINOZA 1632-1677	Monist; pantheist; "God intoxicated"
JOHN LOCKE 1632-1704	Followed Bacon, Hobbes, Spinoza; education of the English gentleman
SIR ISAAC NEWTON 1642-1727	Cartesian Theory of Universal Gravitation; laws of motion
GOTTFRIED LEIBNITZ 1646-1716	Interpreted universe in dynamic spiritual terms
GEORGE BERKELEY 1685-1753	Objective idealist; to be is to be perceived
BENJAMIN FRANKLIN 1706-1790	American patriot, diplomat, scientist, inventor; Academy at Philadelphia
DAVID HUME 1711-1776	Ideas are the lingering images of sense impressions
JEAN JACQUES ROUSSEAU 1712-1778	"Emile"; education according to nature; "Social Contract"; the Rights of Man
CLAUDE A. HELVETIUS 1715-1771	Original equality of men; morals are relative
EDMUND BURKE 1729-1779	Elected representatives to think independently for good of commonwealth

Koenigsberg could set their watches by his movements, failed to take his customary walk on receiving his copy of the *Emile*. His *categorical imperative* derived from Rousseau's dictum that the only absolute good in the universe is the human will governed by a respect for the moral law and a sense of duty. Fichte, Hegel, and others distorted his notion that man could fulfill himself only as part of an absolute state into a philosophy that ended in totalitarianism.

Rousseau believed that man was neither a machine to be conditioned nor a scientific mind, but a feeling heart. Educationally he influenced Pestalozzi, Basedow, and Froebel, and the whole modern trend toward naturalism and the child-centered school.

He was a transitional thinker. He lived at the opening of new worlds: at the beginnings of the rise of the common man. His works were a protest against what had been and a call to what might be. He was the first of the moderns.

SUMMARY

During the period of rationalism and the Enlightenment the following educational ideas were especially emphasized:

BACON and his followers claimed that education should be built upon reason which he based upon empirical data. Comenius advocated and implemented education through the senses.

LOCKE proved, to his own satisfaction at least, the non-existence of innate ideas and first principles.

DESCARTES developed a metaphysical dualism which has been applied to almost every department of human thought and action.

SPINOZA pointed out the importance of the teacher as part of the curriculum and the necessity for establishing aims in teaching.

LEIBNITZ attempted to refute Cartesian dualism, and described man as an organic, self-contained, self-motivated whole. Berkeley's realistic metaphysic and idealistic epistemology laid the foundation for the work of the phenomenologists in philosophy and psychology.

HUME based his ethical principles upon what is agreeable and disagreeable, thus influencing the utilitarians of the next century.

FRANKLIN displayed the American genius for applying principles to practice.

ROUSSEAU stressed, as had never been done before, the emotional nature of man. He believed that a corrupt society can only renew itself by education according to nature. Much of present day naturalism in education springs from him.

BIBLIOGRAPHY

Bacon, Francis, *The Essays, Colours of Good and Evil and Advancement of Learning* (London: Macmillan & Co., Ltd., 1920).

———, *Novum Organum*, 2nd ed., ed. Thomas Fauber (Oxford: Clarendon Press, 1889).

Berkeley, George, *Philosophical Writings*, select. and ed. E. Jessop (New York: Thomas Nelson & Sons, 1952).

Clark, Donald Lemen, *John Milton at St. Paul's School* (New York: Columbia University Press, 1948).

Comenius, John Amos, *The Great Didactic*, trans. and ed. M. W. Keatinge (London: Adam and Charles Black, 1910).

Davidson, Thomas, *Rousseau and Education According to Nature* (New York: Charles Scribner's & Sons, 1898).

Descartes, René, *Philosophical Works*, trans. Elizabeth S. Haldane and G. R. Ross (2 vols.; New York: Dover Publications, Inc., 1955).

Hobbes, Thomas, *Leviathan, on the Matter, Forms and Power of a Commonwealth, Ecclesiastical and Civil*, ed. Michael Oakeshott (Oxford: B. Blackwell, 1946).

Kuhn, Thomas S., *The Copernican Revolution: Planetary Astronomy in the Development of Western Thought* (Cambridge: Harvard University Press, 1957).

Leibniz, Gottfried Wilhelm von, *The Monadology and Other Philosophical Writings*, trans. Robert Valta (London: Oxford University Press, 1925).

Locke, John, *Conduct of the Understanding*, 5th ed., ed. Thomas Fowler (Oxford: Clarendon Press, 1901).

———, *An Essay Concerning Human Understanding*, with prolegomena, biographical, critical, and historical, by Alexander Campbell Fraser (Oxford: Clarendon Press, 1894).

———, *Some Thoughts Concerning Education*, 2nd ed., with introduction and notes by P. H. Quick (Cambridge: Cambridge University Press, 1927).

Martineau, James, *A Study of Spinoza*, 2nd ed. (London: Macmillan & Co., Ltd., 1883).

Milton, John, *Milton on Education; The Tractate of Education*, with supplementary extracts from other writings of Milton, ed. Oliver Morley Ainsworth (Ithaca, N.Y.: Cornell University Press, 1928).

Mulcaster, *Mulcaster's Elementarie,* ed. E. D. Campagnac (London: Oxford University Press, 1925).

Rabenort, William Louis, *Spinoza as Educator* (New York: Teachers College, Columbia University, 1911).

Rousseau, Jean Jacques, *Emile* (New York: E. P. Dutton & Co., Inc., 1950).

Stephen, Sir Leslie, *Hobbes* (London: Macmillan & Co., Ltd., 1904).

Woody, Thomas (ed.), *Educational Views of Benjamin Franklin* (New York: McGraw-Hill Book Co., Inc., 1931).

Chapter VI

Humanitarianism, Idealism, and Realism

PREVIEW

In Chapter VI we shall trace the development of humanitarianism and the interest in the welfare of the common man in Pestalozzi, Froebel, and Mill. We shall see a growing recognition of the responsibility of the state for the education of its citizens, especially in Fichte and Jefferson. Educational psychology begins to take definite form in Herbart through a systematic study of mental processes and based upon sense realism and the psychologies of Locke and Hume. There is a growing emphasis on a study of the whole child in his total environment especially in Pestalozzi and Herbart. All the thinkers of this period are interested in promoting the good life: Kant by moral precepts, Hegel by conformity to the Absolute, Mill by conditioning, Pestalozzi and Froebel by a mystical interpretation of the child's experiences, and Herbart by pedagogical methods based on psychological principles.

JOHANN BERNHARD BASEDOW

When the Enlightenment came to Germany under the influence of Frederick the Great, King of Prussia (1740–1786), the influence of Rousseau was brought to new philosophical heights by the writings of Kant, and was applied to education in both theory and practice by Johann Basedow (1724–1790).

Born in Hamburg in the humblest of circumstances, Basedow was forced by the harshness of his father to leave home at an early age. His early education was deficient and his character vulgar and unstable, but he was decidedly talented. He prepared for the Lutheran ministry at Leipzig, but abandoned his studies because of his rationalistic and heterodox views. He turned his attention to education and in succession became a private tutor, earned a master's degree, and taught in Denmark. He was particularly impressed by the works of Rousseau, but he was also familiar with Locke and Comenius. His ideas interested his contemporaries who supported him while he wrote two books on method which were published in 1770 and 1774. In them he set forth a complete system of education for boys of the upper and middle classes to the age of eighteen. Under the patronage of Prince Leopold of Anhalt-Dessau he established a small school for boys in Dessau in 1774, which he called the Philanthropinum, where he attempted to carry out the educational ideas of Rousseau. Here he aimed to prepare happy, useful citizens of Europe, to give them knowledge of words and things, morals and reason, social duties and commerce through the method of experience. He recognized the need for industrial training and motor activity, but taught trades not only for practical ends, but also for health and the complete development of the individual. His works were widely read in both Germany and England, and he is sometimes credited with having introduced vocational education as a regular part of the secondary school program.

IMMANUEL KANT

Immanuel Kant (1724–1804) was Professor of Philosophy at the University of Koenigsberg from 1755 to 1797. His early training has been in the tradition of Leibnitz, but later when he read Hume he determined to develop a theory of experience which would avoid the dogmatism of Leibnitz and the skepticism of Hume. This he proposed to do by a careful study (critique) of human reason. His philosophy, often referred to as critical idealism, was brought to completion in his *Critique of Pure Reason* which he published in 1781. In this work he maintained that although all knowledge may begin *with* experience it does not necessarily follow that all knowledge comes *from* experience. The *capacity* for experiencing cannot come from experience *itself*. For example, the capacity to have experiences in time and space is a capacity of the knower and exists before (a priori) the experiences themselves. The content which results is a posteriori (that which follows after) to the experience. Knowledge results from the interplay of both. Just as perception is limited to the number and condition of the sense organs, Kant believed the "perceiving-knowing" relations are determined by the way the mind works. He, therefore, studied and revised the categories of Aristotle's logic, and derived twelve relationships in which experience could be understood. These he arranged in four groups of three.

Quantity: unity, plurality, totality
Quality: reality, negation, limitation
Relation: subsistence and inherence, causality and dependence, reciprocity
Modality: possibility, existence, necessity

These Kant believed to be the general forms (categories) of thought.

Kant demonstrated that since perception and knowing are dependent upon the structure of the knower there can be no knowledge of reality (the thing-in-itself, *das Ding an sich*) beyond experience. In the *Critique of Pure Reason*, Kant thought he had answered the question, "What can I know?"

In the *Critique of Practical Reason* (1788) Kant addressed himself to the question, "What ought I to do?" Kant believed that morality is concerned with what ought to be, not with what is. It is, therefore, not descriptive of human behavior, but is prescriptive and based upon the highest principles. Not pleasure, but duty is the key word; and the call to duty is not conditional, but categorical. This principle of Kant's is known as the *categorical imperative*. Man must feel a moral obligation to the universal moral law. Although he is free to act according to natural desires, he should act because of an inward compulsion to do the right and not because of expediency.

In the *Critique of Judgment* (1790) Kant attempted to answer the question, "What may I hope?" Here again the feeling of the sublime is innate (a priori), and can be awakened by art, nature, and religion. Kant believed in God and the immortality of the soul, but not through a process of reason, but through an act of faith. He had great respect for the human personality as an end in itself and believed that it should not be used by groups for political purposes. He recommended republican civil constitutions for all states, guaranteeing national rights, and the condition of universal hospitality to limit the rights between nations.

Kant gave considerable attention to education in his university lectures and here the influence of Rousseau is most clearly seen. Both agree that pedagogy is a form of human endeavor whose foundation must lie as deep as the nature it attempts to modify; that a fresh start must be made in establishing educational principles beginning with child study; that self-activity is a potent force in education; that natural punishments are most effective, but Kant adds that artificial modes of discipline are also important.

Rousseau starts with society and works back to nature: Kant examines nature and constructively builds upward to an ethically constituted social whole in which moral idealism alone encloses the secret goal of man's pedagogical development. In contrast to Rousseau's statement that "all is good as it comes from the hand of God," Kant believed that man is neither good nor bad at birth, but that the origin of evil is due to the lack of rules in his formative training. For Kant education is a positive constructive force in the formation of human character. Rousseau would ban formal study and schools; Kant regarded the school as a welcoming shelter for a youthful humanity growing into its highest values and beauty.

Regarding the nature of education he wrote: "Pedagogy, or the Science of Education, is either physical or practical. Physical education includes that maintenance which man has in common with animals. Practical or moral education is that by which man is being so formed that he can live as a freely acting being." [1]

"Man needs scholastic culture, or instruction, in order to become qualified for the attainment of all his ends. It gives him a value considered as an individual. But through the culture of prudence he is formed for citizenship; then he attains a public worth. Then he learns not only to use civil society for his purposes, but also to

[1] Edward F. Bucher, *The Educational Theory of Immanuel Kant* (Philadelphia: J. B. Lippincott Company, 1904), p. 134.

conform himself to civil society. Through moral culture he finally attains a value with reference to the whole human race." [2]

With regard to the importance and the aims of education, Kant wrote: "Man can become man through education only." [3] "Behind education lurks the great secret of the perfection of human nature." [4] And he continues, "Man is to develop first his native capacities for the good." [5] "Children should be educated, *not* with reference to their present condition, but rather with regard to a possibly improved future state of the human race,—that is, according to *the idea of humanity* and its entire *destiny*." [6] "The child must also learn to distinguish clearly between knowledge and mere opinion and belief." [7] And finally, "Good education is exactly that whence springs all the good in the world." [8]

In regard to the curriculum, Kant first asked himself: "How long should education continue? Until that time when nature herself has arranged that the human being shall guide himself,—until the development of the sexual instinct,—until the youth himself can become a father and can educate,—until about the sixteenth year." [9] He divides the school into two epochs. "The first epoch—that in which he must show submissiveness and positive obedience; the *second*—that in which he is permitted to make use of his powers of reflection and of his freedom, but under laws. Former—mechanical, latter—moral constraint." [10] The curriculum should be adjusted to the learner. The child "should be instructed only in such things as are suitable for his age." [11] But he was opposed to superficial education. "Thoroughness should be a quality of skillfulness, and gradually become a habit of the mind. . . . It is better to know little, but to know this little well, than to know much and to know it superficially." [12] Although he spoke of intellectual, practical, and moral education he did not conceive of these as special entities for

[2] *Ibid.*, p. 136.
[3] *Ibid.*, p. 107.
[4] *Ibid.*, p. 109.
[5] *Ibid.*, p. 113.
[6] *Ibid.*, p. 116.
[7] *Ibid.*, p. 117.
[8] *Ibid.*, p. 118.
[9] *Ibid.*, p. 129.
[10] *Ibid.*, p. 130.
[11] *Ibid.*, p. 197.
[12] *Ibid.*, pp. 198, 201.

he wrote: "no power of the mind shall be cultivated in isolation, but each with reference to the others; for example, the imagination only for the benefit of the understanding." [13]

With regard to the "work-play" dichotomy he believed that "man is the only animal that must work," [14] but that the adult rides "other hobby-horses." "The child," he wrote, "should play . . . but he must also learn to work." [15] "The school is a forced culture. To lead the child to look upon everything as play is very injurious. There must be a time for recreation, but there must also be a time for work." [16]

Educational method, he maintained, must be transformed from a mere exercise of mechanical rules into a science. "We must have *experimental schools* before we can establish *normal schools*. Education and instruction must not be merely mechanical, but must rest upon principles." [17] There are two kinds of education: negative, which merely prevents faults, and positive which is "guidance in the execution of that which has been taught." [18] He also writes about positive and negative discipline. About the former he writes: "I ought to accustom my pupil to tolerate a restraint upon his freedom, and at the same time lead him to make good use of his freedom." [19] "The will of children should not be broken," but they "are *badly* educated if their wills are gratified, and quite falsely educated if one acts directly contrary to their wills and desires." [20] "The child should be left perfectly free, from earliest childhood, in everything . . . unless the manner of his freedom interferes with that of others. . . . [he] must be shown that he can attain his aims only as he permits others to reach theirs . . . that he is under such constraint as will lead him to the use of his own freedom." [21]

Man is by nature neither moral nor immoral; "he becomes a moral being only when his reason raises itself to the concepts of duty and of law. . . . Everything in education depends upon one thing: that good principles be established and be made intelligible and ac-

[13] *Ibid.*, p. 170.
[14] *Ibid.*, p. 167.
[15] *Ibid.*, p. 166.
[16] *Ibid.*, p. 168.
[17] *Ibid.*, p. 125.
[18] *Ibid.*, p. 127.
[19] *Ibid.*, p. 131.
[20] *Ibid.*, p. 154.
[21] *Ibid.*, p. 132.

ceptable to children. . . . It is discipline and not instruction that should appear first."[22]

Kant's influence on European thought has been great. Herder (1744–1803), the German philosopher and poet, was his pupil. Fichte (1762–1814), Schelling (1775–1854), and Schopenhauer (1788–1860) were stimulated by his ideas. In England, Coleridge (1772–1834) and Carlyle (1795–1881) were his disciples.

THOMAS JEFFERSON

Possibly no man influenced the course of public education in colonial and early federalist America so much as did Thomas Jefferson (1743–1826). He was well educated in the classical and modern languages and in mathematics. Although trained in the law, he was more interested in politics than in legal practice. His religious and humanitarian ideas derived from Joseph Priestly (1733–1804) and his political theories followed the ideas of John Locke and the English liberals rather than those of Rousseau. He was one of the outstanding liberals of his day and was a strong advocate of democracy and the rights of the individual. He "planned the University of Virginia (1818) on the elective principle and when it opened (1825) students were left to choose their studies on the basis of their interest rather than follow a prescribed course, as had been done in other American colleges previously."[23]

He also advocated a system of public education for the state of Virginia. The plan recommended the establishment of local elementary schools open free to all boys and supported by local and state taxes. Secondary schools in each district and a state university were to be built by state funds and supported by tuition and a generous number of state scholarships for poor boys of unusual talent.

Jefferson's thinking with regard to democracy has been one of the strongest influences in the development of American life and thought. He had a firm faith in the ability and goodness of man, in human freedom, and in the possibility of improving human life through law, government, and education.

[22] *Ibid.*, pp. 210, 211, 162.

[23] James Mulhern, *A History of Education* (New York: The Ronald Press Company, 1946), p. 418.

JOHANN HEINRICH PESTALOZZI

Pestalozzi's (1746–1827) writing and work were concerned with the fundamental problem of control: the individual vs. the group, social control vs. natural forces. He believed that the individual was superior to the group, although all should work together for the common good, and that control by the ways of nature took precedence over control by men. His thought was influenced by Rousseau's *Emile* and the works of Kant with which he became acquainted through his friend, Fichte, who in turn formulated a plan for the Prussian system of education based on the principles of Pestalozzi. He was born at Zurich, Switzerland. When the boy was five years old, his father, a competent physician, died leaving him to be brought up by a devoted mother. His early contacts with poverty through visiting his grandfather's parishoners during his summer vacation made him determined to raise the level of the poor from a state of abject poverty to humanity, and to secure a happier and more virtuous life for every individual. After unsuccessful attempts at the ministry and the law he came into possession of a property of considerable size at Neuhof where he decided to become a farmer and to establish an industrial boarding school in 1774. This venture failed in 1780. He had a school at Stanz in 1798, at Burgdorf from 1799 to 1804, and at Yverdon from 1805 to 1825. During much of his life he lived on the edge of poverty. He wrote: "Long years I lived surrounded by more than fifty beggar children. In poverty I shared my bread with them. I lived like a beggar in order to learn how to make beggars live like men." [24]

In his two principal works, *Leonard and Gertrude* (1782) and *How Gertrude Teaches Her Children* (1801), he tells how a proper education reforms a Swiss village and how education according to nature mingled with human affection is practical. Man is a natural (not a supernatural) being; he is the same whether on the throne or in the hut. All must follow the road of nature, but it is not the same road for everybody. He constantly worked against the ignorance, poverty, and injustice of his day. "Man," he wrote, "creates organizations, laws, customs, even religion, but uses

[24] J. H. Pestalozzi, *How Gertrude Teaches Her Children,* trans. L. E. Holland and F. C. Turner (Syracuse, N.Y.: C. W. Bardeen, 1894), p. 9.

them for his own personal and selfish ends rather than for the good of all. We live in a state of institutionalized injustice."[25] He believed that reform begins with the individual and not with the group. The individual must be given the chance and the power to help himself to a harmonious functioning of head, heart, and hand. Pestalozzi was among the first to view education as organic development. He inveighed against the traditional education with its overemphasis on mental discipline and memorization. In his *Swan Song* he wrote, "only that which affects man as an indissoluble unit is educative in our sense of the word."[26] By organic development he implied that general education must precede vocational education, that education should be concerned with growth in knowledge and power rather than with the acquisition of knowledge, that the child's innate capacities should be awakened by a series of experiences arranged according to his maturation, and that method should follow the order of nature.

It is like the art of the gardener under whose care a thousand trees blossom and grow. He contributes nothing to their actual growth; the principle of growth lies in the trees themselves. He plants and waters, but God gives the increase. . . . So with the educator; he imparts no single power to men. He only watches lest external force should injure or disturb. He takes care that development runs its course in accordance with its own law. . . . The moral, the intellectual and practical powers of our nature must, as it were, spring out of themselves for themselves.[27]

Pestalozzi recommended that the curriculum correspond with the three constituents of human nature which he listed as intellectual, practical power, and morality and religion. He stressed the cultivation of the emotions and the need for religious experiences which he said are to be experienced by the example of the teacher and the activity of the learner. Faith, not reason, is the faculty by which man apprehends his Maker.

Basing all learning on sense perception and activity, Pestalozzi developed a curriculum made up of object lessons, development of language skills, arithmetic, geography, music (especially singing), drawing, modeling, geometry, gymnastics, and manual training. He

[25] From *The Evening Hour of an Hermit,* quoted in Robert Ulich, *History of Educational Thought* (New York: American Book Company, 1945), p. 258.

[26] Quoted in Frederick Eby and Charles Arrowood, *The Development of Modern Education* (New York: Prentice-Hall, Inc., 1947), p. 638.

[27] J. H. Pestalozzi, "The Swan Song," in *Pestalozzi's Educational Writings,* ed. J. A. Green (London: Edward Arnold Ltd., 1916), p. 195.

rejected, as did Rousseau, the study of history, myth, and literature since they had no direct connection with sense perception.

His views on education were not clearly stated because he was not always sure of them himself. Eby and Arrowood[28] list his influence as follows:

1. He had an unshakable faith in the power of education.
2. He showed the importance of psychology in education.
3. He demonstrated the organic character of education.
4. He believed that intellectual life begins with sense impressions.
5. He taught that the concrete must always precede the abstract.
6. He believed that human development is a gradual building of power.
7. He considered religion to be a matter of faith and action.
8. He introduced new teaching devices.
9. He based discipline on mutual empathy and understanding between teacher and pupil.
10. He advocated a new system of teacher training.

Pestalozzi has been called "education's most successful failure." He died, revered by all who knew him, but without a full realization of how widespread his influence was to be. He gave rise to the manual-labor movement in education in Europe and America through his friend and associate, Fellenberg (1771–1844). After the Swiss reforms of 1830 his principles were introduced into the educational practice of many cantonal schools. Although there was not much interest in his theories in England and France because of the weight of tradition, the influence of a small group made his ideas known in America where his methods were introduced as early as 1806. The great interest in his method and the growth in its application, however, occurred after 1860. Pestalozzian principles were introduced into the schools of Germany at the insistence of Fichte after 1806.

JOHANN GOTTLIEB FICHTE

Johann Gottlieb Fichte (1762–1814), born in Saxony, studied theology and philosophy, became professor of philosophy at Jena in 1794 and helped to found the University of Berlin where he

[28] Eby and Arrowood, *op. cit.*, pp. 662–666.

served as rector from 1810 to 1812. Like his fellow countryman and philosopher, Kant, Fichte was seeking to find in a new idealism a justification for the deepest yearnings and highest hopes of mankind. He was a friend of Pestalozzi and had visited the great Swiss educator and observed his work. At the height of his career, Prussia was suffering under the defeat inflicted by Napoleon at Jena in 1806. Fichte concluded that the nation had come to this state of abject subjection and humiliation because of the lack of moral and religious convictions. In his *Addresses to the German Nation* (1807) he attempted to rouse his people to a new sense of self-esteem, to a new sense of patriotism, and to a recognition of their destiny.

Beginning with Spinoza's idea that there is one substance in the universe, God, which Fichte interpreted as Spirit, he accepted Berkeley's doctrine that what is beyond us is Absolute Mind, and Kant's dictum of the supremacy of the will. Men, he believed, walk by faith and not by sight; they live by what they believe rather than what they know. These moral interests take precedence over the scientific. Basic reality resides in man's will which is a microcosmic representation of the universal ego, God. The world of experience in space and time is posited by the Absolute Spirit as the objectification of its will. When finite selves come into conflict with each other they must be regulated by morality and law which is the manifestation of this Will. Intelligent citizens, therefore, freely accept the restraining influence of the law as self-limitation and not as externally imposed obstacles to action. Freedom is meaningless unless there is resistance to the exercise of freedom. In every age the Absolute Spirit expresses itself fully in the leading culture. Fichte urged the German people to unite and become the manifestation of this Absolute Will. Such reasoning gave the state a divine purpose and made patriotism a religion. He was the first of the absolute idealists.

Fichte's educational theories derive from the educational writings of the Lutheran reformers, and reflect the rising tide of nationalism. The universal morality of Kant and the humanitarianism of Pestalozzi caused him to state the aims of education in terms of morality with a nod to universal brotherhood, under the leadership of the German people, and to rebel against the bookishness and the harsh and inhuman discipline of the schools.

His efforts in behalf of education served to justify the existing class system of schools, to extend the common school opportunities more widely, and to place the national government in complete charge of education. Although he is said to have advocated the "Einheitsschule," an organization similar in some respects to the American comprehensive high school, it took about a century and a half to come into existence on German soil.

With regard to education and the state, he believed that, although the chief aim of national education is to produce men, not scholars, the scholars are to lead and the others to follow. The state has a right to see that every child is educated. It enforces good manners negatively by legislation and positively by establishing equal rights for all. Nationalism and patriotism, he wrote, are not the final ends of education. It must extend to the whole human race. The state is supreme, and therefore, the school which it establishes is the only educational institution. The state has a right to demand that every child be educated by it.

Education should begin with training the power of sensation, then perception, then abstract relationships, and finally, should equip the child to think and judge for himself. All men have an innate love of the good. Education must eventually turn all men to religion. Education aims to regenerate society and to ennoble the whole human race so that it will be animated by the highest morality and order its affairs according to reason.

The progress of the pupil is not to be measured in terms of what he can repeat, but how fully and independently he can use what he has learned. In *Aphorisms on Education* (1804) he wrote: "To educate a man means to give him the chance of becoming completely master and lord of *all* his powers." [29]

With regard to the curriculum, Fichte believed that education should keep pace with the child's powers. Drawing (perspective), singing, musical instruction, classical languages, ancient history, geography, mathematics, especially Euclid, and modern languages were to be included. The university was to be the most important institution in the state, because it is the visible representation of the unity of the world and the manifestation of God himself.

Mental development and knowledge are only means to practical

[29] G. H. Trumball, *The Educational Theory of J. G. Fichte* (London: The University Press of Liverpool, Hodder and Stoughton Ltd., 1926), p. 154.

moral training. The student should be accustomed by practice to speak the truth and to obey. "Once obedience exists it can be strengthened and elevated by freedom. . . . Obedience is demanded . . . till the ends of education have been achieved."[30] The instinct of respect is ineradicably fixed in human nature. Deliberate attempts to educate the child in virtue will cause hypocrites. By good example he will gradually form standards of self-respect. No rewards, not even praise, should be expected or bestowed. The voluntary worker must learn that he is only doing his duty. His reward is the pleasure of having done something for his community.

Like Plato, Fichte would put educators in place of parents even to the extent of separating the children from their parents to live in an ideal community. If they remained at home, however, he wrote, "it is the duty of parents to limit the freedom of children in so far as it might be detrimental to the aim of education."[31]

Fichte suggested that schools be co-educational at the lower level, but women are not to attend higher institutions. They are not inferior to men, but different. "The wish to make a woman really learned can scarcely occur to any reasonable person."[32]

The teacher, he thought, should be able to control children and should know how to behave before them with restraint. His function is twofold; first, to influence the child's moral development, and second, to train him to see the ideal and to comprehend it by his own efforts. The primary teacher should have a pious heart and a love of mankind; the teacher in the "gymnasium" should be a true scholar. The relation between the teacher and the pupil should be one of continuous conversation.

The influence of Fichte on the thought and the educational systems of the western world has been considerable. In Germany he gave hope and inspiration to such poets and creative geniuses as Herder, Lessing, and Goethe: philosophers such as Schlegel and Hegel extended his philosophy of absolute idealism. Carlyle's *Heroes and Hero Worship* echoes his concept of the incarnation of the absolute Spirit in great human personalities. In America, James expanded his idea that the kind of philosophy one has represents the kind of person one is.

[30] *Ibid.*, pp. 130, 132.
[31] *Ibid.*, p. 128.
[32] *Ibid.*, p. 147.

Within three years after his "addresses" the Prussian school system was an established fact and a model to the world. Mann, Harris, and others studied it and adapted it to the American scene. Illiteracy had all but disappeared, teachers were well selected and trained, humane methods were adopted, and compulsory attendance was required from six to fourteen.

GEORG WILHELM FRIEDRICH HEGEL

G. W. F. Hegel (1770–1831) was born of well to do parents in Stuttgart. He was a fellow student of Schelling at Tübingen and in 1805 attained to a professorship at Jena, a position which he held for one year until the defeat by Napoleon in 1806. He was employed as a newspaper editor and as headmaster of a boys' school until he became a professor at Heidelberg in 1816. Two years later he went to Berlin where he remained until his death. As he was everywhere regarded as the greatest philosopher of Germany, many Americans came to study with him, among whom were Horace Mann, Henry Barnard, and G. Stanley Hall.

His philosophy stemmed from Neoplatonism and derived from Leibnitz. He studied Kant whom he considered too subjective. Fichte had reinterpreted Kant's "thing-in-itself" as an "ego-in-itself," an absolute reason manifesting itself from generation to generation in a superior race. Hegel accepted the idea of universal Will, but concluded that it operated through relationships and that each individual must be considered in relation to this all inclusive "ground-of-the-universe." Universal reason is the "Absolute" moving through eternity in a logical process of evolution and embodying itself in the active universe, creating and realizing itself in objects and institutions.

The all-inclusive "ground-of-the-universe" takes many diverse and even opposing forms, and in the course of history these opposites become reconciled. Reality is thus *process*, moving from the unclear to the more clear. Thinking is an inductive process, new content being assimilated into the old. The true is the whole, a totality which is never reached, but which drives thought on in an endless process. Its method of reconciling contradictions is called "dialectic." In the process of thought man arrives at a concept: for example, "idea." This is called the "thesis." He must now search for its exact opposite, the "antithesis," which in this case Hegel declared to be "nature." We have then "idea" or "spirit" on the one hand and "nature" or "matter" on the other. These opposites can be brought together in a synthesis called "mind." Another example takes as its thesis, "evil." The antithesis is "innocence," that which is non-evil. To possess a knowledge of evil and yet to will to do what is good gives us the synthesis, "virtue."

Other examples are: thesis, "War is evil"; antithesis, "War is good"; synthesis, "Despite the evils of war good comes of it." Thus, Hegel argued that war is justified because it is the way progress is made. The Prussians believed that their state was the instrument for the realization of universal reason which would eventually conquer the world.

Similarly, Hegel argued, man is a microcosm of the macrocosm, God, or Absolute Mind, one of whose attributes is freedom. Man is therefore free to realize himself to the fullest in the development from the primitive toward Absolute Mind. Since an individual can only be considered in relation to others, it follows that the highest freedom is attained when free individuals subordinate individual reason to universal reason. By substituting a materialistic metaphysic for Hegel's idealism, as did Karl Marx, it is easy to follow the Soviet argument that the individual attains his greatest freedom through the state.

Hegel's educational theories grew directly out of his absolute idealism. He considered education to be a life process, a mental discipline which makes man religious, moral, cultured, and rational. Education should be compulsory through the state and for the state because only through education is the Will of God transmitted.

The aim of education is utilitarian in the sense that it is necessary to bring about an understanding of the unity of man with the universal spirit. Education must lead man to break from the natural order to be at home in the intellect. "With the schools begins the life of universal regulation, according to a rule applicable to all alike. For the individual spirit or mind must be brought to the putting away of its own peculiarities, must be brought to the knowing and willing of what is universal, must be brought to the acceptance of that general culture which is immediately at hand." [33]

[33] Georg Wilhelm Friedrich Hegel, *Werke* (Berlin: Duncker, 1832), VIII, 82. Quoted in William M. Bryant, *Hegel's Educational Ideas* (Chicago: Werner School Book Co., 1896), p. 38.

While others in his day were writing about elementary education, Hegel championed the secondary school. He believed that the aim of the school should determine its curriculum. Languages, literature, history, philosophy, and logic were recommended as the best subjects, the latter especially for its mental discipline. Latin and Greek he considered to be especially good, because being dead languages, they impose a barrier between the natural self and the developing mind.

Method, he taught, should be through the child's self-activity, and should be rational, because the child is naturally a rational being, although only potentially so. Learning should be vital and spontaneous and should achieve a synthesis of the child's self-motivation and his respect for the discipline of the school. In the classroom the mind of the teacher and the mind of the pupil are bound together by a principle of knowledge to be taught and learned which constitutes the spiritual mind, the synthesis of the other two minds.

Hegel believed that he had brought about a perfect synthesis of the philosophies of Kant and Fichte and all those who had preceded them. He has been compared to Aquinas for his powers of systematization. His influence has been felt in the thought of the modern world until today. After a temporary eclipse at the beginning of the present century his ideas are experiencing a revival in neo-Hegelianism. In France, Henri Bergson (1859–1941) developed a theory of "creative evolution" and of the *elan vital* (vital force) which derives from Hegel's evolutionism. In Italy, Giovanni Gentile (1875–1944), the facist, and Benedetto Croce (1866–1952), the aesthetician and anti-facist, presented opposite interpretations of Hegel's idealism. His most famous German disciple, Karl Marx (1818–1885), developed what has been called Hegelianism of the left in *Das Kapital.* In Great Britain Samuel Taylor Coleridge (1772–1834), the philosopher and poet, Thomas Carlyle (1795–1881), the historian and essayist, Benjamin Jowett (1817–1898), the classicist, and the philosophers Edward Caird (1875–1908), Edward Herbert Bradley (1846–1924), and George Sylvester Morris (1840–1889) were among his most ardent followers.

In America, Ralph Waldo Emerson (1803–1882) expanded and modified Hegel's idealism into New England transcendentalism in accordance with the intellectual climate of America. Among professional philosophers who wear the tag of Hegelianism were Josiah Royce (1855–1916), Mary W. Calkins (1863–1930), and Henry Harrell Horne (1874–1946). Among American educators who incorporated Hegel's thoughts into American educational theory and practice were Horace Mann (1796–1859), Henry Barnard (1811–1900), and William T. Harris (1835–1909). John Dewey (1859–1952) incorporated Hegel's social evolution into his instrumentalism.

JAMES MILL

James Mill (1773–1836) was born in Scotland and was graduated from the University of Edinburgh. In 1802 he went to London where he supported himself as a journalist and became associated with Jeremy Bentham (1748–1832). In *Analysis of the Phenomena of the Human Mind* (1802) he set forth his psychology which shows clearly the influence of Hume, Hartley, and Locke. He explained all consciousness as the association of ideas, and with Bentham he set forth a utilitarian and hedonistic ethic. According to Mill, there were three stages of moral development; (1) Pleasure or Pain, (2) Praise or Blame, and (3) the Anticipation of Praise or Blame. Thus he made moral values contingent upon consequences in contradistinction to Kant and the German idealists who based morals on principles. With Bentham he supported Bell in the establishment of monitorial schools under the auspices of the National Society for Promoting the Education of the Poor in the Principles of the Established Church throughout England and Wales, and opposed a similar non-conformist organization inspired by Lancaster.

Mill considered education to be a life process, a mental discipline which makes man religious, moral, cultured, and rational. Education should be compulsory through the state and for the state because only through it can the will of God be transmitted. The aim of education is utilitarian. Man should be understood as one with Universal Spirit. He must break with the natural order in order to be at home in the intellect. ". . . the end of education is to render the individual as much as possible an instrument of happiness, first to himself and next to other people." [34]

[34] Quoted in F. A. Cavanaugh, *James and John Stuart Mill on Education* (London: Cambridge University Press, 1931), p. 1.

He conceived of education as an instrument for rendering the mind, as much as possible, an operative cause of happiness. Education must make man cognizant of real knowledge, the properties of objects, in contradistinction to supposed knowledge which does not correspond to physical reality. Thus education should promote a knowledge of things. The business of education is to make certain feelings or thoughts take place instead of others. Education is the best means for rendering the human mind the cause of human happiness.

Mill believed that everything should be taught through the "universal principle of association." Since the child is naturally a rational being, although only potentially so, method should be rational, but should be vital and spontaneous, encouraging the child's own initiated activity. Mill also believed that instruction was a personal matter between the instructor and his pupil, and that by manipulating the pupil's experience the teacher could control his entire development. Seldom does an educational theorist have an opportunity to put his ideas to the test in so intensive a fashion as did James Mill in the education of his son, John Stuart Mill (1806–1873).

JOHN STUART MILL

Mill and Bentham had a concerted plan to leave "the poor boy a worthy successor to us both." Young Mill began the study of Greek at three and read difficult historical and philosophical works before the average British boy was ready for the public schools. The father devoted much individual attention to the education of his son, believing that by manipulating the pupil's experiences one could control his entire development.

To a certain extent, John Stuart Mill became the sort of man his father intended. He was intellectually a generation ahead of his time, a great logician and a political thinker. But he was underdeveloped sensually, lacking in human sympathy, highly emotional, and insensitive to nature, art, and beauty. A nervous breakdown at twenty proved that, for him, intellectual training was not sufficient. Wordsworth's poetry came as a revelation and showed him that education which appealed only to the intellect was not enough. Of his own education he remarked that it was more fitted to train him to know than to do.

Although he had little personal acquaintance with universities, he was elected rector of St. Andrews in 1865 because of his great reputation as a scholar. In his inaugural address he advocated a broad concept of education, warned against overspecialization, and extolled the four cardinal virtues of the ancients: knowledge, temperance, justice, and generosity. "The proper function of a university in national education . . . is not to make skillful lawyers, or physicians, or engineers, but capable and cultivated human beings." [35]

And of higher education he concluded:

This last stage of general education, destined to give the pupil a comprehensive and connected view of the things which he has already learnt separately, includes a philosophical study of the methods of the sciences, the modes in which the human intellect proceeds from the known to the unknown. We must be taught to generalize our conception of the resources which the human mind possesses for the exploration of nature; to understand how man discovers the real facts of the world, and by what tests he can judge whether he has really found them, and doubtless this is the crown and consummation of a liberal education.[36]

JOHANN FRIEDRICH HERBART

Johann Friedrich Herbart (1776–1841) was born in Aldenberg in northwestern Germany. After attending the University of Jena (1794–1797), he became tutor to the three sons of the governor of Interlocken, Switzerland. While there he visited Pestalozzi and was much impressed by the great Swiss educator, especially by his views on psychology. The two men, however, offer considerable contrast; Pestalozzi was active, impulsive, and developed his psychology in actual practice; Herbart, on the other hand, was thoughtful, scholarly, systematic, and developed his theory of psychology in connection with his teaching of philosophy. While Pestalozzi was interested in the education of childhood and youth through sense perception, Herbart was interested in the intellectual development of the secondary school pupil and the university student. Herbart taught at Göttingen from 1802–1809, in which year he became successor to Kant in the chair of philosophy at Koenigsberg

[35] *Ibid.*, p. 133.
[36] *Ibid.*, pp. 135–136.

where he remained until 1833. Returning to Göttingen in 1833, he remained there until his death in 1841. His careful and systematic mind caused him to avoid the subjective and romantic interpretation of many of his contemporary German philosophers and to combine the rigorous method of Kant and the observational techniques of the English to the sense impressions, which he believed, with Pestalozzi, to be at the basis of all human experience.

The whole work of education, he taught, was to produce the man of culture whose actions would be constantly motivated by the highest ethical values of life. With Rousseau he believed that youth wills the good constantly and consistently, but he believed that youth did not know the good until the teacher had represented it to him and made him aware of it. The purpose of education, therefore, is to develop insights, to instill the proper interests and desires, to give a complete experience of life in its many phases, to mature the judgment, and to impart inner control. The teacher must prepare the learner to accept these aims and help him to realize them through a scientific method of procedure. Then youth will do good because it is his very nature to do so and *morality* which is the end of education will be achieved.

Herbart's idea of "conditioning" the learner to "right action" according to absolute moral principles led him to criticize the "soft pedagogy" of Locke, Montaigne, and Rousseau (see Chapter IV, pp. 72, 102–103, 112).

With regard to the curriculum, Herbart maintained that there were two sources of knowledge—experience with things and social intercourse. From things one gained empirical knowledge and learned the laws of nature; from people one learned the nature of man and man's achievements as recorded in history and geography. He accepted the traditional curriculum of the early nineteenth-century gymnasium: mathematics, history, languages, literature, and religion. Through these subjects the learner's mind was to be lifted from the sensory and concrete level to concepts and judgments. Education was to proceed from the particular to the general. From sympathy for the individual the pupil should learn sympathy for mankind; from relationships with a few, to relationships with society and with God.

Much knowledge, he declared, was acquired before the child came to school and much of this was inaccurate, incomplete, and unsystematic. The amount, kind, and quality of knowledge would vary with each individual. The teacher, therefore, must take individual differences into account when selecting subject matter to correct and supplement the learner's experiences. Herbart gave support to the then popular "cultural epochs theory" that the child's education should recapitulate the history of the race. Accordingly the sequence in history and literature included Homer, the Greek and Roman period, the stories of the Old and New Testatments, the medieval romances, and modern history and literature.

Although Herbart held chairs of philosophy at two distinguished German universities and wrote a number of treatises on the nature and method of philosophy, he is chiefly known for his works on psychology and education. Two views of psychology were current in the early nineteenth century. One held that the soul or mind had certain capacities, functions or activities, instincts, and impulses which gave rise to sensations, perceptions, and intellectual processes. Among those who maintained this position were Spinoza, Rousseau, Pestalozzi, and Froebel. The other viewpoint, held by the English and French associationists and derived from Locke, considered the soul or mind to be empty and devoid of content, nothing being present until the first sensation. Herbart held the latter point of view, although he differed from the strict materialistic interpretation. He carried on his analyses in great detail, agreeing with Locke on the indispensability of sense perceptions. To pure psychology he made four significant contributions: He turned from speculative philosophy to empirical observation and rejected faculty psychology. He demonstrated the physiological basis for psychology, and applied mathematical procedures to the analysis and description of psychological phenomena. His psychology recognized three basic states: feeling, knowing, and willing.

Herbart's theory of mind admitted two states, the conscious and the unconscious. Between the two, Herbart described a threshold which he called the "limen." An object presented to the mind does not remain long in consciousness, but drops into the unconscious which is always active and contains all past experiences, for no object once presented to consciousness is ever forgotten.

Interest is basic to Herbart's principles of learning, because it is the inner force which determines what ideas and experiences will be brought into consciousness and how long they will be retained there. For example, a person is reading a historical novel. Those of his past experiences which bear a relationship to the events about which he reads are brought into consciousness and form a cluster of ideas around the center of interest. The doorbell rings and a stranger asks directions to a nearby address. Historical incidents are put aside and the new center of interest brings forth known facts about the distance, the direction of turns, familiar landmarks, and perhaps incidents and acquaintances along the way. When the stranger leaves and the reader returns to his book, the historical associations again come to the fore, but the experiences of the stranger persist in consciousness for a time, perhaps with mental queries as to whether the information given was accurate and easy to follow before they slip into the unconscious. Thus each center of interest draws from the unconscious whatever past experiences bear a relation to it. This unconscious state has come to be known as the "apperceptive mass" and is related to Herbart's steps of learning: clearness, association, system, and method.[37]

The teacher should frequently bring into consciousness those ideas which he wishes to be cultivated and learned. He should present new material in terms of former experiences so that associations can be formed, and concepts can be clearly formulated. Perceptions in the unconscious are in a highly disorganized state. It is the function of education to systematize them and to derive generalizations for easy recall and action. Thus a right method of instruction will develop readily available systems of thought and action in the stream of consciousness. Herbart, foreshadowing Dewey, made no distinction between content and process. He held that the mind developed by expanding percepts into concepts. Perceptions are primary. Feeling and willing are secondary or derived mental states springing from objects known and the relationship between them. "The circle of thought contains the store of that which by degrees can mount by the steps of interest to desire, and then by means of action to volition."[38]

Herbart is often called the father of the modern science of educa-

[37] See Robert Ulich, *History of Educational Thought* (New York: American Book Company, 1945), pp. 279–280.

[38] Johann Friedrich Herbart, *The Science of Education* (Boston: D. C. Heath & Company, 1902), p. 213. Quoted in Eby and Arrowood, *op. cit.*, p. 772.

tion and of modern psychology. His method of learning was expanded into the five "formal steps" of teaching and learning: preparation, presentation, association, generalization, and application, which became the basis for teaching methods in teacher-training institutions. Zeller and Rein developed a system of Herbartian pedagogy for the elementary school in Germany, and Frank and Charles McMurry popularized and somewhat distorted the method in the United States. James' psychology, especially the theory of the stream of consciousness, owes much to Herbart as does much of Dewey's early writing in the fields of educational philosophy and psychology, although with Colonel Parker he was skeptical of applying the Herbartian pattern strictly to American education. Herbart's influence on American pedagogical thought and practice has been profound. One may say that all essentialists are in his debt and that all who follow the unit method of teaching as developed by H. C. Morrison are modern Herbartians.

FRIEDRICH WILHELM AUGUST FROEBEL

Friedrich Froebel (1782–1852) was born in Oberwiesbach in the Thuringian mountains of southern Germany. His mother died when he was nine months old and his father, the pastor of a large parish, paid little attention to the boy or his education. His stepmother treated him with noticeable contempt. This early unfortunate childhood probably shaped the whole course of his life and was influential in centering his interest on early childhood education, making him sympathetic to and understanding of the problems of the very young. He received his only formal education during the four happy years he lived with his uncle, Pastor Hoffman, from whom he received his religious training and his profound spiritual convictions. After some years of study at Jena he successively taught drawing at the normal school at Frankfort and served as tutor for three boys while he lived and studied with Pestalozzi at Yverdun. In 1817, after having studied at Göttingen and Berlin where he began his attempt to form a synthesis of existing philosophies, he established a school for boys at Keilhaus in Thuringia. He founded the first kindergarten at Blankenburg in 1837 and devoted the rest of his life to early childhood education and the preparation of teachers.

His idealism was in accord with Plato and Goethe, and he absorbed the romantic pantheism of Schelling which identified man and nature. He was a Christian mystic in the primitive sense of that term and revived the early Christian interest in the very young. Although differing in many respects from Rousseau and his teacher Pestalozzi, he shared with them a concern for the continuous development of the individual from infancy. He aimed to rear free-thinking, independent men through developing the inner nature of the child, and believed that all learning should be oriented in the direction of the child's interest and capacities. "Education" for him "consisted in leading man, as a thinking, intelligent being, growing into self-consciousness, to a pure and unsullied, conscious and free representation of the inner law of Divine Unity, and in teaching him the means thereto."[39]

Central to his philosophy of life and education was the unity of all things. In order that the child experience this organic unity of man and nature and learn their interrelationships, he must have experience with things. He must study man in nature, learn the art of cooperation rather than competition, and develop mind and hand simultaneously. For him childhood was an essential phase of human development, a recapitulation of the childhood of the race, and was therefore to be studied and lived for its own sake rather than as a prelude to maturity.

Believing that education must give man free play to develop his creative powers and that "in the development of the inner life of the individual man, the history of the spiritual development of the race is repeated,"[40] Froebel selected materials and activities to this end. Natural science was included in his curriculum because it revealed the workings of God's law; mathematics and languages linked the mind and the natural world; and the arts, drawing and music, were a means for the soul to express itself. All these he approached with religious mysticism. He refused to believe that the child possessed evil tendencies at birth, for God and man were one. Therefore education was an epigenetic unfoldment of the spirit of God within man. He likened education to a garden and believed that the school should cultivate and develop the potential

[39] Friedrich Froebel, *The Education of Man*, trans. William Hailmann (New York: D. Appleton and Co., 1892), pp. 1–2. Quoted in Robert Ulich, *op. cit.*, p. 287.

[40] Froebel, *ibid.*, p. 160.

in each child as a horticulturist tends each tender plant. To this end he used color, motion, spheres, cubes, and other geometric forms and figures for their symbolic meaning. For example, a sphere taught the child the unity of mankind in God.

The idea of growth in a garden was incorporated into the name "kindergarten" which he gave to the institution with which his name is most frequently associated. In fact he recommended that a garden of living things be a part of every kindergarten. Trades were also given a prominent place in his school at Keilhau to show the unity and equality of mental and physical occupations among men.

Possibly Froebel's greatest contribution to educational method was the doctrine that play was itself educational. He believed that play and free self-activity were nature's way of developing the child and that the child's activities should be prompted by the development of his own nature. The parent-teacher role was to keep the child from the possible evil effects of the environment; it was protective rather than prescriptive. With Comenius and Pestalozzi he recognized the importance of the mother in the child's early training. Froebel wrote a songbook for mother and child to sing together, and he showed the value of women as teachers especially in the early grades. All learning, he believed, should take place in a social setting and in harmony with the society to which man belongs, for every act of man has social implications.

Rusk[41] calls Froebel "one of the most idealistic of educational philosophers," and Brubacher[42] writes that the "*Education of Man* is idealism's most notable innovation in education." A comparison with the educational philosophy of Hegel, generally acknowledged to be the greatest idealist philosopher of his day, however, shows interesting points of difference.

HEGEL	FROEBEL
Education helps man break away from his natural self, from the world of nature. (Hegel	Education promotes the harmonious development of the child according to the laws of

[41] Robert R. Rusk, *The Philosophical Bases of Education* (Boston: Houghton Mifflin Co., 1956), p. 8.

[42] John S. Brubacher, *A History of the Problems of Education* (New York: McGraw-Hill Book Company, 1947), p. 124.

HEGEL (*cont.*)	FROEBEL (*cont.*)
limited "nature" to the world of sense experiences, the antithesis of the spirit.)	nature. (Froebel understood nature to cover all the phenomena of the unfolding life of the individual mind.)
The teacher should not study the individual child but seek to bring him out of himself, to seek a new birth through obedience.	The teacher studies the individual following the laws of nature, thus warding off evil. He helps the child's nature unfold to mental and moral maturity.
Latin and Greek are especially good subjects, because, being dead languages, they impose an effectual barrier between the natural self and the developing mind.	The harmonious study of nature, of man in nature, and of man in society is stressed.
Emphasized antagonisms.	Emphasized reconciliation.
The child is to learn the seriousness of work as opposed to play. The two should never be combined.	Child's play is his serious attempt to understand life. His natural expression is a guide to the teacher's methods.
Education for the few. (He knew only boys from 14 to 18).	Chiefly concerned with universal education for young children.
Uncertain about the education of women.	Advocated the education of girls. Recommended the training of young women for teaching.
Hegel's intellect was logical and scientific.	Froebel's method was more intuitive.

Both aimed at giving the young man to himself so that he might attain "true freedom" by realizing his oneness with the universe.

In the same manner it will be interesting to show the points of difference between the idealistic philosophy of Froebel and the realism of Herbart.

HERBART	FROEBEL
Directed the education of adolescents of superior mentality.	Developed (unfolded) the life and powers of the pre-school child.
Herbart's realistic education placed emphasis on factors external to the individual. His psychology suggested the connectionism of the twentieth century.	Froebel's idealism emphasized the unfolding of the inner potential of the individual. His psychology was the forerunner of present day gestalt psychology.
Herbart's method manipulated the reals (externals) with which the mind comes into contact.	Froebel's method was a mystical becoming or unfolding of the inner reality and unity of the individual, an unfolding of what was already enfolded in the germ.

While Herbart influenced the essentialist educators of the twentieth century, Froebel gave considerable impetus to the progressive education movement. His principles of trade training inspired a similar development in Sweden, and in America Felix Adler's Workingman's School introduced the Swedish method where individuals could shape objects to serve human purposes.

His work at Blankenburg inspired the development of early childhood education in America. The first American kindergarten was established in 1855 in Watertown, Wisconsin by Mrs. Karl Schurz who came from Germany with her husband after the abortive Stuttgart revolution of 1848. Five years later, Elizabeth P. Peabody established the first English-speaking kindergarten in Boston.

He inspired Dewey's faith in the importance of play and the creative possibility of activity. However, Dewey did not use objects to develop mystical meanings, nor did he believe that facts must be understood before they could be used, but rather he maintained that facts could be understood through their use.

Froebel, together with Comenius, Pestalozzi, Locke, and Herbart helped to lay the psychological and sociological foundations of education.

Twenty-five Centuries of Educational Thought

CHART 5: HUMANITARIANISM, IDEALISM, AND REALISM

1700 1800 1900	
JOHANN B. BASEDOW 1723-1790	Vocational education
IMMANUEL KANT 1724-1804	Critical idealism; Categorical Imperative
THOMAS JEFFERSON 1743-1826	Followed Locke; founded University of Virginia
JOHANN HERDER 1744-1803	Followed Spinoza; unity of mind and matter
JOHANN HEINRICH PESTALOZZI 1746-1827	Followed Rousseau; combined naturalism and religious mysticism
COUNT DE SIMON 1760-1825	Utopian socialism
JOHANN G. FICHTE 1762-1814	Absolute idealism; Prussian educational system
FRIEDRICH SCHLEIERMACHER 1768-1834	Emotions the fundamental seat of human behavior
GEORG W. F. HEGEL 1770-1831	Absolute idealism; dialectic
FRIEDRICH SCHLEGEL 1772-1839	Romantic school of literature
SAMUEL TAYLOR COLERIDGE 1772-1834	Introduced Kant to England
JAMES MILL 1773-1836	Followed Hume; utilitarianism; friend of Bentham
FRIEDRICH W. J. SCHELLING 1775-1854	Absolute idealism
JOHANN FRIEDRICH HERBART 1776-1841	Realist; educational psychology
FRIEDRICH FROEBEL 1782-1852	Kindergarten
JEREMY BENTHAM 1784-1832	Ethics based on regard for consequences (pleasure-pain)
ARTHUR SCHOPENHAUER 1788-1860	Pessimism
THOMAS CARLYLE 1795-1881	Studied German philosophy, especially Fichte
AUGUSTE COMTE 1798-1857	Positivist; father of sociology
CARDINAL JOHN HENRY NEWMAN 1801-1890	Oxford movement; Roman Catholicism
RALPH WALDO EMERSON 1803-1882	Transcendentalism
LUDWIG A. FEUERBACH 1804-1872	Religious humanism
JOHN S. MILL 1806-1873	Utilitarianism; happiness is the pleasure of enlightened minds

SUMMARY

Chapter VI has shown:

1. How the development of German idealism, through Kant's critical idealism and the absolute idealism of Fichte and Hegel, directly influenced educational thought in England and America, and indirectly inspired fascism, communism, nazism, and existentialism.
2. The importance of early childhood education.
3. The value of free public education by the state for the education of its citizens.
4. The development of an educational psychology based on sense realism and its influence on the connectionist school of psychology and the method of essentialist educators in America.

BIBLIOGRAPHY

Arrowood, Charles Flinn (ed.), *Thomas Jefferson and Education in a Republic* (New York: McGraw-Hill Book Co., Inc., 1930).

Bryant, William M., *Hegel's Educational Ideas* (Chicago: Werner School Book Co., 1896).

Bucher, Edward F., *The Educational Theory of Immanuel Kant* (Philadelphia: J. B. Lippencott Co., 1904).

Burtt, Edwin A., *The English Philosophers From Bacon to Mill* (New York: The Modern Library, 1939).

Cavenaugh, F. A. (ed.), *James and John Stuart Mill On Education* (Cambridge: Cambridge University Press, 1931).

Froebel, Frederick, *The Education of Man,* trans. William Hailmann (New York: D. Appleton and Co., 1892).

———, *Pedagogics of the Kindergarten,* trans. Josephine Jarvis (New York: D. Appleton & Co., 1917).

Green, J. A., *The Educational Ideas of Pestalozzi* (Baltimore: Warwick and York, Inc., 1907).

Henderson, J. C., *Thomas Jefferson's Views on Public Education* (New York: G. P. Putnam's & Sons, 1890).

Herbart, Johann Frederick, *The Science of Education,* trans. Henry M. and E. Felkin with a preface by Oscar Browning (Boston: D. C. Heath & Co., 1895).

Kant, Immanuel, *Kant on Education,* trans. Annette Churton (Boston: D. C. Heath & Co., 1906).
Kilpatrick, William Heard, *Froebel's Kindergarten Principles Critically Examined* (New York: The Macmillan Company, 1916).
Lang, O. H., *Basedow, His Educational Work and Principles* (New York: E. L. Kellogg & Co., 1891).
Luquier, Frederic Ludlow, *Hegel as Educator* (New York: The Macmillan Company, 1896).
Mackenzie, Millicent, *Hegel's Educational Theory and Practice* (London: S. Sonnenschein, 1909).
Pestalozzi, Johann Heinrich, *The Education of Man, Aphorisms,* trans. Heinz and Ruth Norden (New York: Philosophical Library, Inc., 1951).
———, *How Gertrude Teaches Her Children,* 5th ed., trans. Lucy E. Holland and Francis C. Turner and ed. Ebenezer Cooke (London: George Allen & Unwin, Ltd., 1915).
———, *Leonard and Gertrude,* trans. and abr. Eva Channing (Boston: D. C. Heath & Co., 1885).

Chapter VII

Post-Hegelianism and the Century of Darwin

PREVIEW

In Chapter VII we shall trace the development of American philosophies through the writings of six outstanding educational thinkers. Ralph Waldo Emerson was a leader among the New England Transcendentalists who adapted German idealism to American life and thought. American education seized upon Herbert Spencer's social Darwinism to state the aims of education in terms of individual and social welfare. The scientific method began to be applied rigorously to the study of educational problems as in the other behavioral sciences. William James' original mind explored new paths of interrelationship between philosophy, psychology, medicine, and education, and made his theories about the psychology of learning available to the classroom teacher.

Dewey showed the relationship of philosophy to education, and called for a constant reconstruction of education in terms of an ongoing society. His rather conservative and intellectual philosophy has not been universally understood or accepted. Jacques Maritain applies Thomism to education and pleads for civil pluralism and religious monism. Finally, Alfred North Whitehead attempts a synthesis of these conflicting ideas in his philosophy of organism, of process, of interaction between men and their environment.

The nineteenth century, more than any other period in history, saw the rise and fall of many philosophical systems. Kant's critical idealism was succeeded by the absolutism of Fichte and Hegel which gave rise to the writings of Nietzsche, Schopenhauer, and Karl Marx. At the same time Comte developed his logical positivism in France, Bentham and Mill, the philosophy of utilitarianism in England, and Søren Kierkegaard, his Christian existentialism in Denmark.

Although these philosophies differ from each other in many ways, they had one thing in common. They sought to establish systems which would be prescriptive of human conduct rather than to give a description of reality akin to, but more inclusive and more profound than, the physical and biological sciences.

As important as the Copernican revolution which had dislodged the earth from the center of the universe, was the joint statement regarding biological evolution by Wallace and Darwin in July, 1858, and the subsequent publication in the next year of *The Origin of Species*. Kierkegaard had died four years before, August Comte in 1857, and Schopenhauer was to die one year later, in 1860. But with *The Origin of Species* three important philosophers made their debut into the world. John Dewey, the instrumentalist, Edmund Husserl, the phenomenologist, and Henri Bergson, chiefly known for his *Creative Evolution*, were all born the same year.

Biological evolution further dislodged man from his unique place as lord of creation by positing that he was the last, not necessarily the ultimate, in a long line of descent from the single cell, that he was closely related to the other primates, and that he was part and parcel of an inscrutable struggle through the survival of the fittest.

Even though one did not accept the new doctrine completely, one found it necessary to live with it. Emerson sought to ignore it; Spencer accepted it and applied it to the social sciences; and Bergson interpreted it according to Christian principles.

Almost every important philosophical work of the late nineteenth and early twentieth century began with an attack on Hegel. Marx and Kierkegaard came into contact with Hegel's work directly while Emerson, James, Dewey, and Russell knew him chiefly through the influence of English and American writers such as Coleridge, Carlyle, Bradley, McTaggart, and Royce.

Marx applied the doctrine of historical determinism and the method of dialectic to a materialistic metaphysic to develop the doctrine of the inevitable class struggle upon which much communistic doctrine is based. On the other hand, Kierkegaard's existentialism was an emotional, outraged cry against the historical determinism of the Absolute and an emphasis on the importance of the existent individual.

Hegel held that the universe reveals the work of the Absolute. Historical events and change are embedded in the cosmic forces which lead ultimately to the realization of the world spirit. Henri Bergson (1859–1941) rejected both the absolutism of Hegel and the scientism of the post-Darwinians for a philosophy in which living was a more basic process than knowing, and where the course of evolution is determined in process by the intelligent cooperation of man.

James and Dewey accepted Hegel's synoptic view of philosophy, but not his historical determinism or his dialectic. The philosophy which they developed, variously known as pragmatism, instrumentalism, and experimentalism, aspired to present a total view of reality in a setting of the findings of modern science and of the problems of men. It stands between the world view of Hegel and the analytical philosophers of the present day.

Jacques Maritain, a convert to Catholicism, has devoted his brilliant career to an exposition of St. Thomas Aquinas and to a defense of Thomism against all secular philosophies. Alfred North Whitehead, mathematician, scientist, metaphysician, has sought to form a synthesis of existing philosophies in his theory of organism. Of the great number of writers on education during the last hundred years, six have been selected for special study. They are Emerson, Spencer, James, Dewey, Maritain, and Whitehead.

RALPH WALDO EMERSON

Ralph Waldo Emerson (1803–1882), born in Concord, Massachusetts, achieved fame as a poet, essayist, lecturer, and minister of the Old North Church in Boston. Although he studied briefly at Göttingen in 1824, his best contact with German thought was through English sources. As an idealist he believed that man lives in an innately moral and friendly world. As a Protestant, he believed that only the most personal contacts between man and God were religious. His philosophy descended in a direct line from Plato, through Plotinus, Eckhart, Bruno, and Leibnitz, to Goethe and Coleridge. He had a great regard for the poetic and symbolic works of Plato. For the philosopher-king he substituted the scholar whom he called the guide to mankind because he lived the examined life.

He was acquainted with oriental philosophy through the *Upanishads,* and based many of his moral utterances upon the stoicism of Marcus Aurelius and the *categorical imperative* of Kant. He was a great admirer of the educational theories and humanity of Pestalozzi and of the poetry and thought of Goethe. As a leader among the New England Transcendentalists he did for America what Carlyle and Coleridge had done for English thought.

He held that reason is greater than empirical science. In "Worship"[1] he wrote: "It is a short sight to limit our faith in laws to those of gravity, of chemistry, of botany, and so forth. Those laws do not stop where our eyes lose them, but push the same geometry and chemistry up into the invisible plan of social and rational life." Rather, he maintained, truth, reason, and virtue are lodged in the *over-soul* of which all men are a part. Nature is purposive, and all men are innately moral. Each individual aspires to realize, through insight, the moral perfection within himself, for to be good is also to be wise.

Since man's destiny does not lie in the material but in the spiritual world, education, he believed, is a sort of spiritual dedication. Therefore it should teach moral and spiritual self-reliance. It should be as broad as man. The schoolroom is only an insignificant part of education. After describing the eager curiosity, the initiative, and activity of boys in the community in his essay on *Education,* he concludes: "They are there only for fun, and not knowing that they are at school, in the courthouse, or the cattle show, quite as much and more than they were, an hour ago, in the arithemetic class."[2] Emerson believed that all subjects in the school should be taught to give insight into the symbolic character of life, for education is a communication of a spiritual attitude or way of looking at life

[1] Ralph Waldo Emerson, "Worship," in *Conduct of Life,* Vol. VI of the Centenary Ed., *Complete Works,* ed. Edward Waldo Emerson (Boston, 1903), pp. 218–219. Quoted in Robert Ulich, *History of Educational Thought* (New York: American Book Company, 1945), p. 303.

[2] Ulich, *ibid.,* p. 305.

rather than a communication of knowledge. Facts, therefore, are to be subordinated to values, all knowledge should be applied, and correct habits should be formed as the basis for genuine freedom.

The true teacher should realize the greatness of children. He should believe that even the most perverted human being can be raised up to the society of men. His chief duty is to direct the child toward the Eternal Truth, to which every individual aspires, to give him a standard of moral judgment, and to strengthen the power of his will.

Emerson's advice to the teacher can be stated briefly as follows:

1. Possess a great ideal.
2. Respect your pupil as you respect yourself.
3. Develop an enthusiam derived from inspiring values.
4. Combine drill and discipline with initiative and self-expression for accuracy and inspiration complement each other.
5. Have high standards and do not compromise with the vulgar.
6. Relate all things to the divine plan of the universe.
7. Relate school work to all of community living.[3]

Emerson was a poet and essayist rather than a philosopher in the technical sense. His many lecture tours and his published works gave his ideas great currency, so that his influence, while indirect, was widespread. The idealistic tradition in American education has been carried on by such men as Henry Harrell Horne, Edgar S. Brightman, William E. Hocking, and J. Donald Butler.

HERBERT SPENCER

Herbert Spencer (1820–1903) was born in Derby, England, the son of a non-conformist schoolmaster. He was educated at home and had few contacts with other boys. At seventeen he became a civil engineer for a railway company, but soon turned to journalism. In 1850 he published his *Social Statics,* and shortly thereafter conceived his idea of developing a synthetic philosophy to which he devoted forty years of his life, publishing the entire work complete in ten volumes in 1896. In 1861 he published *Education, Intellectual, Moral, and Physical* upon which his fame as an educational theorist rests.

[3] See *ibid.*, pp. 312–313, for an excellent treatment of these points.

He was largely self-taught. Reading Kant he regarded as a waste of time, and he was bored by Plato, Locke, and John Stuart Mill. He was greatly influenced by the works of Bacon, the positivism of Comte, and the evolutionary and biological writings of Lamarck and Darwin. He adopted a naturalistic metaphysic similar in many respects to that of Democritus and Epicurus, and is known as the chief exponent of the philosophy of evolution which he applied to biology, psychology, sociology, and ethics. Philosophy, he said, arranges the material of the sciences systematically.

He maintained that human knowledge deals with phenomena which can be divided into *outer*, explained in terms of time, space, matter, motion, and force, and *inner*, explained in terms of sensation and states of consciousness. Both are aspects of an absolute reality which we cannot know, but in which we are constantly involved and in which we have an indestructible belief. Religion is an affirmation of this inscrutable power which is beyond the range of human knowledge and cannot, therefore, be displaced by science. Accordingly, science and religion complement each other in peaceful harmony.

In his classification of the sciences, physics deals with the basic laws of nature, biology, with the relations between the organism and the environment, sociology, with society as an evolving organism from uniformity to multiformity, and politics as the balance between the ideal and the state.

In his consideration of ethics he regarded "good" as that type of conduct which is relatively more involved in society, and "bad" as that which is relatively less involved. That is, a good act would be concerned with the welfare of the social group, while a bad act would be motivated solely by selfish interests. Evolution, he contended, furnishes the major criterion for moral judgment, because it guarantees that life will become fuller, more complete, and more harmonious. Egoism is the original or primitive nature of man, but as society evolves and becomes more complex, egoism must give way to altruism.

He divided all of reality into science which deals with the knowable, and religion which deals with the unknowable. For Spencer there were three levels of knowledge: the lowest, common sense, unorganized knowledge; second, the sciences; and third, philosophy, which organizes all knowledge into a single comprehensive system.

Although he interpreted "the survival of the fittest" to mean the dependence of the individual on the life of the group, he would not accept the socialism of Mill. He wished to restrict the powers of the state, and defended the economic doctrine of *laissez faire.*

In *Education, Intellectual, Moral, and Physical,* Spencer introduced naturalism into education and was among the first to develop its scientific study. As an advocate of the phylogenetic theory he wrote: "The education of the child must accord both in mode and in arrangement with the education of mankind considered historically. In other words, the genesis of knowledge in the individual must follow the same course as the genesis of knowledge in the race." [4]

Believing that science excelled languages as an intellectual discipline, and that practical subjects were of greater value than cultural subjects, he attacked the traditional curriculum. He replaced the Latin of the classicists and history of the Herbartians with science as the core of the curriculum which was to provide a liberal education.

That education is of most worth, he believed, which is centered in human welfare and prepares the child for complete living, for education should aim to enable a person to perform his function in society as efficiently as his social and economic position demands. These activities include: self-preservation, securing the necessities of life, rearing and disciplining offspring, maintaining proper social and political relations, and performing a miscellany of leisure-time activities.

In method he followed Pestalozzi, but proposed that the object lesson should be continued throughout education until it merged into the methods of science. Children, he thought, should be told as little as possible, and should discover much by themselves. In discipline he followed Rousseau's theory of natural consequences, but where Rousseau would supplement this by direct moral training in adolescence, Spencer believed that it should provide complete moral training. As a hedonist, he held that thus the student

[4] Herbert Spencer, *Education, Intellectual, Moral, and Physical* (London: Williams and Norgatte, 1906), p. 90.

would refrain from that which produced pain and tend to repeat those experiences which gave him pleasure.

Spencer enunciated eight principles of education which may be listed as follows:

1. Education must conform to the natural processes of growth and mental development.
2. Education should be pleasurable.
3. Education should engage the spontaneous activity of the child.
4. Education should be concerned with the acquisition of knowledge.
5. Education is for the body as well as the mind.
6. Education should practice the art of delay.
7. Education should use an inductive method of instruction.
8. Education should develop moral conduct through natural consequences, tempered with sympathy.[5]

Spencer's influence was widespread. Bergson was partly his disciple, and James taught a course about his philosophy at Harvard; Santayana remarked, "I belong to Herbert Spencer's camp," and traces of his philosophy can be found in the writings of Woodbridge and Caird. His educational writings began a complete reorganization of educational thought, especially with regard to the curriculum and the aims of education. The now famous "Cardinal Principles of Secondary Education," presented by The Commission on the Reorganization of Secondary Education in 1918, clearly shows the influence of Spencer's thought, as indeed do most restatements of aims of education since his time.

WILLIAM JAMES

William James (1842–1910) was born in New York City of wealthy and cultured parents. He traveled widely and lived and studied both in England and America. He had wide interests in art, biology, medicine, psychology, and philosophy. His thought was influenced by the materialism of John Stuart Mill, the biology of Louis Agassiz, the positivism of Auguste Comte, the psychology of

[5] See J. Donald Butler, *Four Philosophies* (New York: Harper and Brothers, 1957), pp. 110–113, upon which this list is based.

Wilhelm Wundt, and the philosophy of Charles S. Peirce. He accepted Darwinian evolution but insisted on provision for individual initiative. He dubbed Spencer's theory of automatic progress an "obsolete anachronism" and broke with Hegel's block universe, calling his dialectic a "mousetrap" in which those who enter "may be lost forever." He was a prophet of individualism and of voluntarism. He never accepted a scientific conclusion as final truth, but always insisted on leaving room for exceptions.

Philosophy for James is connected with the solution of social problems and of social issues; it is our more or less dumb sense of what life honestly and deeply means. The real world is the world of human experiences beyond which the human mind cannot go. It is an unfinished lot of things, and man is in the center of it because what he experiences is real. This world of our knowledge lies within a larger unseen world. Belief in God is necessary for the satisfaction of man's nature. The will to believe is man's greatest companion and helper. Man wants to believe in a certain way because these beliefs seem to satisfy him. If this will to believe is fundamental, man cannot be bound by immutable laws, but must be free to build his own ideas, and to risk everything on their fulfillment.

Truth, in the long run, he believes, is the over-all expediency in ways of believing as goodness is in ways of behaving. The good is that which serves the ends of the group and the individual in the group, for the individual is an end in himself and not a means to an end. The ultimate measure of the good is the human individual as a social unit.

With regard to cherished formulas, he holds that they are often obstacles rather than aids to thinking. Theories and ideas should be instruments and plans for action. Beliefs are not pictures of the past but factors we can rely on for the future. To think is to be prepared to do. We must have confidence in the future. Absolute truth is a distant vanishing point to which our contemporary truths converge.

For Charles S. Peirce (1839–1914), pragmatism was a logical theory that the meaning of an idea is the sum of all the practical consequences which might conceivably ensue from the truth of that idea. For James, pragmatism was a theory of meaning and of truth. "An idea is true if it works," he declared, "if it leads to satisfactory outcomes." His pragmatism offers a theory of the middle of the road which allows a man to choose and to live by the philosophy that fits him best and works most satisfactorily for him.

James' psychology, published in 1890, was written in his usual vivid, concrete, and pragmatic style. Mind, he said, is a kind of behavior, and is a latecomer in the evolutionary series. It aids man to make better practical adjustments to his environment. He showed the neurological, physiological, and organic bases for psychology and maintained that there was "no psychosis without neurosis," that is, that mental life was grounded in experience. A famous example of this is the James-Lange theory of the emotions with its sequence, "I see a bear; I run; I am afraid," by which he attempted to illustrate his hypothesis that emotional states were the result of mental and organic activity arising from an external stimulus.

While he held that there was no reception of external stimuli without reaction, and no impression without expression, he rejected the "tabula rasa" theory of Locke and the environmental theory of Herbart for the theory of unlearned native endowments or instincts of Aristotle. He listed these instincts as: fear, love, curiosity, imitation, pride, ambition, pugnacity, ownership, and constructiveness. His belief that every acquired action supplements or supplants a native one anticipated present day theories of conditioning and associative shifting. To develop habits he recommended beginning with strong initiative, permitting no exceptions, and seizing upon every opportunity for practice.

Among his most important contributions to psychology was his description of consciousness as awareness of experience and as experience in a medium in which objects and organisms are related. He did not believe that consciousness could be described in terms of individual sensations, but that it was a continuous stream, always flowing, always changing, appearing in new concepts, always impulsive, affective and personal, and only sometimes intellectual. It is much more than the brain, which consciousness uses as an instrument to localize our purposes and to act efficaciously upon the world. With Kant, he believed that mind contributes to the structure of experience.

"We think for a purpose," wrote James. Thought was process, and the business of the psychologist and educator was to discover how thinking could be done more efficiently, for it is no better than the service it can render in a situation.

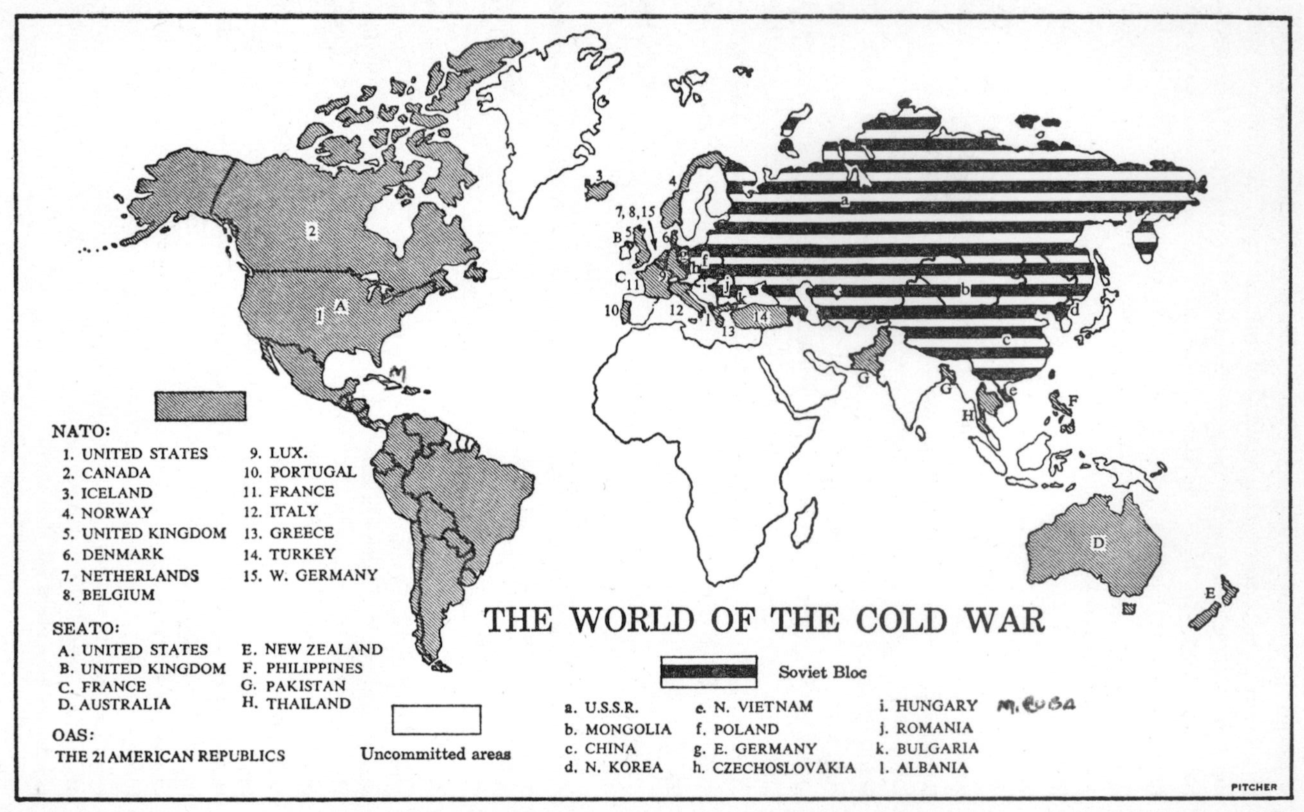
THE WORLD OF THE COLD WAR
NATO:
1. UNITED STATES
2. CANADA
3. ICELAND
4. NORWAY
5. UNITED KINGDOM
6. DENMARK
7. NETHERLANDS
8. BELGIUM
9. LUX.
10. PORTUGAL
11. FRANCE
12. ITALY
13. GREECE
14. TURKEY
15. W. GERMANY
SEATO:
A. UNITED STATES
B. UNITED KINGDOM
C. FRANCE
D. AUSTRALIA
E. NEW ZEALAND
F. PHILIPPINES
G. PAKISTAN
H. THAILAND
OAS:
THE 21 AMERICAN REPUBLICS
Uncommitted areas
Soviet Bloc
a. U.S.S.R.
b. MONGOLIA
c. CHINA
d. N. KOREA
e. N. VIETNAM
f. POLAND
g. E. GERMANY
h. CZECHOSLOVAKIA
i. HUNGARY
j. ROMANIA
k. BULGARIA
l. ALBANIA
PITCHER

James is a universal genius, and therefore defies classification. His many works show the variety of his interests. Beginning with his *Psychology* in 1890, he forged new paths by bringing his medical knowledge to bear on this new science. He popularized his psychology and applied it directly to teaching situations in his popular *Talks to Teachers About Psychology* published in 1899. These works have not only influenced the development of educational psychology, but have had a profound effect on teaching methods.

White characterizes the triumvirate of pragmatists when he writes: "Peirce is the pragmatic philosopher of science, James the pragmatic philosopher of religion, and Dewey the pragmatic philosopher of morals, only it must be clear by now that it is not the same pragmatism that they apply to these different problems."[6]

His two works on the philosophy of religion, *The Will to Believe* and *The Varieties of Religious Experience,* were published in 1897 and 1902 respectively. Religion, for James, is the cause of the individual's striving for the unknown. On the other hand, for Emerson, it springs from our being embedded in something greater than man. For both there was the universal will to believe.

Possibly his best known work is *Pragmatism* (1907), which he described as a new way to express old ideas, and which he claimed

[6] Morton White, *The Age of Analysis* (New York: Mentor Books, The New American Library, 1955), p. 154.

Figure 4. In Figure 2 (p. 74) we saw the encroachment of a foreign power and a conflicting ideology upon the Christian West. Figure 4 shows the world which philosophy and education must consider today. Here again a much expanded Christian West is confronted with a strong military force and a new ideology as represented by the Soviet Bloc.

Some of the uncommitted countries remain neutral by long established policy, others because their territory lies adjacent to the communist world. Many of these countries represent new governments who are having their initial experience with self-government. Their status requires a display of independence, and they shun assistance of any kind from their former overlords for fear of returning to colonial status. Many of these countries are attempting to build democracy upon a base of mass illiteracy. They need help in setting up a program of education to meet their needs, an education for free men.

must be constantly redefined or it will become a dogma instead of a "living vision." His *Essays in Radical Empiricism* was published posthumously in 1912. Almost every psychologist and philosopher since G. Stanley Hall who studied with him at Harvard has come under his influence at some time. Through his greatest interpreter, Ralph Barton Perry, he has had a profound influence on the "new-realism" in philosophy. Morton White says of him:

James . . . was no second-rate imitator or satellite of British or continental philosophy; he was a major philosophical planet who whirled on his own axis and drew all of the other pragmatic luminaries into his powerful field. His pragmatism was anticipated by Peirce and revised by Dewey, but he was unquestionably the central literary figure in the pragmatic movement, an "adorable genius" as Whitehead called him, and the man of whom Russell said: "No degree of democratic feeling and of desire to identify himself with the common herd could make him anything but a natural aristocrat, a man whose personal distinction commanded respect." [7]

JOHN DEWEY

John Dewey (1859–1952), born in Burlington, Vermont, on October 20, 1859, was descended from a long line of Vermont farmers who came from Flanders to Massachusetts in 1630. He attended the local schools and the University of Vermont. After three years of teaching in high school, he went to Johns Hopkins University where he studied with George S. Morris and G. Stanley Hall, and took his doctorate in 1884. He taught philosophy at the Universities of Michigan and Minnesota, was professor of philosophy and pedagogy at the University of Chicago from 1894 to 1904, and was professor of philosophy at Columbia University from 1905 until his retirement in 1931. Edman writes of him:

It might be said, that if Dewey is recognized as a peculiarly American philosopher, it is because he caught the voice, accent and temper of the American tradition and the nature of the special contingencies and choices before it in his own era. He did not, it may be argued, make the tradition, or, for that matter, remake it. The expanding forces of technology, the intervolvement of public and private affairs, the rising tide of the labor movement, the revolt against authoritianism in religion

[7] *Ibid.*, p. 155.

and in education—all these play a large part in and color his social philosophy—were, it may be argued, themes he translated into general terms of philosophical analysis; they were *not* consequences of his published ideas.[8]

During all of his life, he retained much of the quiet simplicity and the wholesome regard for facts of the Vermonters among whom he grew up, and the respect for the private dignity of the individual so characteristic of his fellow New Englander, Emerson.

Among Dewey's chief philosophical problems were an analysis of the thinking process and the establishment of a medial position which would show the relation between the great number of dualisms, such as mind and body, interest and effort, change and permanence, with which many of the philosophers who preceded him had been concerned.

To Plato, Kant, and many others, time and change were mere illusions, mere opinions with respect to reality. In ancient Greece, on the other hand, Heraclitus had said that the only certainty was the law of change. Dewey accepted this idea, except that he believed with James in a constant flow or continuity of experience which, while always changing, contained elements from the past as well as for the future. Also, he maintained that man's ability to think can be and should be instrumental in affecting the direction of change. For Dewey, then, reality is *change*, the universe is *process*, and man is coexistent with nature.

Instead of the absolute and universal he wrote in terms of the relative and contingent. Facts became knowledge only through activity in social situations. Knowledge itself was fractional and situational, being true only for one place, at one point of time, under certain circumstances. It was a sort of hypothesis, born in perplexity and proved through experience. Changes cause conflicts between new problems and old patterns, and call for constant reevaluation and reconstruction of experience. The key to life is growth which is a kind of alertness to the changing patterns of life. Intelligence is man's means of evaluating and of adapting himself to his environment, and his environment to himself. This and man's use of symbols to preserve past experiences are man's distinctive

[8] Irwin Edman, *John Dewey* (New York: The Bobbs-Merrill Company, Inc., 1955), pp. 21–22. Copyright © 1955 by The Bobbs-Merrill Company, Inc., and used by special permission.

characteristics. Thus history may be said to be the mother of civilizations. But not all of human events are recorded, and Dewey points out that those possessed of the use of symbols select the events which are most favorable to them and which advance their position among those who pursue only manual occupations. In time there arose class distinctions with all their attendant circumstances between the thinker and the doer, and as laws codified and strengthened customs, these distinctions became fixed and similar types of dualisms became accepted modes of thought. Such dualisms as work-play, mental-physical, liberal-vocational, are conventions which must be re-examined in the light of the on-going process of change. Intelligence is instrumental to this examination of values.

Thinking arises, says Dewey, in a forked-road situation. It is "in the first instance the up-welling of a suggestion, and imaginative rehearsal, a leap into some envisioned possibility, an enactment in imagination, of what may be done."[9] Or more specifically, the problem, which arises in activity (which may, of course, be entirely mental), calls for the assembling, organization, and comparison of data, the vicarious exploration of the bearings of the situation, and the formulation of a tentative hypothesis which is tested, modified, and probably discarded through experience.

This formula is also the basis for establishing ethical standards. Values are determined not by intention, but by their salutary effect on the social group they concern. This shared life for the good of the individual and the community—and Dewey thought in terms of the world community—is the ideal of democracy, an ideal which was for Dewey at once moral, religious, and esthetic. He wrote:

The most penetrating definition of philosophy which can be given is that it is the theory of education in its most general phases. . . .

A democracy is more than a form of government: it is primarily a mode of associated living, of conjoint communicated experience. . . .

Men live in a community in virtue of the things which they have in common, and communication is the way in which they come to possess things in common. What they must have in common in order to form a community or a society are aims, beliefs, aspirations, knowledge, a com-

[9] *Ibid.*, p. 29.

mon understanding—likemindedness, as the sociologists say. Persons do not become a society by living in physical proximity. . . . Individuals do not even compose a social group because they all work together for a common end . . . . If, however, they were all cognizant of the common end, and all interested in it so that they regulated their specific activity in view of it, then they would form a community. . . . Consensus demands communication . . . . To be a recipient of a communication is to have an enlarged and changed experience. Except in dealing with commonplaces and catch phases one has to assimilate, imaginatively, something of another's experiences in order to tell him of his own experience. . . . Not only does social life demand teaching and learning for its own permanence, but the very process of living together educates.[10]

Dewey stigmatizes the type of interest which is an attempt to secure effort and attention by offering a bribe as "soft pedagogy, soup-kitchen theory of education." "Interesting by extraneous and artificial inducements deserves all the bad names which have been applied to the doctrine of interest in education."[11] In learning, interest is necessary to sustain effort during the period between the acceptance of an objective and its realization. The teacher challenges the active interest of the learner by presenting old material in new settings, or new material to challenge old ideas. In the same vein he continues:

In learning, the present powers of the pupil are the initial stage; the aim of the teacher represents the remote limit. Between the two lies *means*—that is middle conditions—acts to be performed; difficulties to be overcome; appliances to be used. Only *through* them, in the literal sense, will the initial activities reach a satisfactory consummation. To be means for the achieving of present tendencies, to be "between" the agent and his end, to be of interest are different names for the same things. When material has to be made interesting, it signifies that, as presented, it lacks connection with purposes and present power; or that if the connection be there, it is not perceived. To make it interesting by extraneous and artificial inducements deserves all the bad names which have been applied to the doctrine of interest in education.[12]

Thus, Dewey explains the intimate relationship between interest and means in education. These means move toward further ends.

[10] John Dewey, *Democracy and Education* (New York: The Macmillan Company, 1916), pp. 386, 101, 5–7. Copyright 1916 by the Macmillan Company and reprinted by their permission.

[11] *Ibid.*, pp. 149, 150.

[12] *Ibid.*, pp. 149–150.

Only, Dewey maintains that these ends must be personal and more or less immediate, and the motivation to these ends must arise from within the individual who governs his course of action in accordance with his goals. This Dewey describes as discipline, saying, "discipline means power at command." [13]

With regard to the relation between work and play Dewey remarks:

When fairly remote results of a definite character are foreseen and enlist persistent effort for their accomplishment, play passes into work. Like play, it signifies purposeful activity and differs *not* in that activity is subordinated to an external result, but in the fact that a longer course of activity is occasioned by the idea of a result. The demand for continuous attention is greater, and more intelligence must be shown in selecting and shaping means. . . . Activity carried on under conditions of external pressure or coercion (namely drudgery) is not carried on for any significance attached to the doing. . . . What is inherently repulsive is endured for the sake of averting something still more repulsive or of securing a gain hitched on by others. . . . Only the hold which the completion of the work has upon a person will keep him going. But the end should be intrinsic to the action; it should be its end—a part of its own course.[14]

Such a reorientation of aims will have a decided effect on the curriculum. In *The Child and the Curriculum* Dewey writes:

Abandon the notion of subject-matter as something fixed and ready-made in itself, outside the child's experience; cease thinking of the child's experience also as something hard and fast; see it as something fluent, embryonic, vital; and we realize that the child and the curriculum are simply two limits which define a single process.[15]

Dewey stresses the importance of the cultural heritage, but warns: "A knowledge of the past and its heritage is of great significance when it enters into the present, but not otherwise." [16] He continues:

An experimental school is under the temptation to improvise its subject-matter. It must take advantage of unexpected events and turn to ac-

[13] *Ibid.*, p. 151.

[14] *Ibid.*, pp. 240–289.

[15] John Dewey, *The Child and the Curriculum* (Chicago: The University of Chicago Press, 1902), p. 14.

[16] Dewey, *Democracy and Education,* p. 88.

count unexpected questions and interests. Yet if it permits improvisation to dictate its course, the result is a jerky, discontinuous movement which works against the possibility of making any important contribution to educational subject-matter. Incidents are momentary, but the use made of them should not be momentary or short-lived. They are to be brought within the scope of a developing whole of content and purpose, which is a whole because it has continuity and consecutiveness in its parts. There is no single subject matter which all schools must adopt, but in every school there should be some significant subject-matters undergoing growth and formulation.[17]

Dewey was a great moral philosopher but not a religionist in the accepted sense of the term. He had great faith in democracy and to that end he thought the public schools should dedicate themselves, directing all studies and activities thereto.

Just because the studies of the curriculum represent standard factors in social life they are organs of initiation into social values. As mere school studies, their acquisition has only a technical worth. Acquired under conditions where their social significance is realized, they feed moral interest and develop moral insight.[18]

He points out further that studies are pursued not only for practical ends but for values inherent in them.

Appreciation . . . denotes an enlarged, an *intensified* prizing. . . . Certain conclusions follow with respect to educational values. We cannot establish a hierarchy of values among studies. . . . In so far as any study has a unique or irreplaceable function in experience, in so far as it marks a characteristic enrichment of life, its worth is intrinsic or incomparable. . . . And what has been said about appreciation means that every study in one of its aspects ought to have just such ultimate significance. It is as true of arithmetic as it is of poetry that in some place and at some time it ought to be a good to be appreciated on its own account—just as an enjoyable experience. In short, if it is not, then when the time and place come for it to be used as a means or instrumentality, it will be just that much handicapped. Never having been realized or appreciated for itself, one will miss something of its capacity as a resource for other ends.[19]

With regard to deferred values in education, he observed:

[17] John Dewey, "Progressive Education and the Science of Education," *Progressive Education*, V (July–September, 1928), 201.
[18] Dewey, *Democracy and Education*, p. 414.
[19] *Ibid.*, pp. 278, 281.

Who can reckon up the loss of moral power that arises from the constant impression that nothing is worth doing in itself, but only as a preparation for something else, which in turn is only a getting ready for some genuinely serious end beyond?[20]

Of the teaching of religion in the public schools he says:

Already the spirit of our schooling is permeated with the feeling that every topic, every fact, every professed truth must submit to a certain publicity and impartiality. . . . It is the essence of all dogmatic faiths to hold that any such "showdown" is sacrilegious and perverse. . . . Our schools, in bringing together those of different nationalities, languages, traditions, and creeds, in assimilating them together upon the basis of what is common and public in endeavor and achievement, are performing an infinitely significant religious work. They are promoting the social unity out of which in the end genuine religious unity must grow.[21]

John Dewey's influence in American education has been considerable, not only in the main stream of public education, but among the traditionalists and essentialists on the one hand who opposed him, and that parody of Dewey, the ultra-progressives who grossly misinterpreted him on the other. The impact of his writings can be traced in the fields of law and art as well as in the social sciences. As a philosopher's philosopher he added considerably to the technical development of this discipline. He was not as analytic as Peirce nor as fluent a writer as James, but his often difficult style has got through to the minds of his countrymen and has influenced every department of American thought.

JACQUES MARITAIN

Jacques Maritain (1882–) was born in Paris of a liberal Protestant family, devoted to political liberty and the spirit of the republic. At the Sorbonne he studied skeptical and phenomenalistic philosophy and biological materialistic science. Then he met his

[20] John Dewey, *Moral Principle in Education* (Boston: Houghton Mifflin Co., 1909), p. 26.

[21] John Dewey, "Religion and Our Schools," *Hibbert Journal,* VI (July, 1908), 804, 807.

future wife and together they determined to work their way out of skepticism and relativism even though suicide were the only solution.

A study of Bergson restored their faith in metaphysics, and under the influence of Léon Bloy they were converted to Catholicism. Maritain studied biology at Heidelberg and at the same time made an intensive study of the *Summa Theologica* of St. Thomas Aquinas. He determined to devote his life to philosophy and to an interpretation of the works of St. Thomas. In 1913 he went to the Institute Catholique in Paris where he was made professor of philosophy. Although he is not alone in developing the neo-scholastic movement initiated by the encyclical letter "On Christian Philosophy" of Pope Leo VIII, August 4, 1879, he is possibly the best known Thomist in America, where he has lectured widely, notably at the universities of Toronto, Harvard, Columbia, Chicago, Notre Dame, Yale and Princeton.

In *Man and the State* he distinguishes between a community which he describes as biological and a society which is more related to the rational and spiritual qualities of man. A community is historical, environmental, and collective and springs from nature. A society springs from individual initiative and imposes patterns derived from law. A nation is a community of people into which one is born. In contradistinction to the nation, both the *Body Politic* and the *State* pertain to the order of society in its highest or "perfect" form.[22] Since in the political society authority comes through the people, it is normal that the society should be made up of tiers one above the other to the top authority of the state.[23]

The state is not the supreme incarnation of the ideal as Hegel believed: it is but an agency entitled to use power and coercion. But man is by no means for the state. The state is for man.[24] The people have the right to self-government.[25] Neither men nor states are sovereign, and since their rulers are from the people they may be deposed by the people.[26] This is different with the Church

[22] Jacques Maritain, *Man and the State* (Chicago: University of Chicago Press, Phoenix Books, 1955), p. 9.
[23] *Ibid.*, p. 11.
[24] *Ibid.*, p. 13.
[25] *Ibid.*, p. 25.
[26] *Ibid.*, p. 50.

where God is sovereign and the Pope rules as his Vicar by divine authority which cannot be denied or deposed.[27]

The laws and standards made by men can be changed. What might be considered a crime in civilized society can be a heroic virtue in a concentration camp. In the laws of the Church, however, there is but one moral standard. Man-made societies must be pluralistic since they do not derive directly from divine authority, but the Church is supreme and must eventually draw all men to it. When states realize that they are not sovereign (according to Maritain's definition), they will be able to cooperate in world government, and men will then live together in freedom.[28] It is by means of freedom that the peoples of the earth will have been brought to a common will to live together.[29] "The cause of freedom and the cause of the Church are one in the defense of man."[30]

In *Education at the Crossroads*[31] Maritain points out what he considers to be the weaknesses of contemporary secular education and explains his theory and system of *true Christian* education according to his interpretation of St. Thomas and the dogma of the Roman Catholic church. The essays were delivered as a part of the Dwight Harrington Terry Foundation Lectures on religion in the light of science and philosophy in 1943.

In the first essay Maritain discusses the "Aims of Education." Education is an ethical art, the chief aim of which is to shape man as man, as an animal of both nature and culture.[32] Present day secular education suffers from seven fundamental misconceptions:

1. A disregard for ends.
2. Incomplete ideas regarding ends.
3. The pragmatic emphasis on activity.
4. Conditioning for social living.
5. Intellectualism (chiefly an over-emphasis on scientific and technical specialization).

[27] *Ibid.*, pp. 49–50.
[28] *Ibid.*, p. 207.
[29] *Ibid.*, p. 206.
[30] *Ibid.*, p. 187.
[31] Jacques Maritain, *Education at the Crossroads* (New Haven: Yale University Press, 1943).
[32] *Ibid.*, pp. 1–2.

6. Voluntarism (making the intelligence subservient to the will to obey irrational forces).
7. The belief that everything can be learned.

Ends are superior to means and the process of achieving ends is a matter of some indifference. The scientific idea of man has no reference to ultimate reality and distorts the idea of man. The religious-philosophical idea is ontological. "Man is a horizon in which two worlds meet." [33] What is most important is respect for the soul as well as the body of the child.[34] "The man of our civilization is the Christian man. When I state that the education, in order to be completely well grounded, must be based upon the Christian idea of man, it is because I think that this idea of man is the true one." [35] He opposes vocational education,[36] and any attempt on the part of the school to impose social or nationalistic patterns,[37] and remarks that "the saints and martyrs are the true educators of mankind." [38] Of the study of educational psychology he says:

> The teacher must be solidly instructed in and deeply aware of the psychology of the child, less in order to form the latter's will and feelings than in order to avoid deforming or wounding them by pedagogical blunders.[39]

Of the purpose of the school he writes:

> School and school life have to do, in an especially important manner, with "premoral" training, a point which deals not with morality strictly speaking, but with the preparation and first tilling of the soil thereof. The main duty of the school is to enlighten and strengthen reason. . . . Thus the paradox of which I have spoken comes to a solution: what is important in the upbringing of man, that is, the uprightness of the will and the attainment of spiritual freedom, as well as the achievement of a sound relationship with society, is truly the main object of education in its broadest sense.[40]

[33] *Ibid.*, p. 5.
[34] *Ibid.*, p. 9.
[35] *Ibid.*, p. 6.
[36] *Ibid.*, p. 23.
[37] *Ibid.*, pp. 15–22.
[38] *Ibid.*, p. 25.
[39] *Ibid.*, p. 27.
[40] *Ibid.*, pp. 27–28.

He begins the second essay "The Dynamics of Education" by saying that education like medicine is an art of ministering, an art subservient to nature. The primary dynamic factor is the internal vital principle in the one to be educated. "Education by the rod is positively bad education. That which reduces the education and progress of man to the mere freeing of the material ego is false." [41]

"Man's perfection consists of the perfection of love. . . . And to advance in this self-perfection is not to copy an ideal. It is to let yourself be led by another where you did not want to go, and to let Divine Love Who calls each being by his own name mold you and make you a person, a true original, not a copy." [42]

The "fundamental norms of education" are:

1. To foster those fundamental dispositions which enable the principle agent to grow in the life of the mind.
2. To lay stress on inwardness and the internalization of the educational influence.
3. To foster internal unity in man.
4. To free the mind through the mastery of reason over the things learned.

He [St. Thomas] knew [that] to raise clever doubts, to prefer searching to finding, and perpetually to pose problems without ever solving them are the great enemies of education.[43]

Thus Maritain would have the pupil free to open his mind to receive the ultimate and eternal truths which the Catholic church has been guarding for centuries, especially those truths which penetrate the here and now.

Finally, he would recast the curriculum along the lines of the medieval seven liberal arts. For the elementary school (called rudimentary period in his third essay) there would be the trivium: (1) eloquence, (2) literature and poetry, and (3) music and the fine arts. For the secondary period (called humanities) there would be the quadrivium to each of which he would give a separate year of study: (1) mathematics, (2) physics and the natural sciences, (3) philosophy, and (4) ethical, political, and social philosophy.

[41] *Ibid.*, pp. 30–32, 35.
[42] *Ibid.*, p. 36.
[43] *Ibid.*, pp. 39–50.

In the third essay Maritain adds poetry to the first year, while in the second year he substitutes fine arts for physics.

His third essay "The Humanities in Education" is a nostalgic recollection of the European system of education for the upper classes. He proposes three layers of education—the rudimentary, the humanities, and advanced studies—which he says correspond to stages of human development. In each the subject matter must be fitted to the learner. College education should be given to all, but to introduce specialization in this sphere is to do violence to the world of youth.[44]

The conclusion of all of the preceding remarks implies a clear condemnation not only of the many preprofessional undergraduate courses which worm their way into college education, but also of the elective system.[45]

He concludes that the highest aim of liberal education is to make youth possess the foundations of wisdom. A course in theology would conclude the last undergraduate year.

In "The Trials of Present Day Education" Maritain presents a rhapsodic prophecy of the future.

> Humanism only will conteract the present day threat of slavery and determinism. . . . Bourgeois individualism is done for . . . and must be replaced by a personalistic and communal civilization grounded on human rights and satisfying the social aspirations and needs of man. . . . Education must remove the rift between the social claim and the individual claim within man himself. . . . The problem of leisure . . . will become particularly crucial. . . . The duty of educators is . . . to maintain the essentials of humanistic education and to adapt them to the present requirements of the common good. Pluralism in education demands the right to form private schools and organizations of schools.[46]

The task of moral re-education is really a matter of public emergency. Democracy needs "some abiding sense of the reality of original sin."[47] There must not only be teaching of natural morality, but supernatural morality. The greatest education comes through trial and suffering. "The renewal of Christian conscience and a new work of evangelization are the primary and unquestion-

[44] *Ibid.*, pp. 58–64.
[45] *Ibid.*, p. 65.
[46] *Ibid.*, pp. 88–92.
[47] *Ibid.*, p. 94.

able conditions for the moral re-education that the man of our civilization needs." [48] Pragmatism will naturally lead to a "strong positivist or technocratic denial of the objective values of any spiritual need." [49]

Maritain concludes his essay by calling upon American youth. He is convinced that America must free itself from an instrumentalist and pragmatist philosophy and suggests that it take refuge in the wisdom of Europe and the truth of the Catholic church.

Dewey and Maritain then represent two contrasting points of view with regard to American education. In order to bring these differences into focus, in the following table we present a number of parallel statements which represent approximately the points of view of these two significant educational theorists.

MARITAIN	DEWEY
Value is found in the thing learned.	Value is found in the process of learning.
The learner is a recipient of the truth.	The learner is a seeker after truth.
Learning comes through precept.	Learning comes through active participation.
Man is the child of the Church.	Man is the child of society.
Truth is absolute and eternal.	Truth is functional, situational, instrumental.
Responsibility for learning lies mainly with the teacher.	Responsibility for learning lies mainly with the pupil.
The pattern for American education is found in Europe and in the middle ages.	The pattern for American education is contemporary and indigenous.
Education should fit universal man to live in an ideal community.	Education should fit man for living in present day society.

[48] *Ibid.*, p. 107.
[49] *Ibid.*, p. 115.

Maritain is not an official spokesman for the Roman Catholic church, but he does speak for a large number of Catholics and for a great many others who are associated with established institutions or systems of thought that look to their established doctrines for ready answers to difficult problems.

ALFRED NORTH WHITEHEAD

Since the foregoing sketch of the development of theories of education began with a quotation from Alfred North Whitehead (1861–1947), it seems fitting that it should conclude with a consideration of his educational theories.

He was born at Ramsgate in Kent, England, of a long line of schoolmasters and Anglican clergymen. He entered Trinity College, Cambridge in 1880 to read mathematics and remained there as a scholar and fellow until 1910. He taught in London till 1924, when he came to Harvard, becoming emeritus professor in 1937. As a mathematician and logician he gained fame through his collaboration with Bertrand Russell in *Principia Mathematica* (1910). While at London he devoted himself to the philosophy of science, but his most famous period was at Harvard where he published such notable metaphysical studies as *Process and Reality* (1929) and *Adventures of Ideas* (1933). The *Aims of Education* was published in 1929.

Whitehead's philosophy has been called Aristotelianism, realism, panpsychism, and idealism. Actually it is a philosophy of organism, an active philosophy of process, in which he tries to show interrelationships between man and his environment, natural, social, and spiritual. Maintaining that modern physics has identified matter with energy in a field of force, he claims that matter is alive and in process. Knowledge, he says, is a blend of primary qualities "out there," and of secondary qualities "in here," and adds, "the pain is in us and not in the knife with which we cut ourselves." A dead nature cannot answer "why" for all ultimate reasons are in terms of aim or value.

In *Nature and Life*,[50] Whitehead assigns himself the task of

[50] Alfred North Whitehead, *Nature and Life* (Chicago: University of Chicago Press, 1934). Quoted in Morton White, *The Age of Analysis*, pp. 86–100 *passim*.

examining the basis for his philosophy. The following paragraphs are a précis of this essay.

The doctrine I am maintaining is that neither physical nature nor life can be understood unless we fuse them together as essential factors in the composition of "really real" things whose interconnection and individual characters constitute the universe. . . . Thus there is a unity . . . of the body and soul into one person. . . . There is a continuity of the soul [through all states of consciousness]. . . . The weakness of the epistemology of the eighteenth and nineteenth centuries was that it based itself purely upon a narrow formulation of sense perception.

The experienced world is one complex factor in the composition of many factors constituting the essence of the soul . . . in one sense the world is the soul . . . an experience of the world involves the exhibition of the soul itself as one of the components within the world. . . . The world is included within the occasion in one sense, and the occasion is included in the world in another sense. . . . The soul is nothing else than the succession of my occassions of experience, extending from birth to the present moment . . . the world for me is nothing else than how the functionings of my body present it for my experience. . . . No event can be wholly and solely the cause of another event. . . . The only intelligible doctrine of causation is founded on the doctrine of immanence. Each occasion presupposes the antecedent world as active in its own nature. This is the reason why events have a determinate status relatively to each other. . . . Descartes' "Cogito, ergo sum" is wrongly translated, "I *think,* therefore I am." It is never bare thought or bare existence that we are aware of. . . . My unity—which is Descartes' "I am"—is my process of shaping this welter of material into a constant pattern of feelings.

The most obvious example of conceptual experience is the entertainment of alternatives. Life lies below this grade of mentality. Life is the enjoyment of emotion, derived from the past and aimed at the future. . . . The emotion . . . is received, it is enjoyed and it is passed along, from moment to moment. . . . It is the conjunction of transcendence and immanence. . . . Philosophy begins in wonder, and, at the end, when philosophic thought has done its best, the wonder remains. There has been added, however, some grasp of the immensity of things, some purification of emotion by understanding.

Whitehead continues,

Education is the art of the utilization of knowledge. . . .[51] The essence of education is that it be religious. A religious education is an

[51] Alfred North Whitehead, *The Aims of Education* (New York: Mentor Books, The New American Library of World Literature, Inc., 1949), p. 16.

education which inculcates duty and reverence. Duty arises from our potential control over the course of events. Where attainable knowledge could have changed the issue, ignorance has the guilt of vice. And the foundation of reverence is this perception that the present holds within itself the complete sum of existence, backwards and forwards, that whole amplitude of time which is eternity.[52]

About the curriculum, he continues: "There is one subject-matter for education and that is Life in all its manifestations." [53] He criticizes the traditional school for teaching ideas without meaning or application, saying: "Education with inert ideas is not only useless: it is, above all things, harmful." [54] He continues: "Do not teach too many subjects, and again, what you teach, teach thoroughly. . . . Do not be deceived by the pedantry of dates. . . . The communion of saints is a great and inspiring assemblage, but it has only one possible hall of meeting, and that is the present." [55]

"There is no course of study which merely gives general culture and another which gives special knowledge. . . . You may not divide the seamless coat of learning. . . . Finally there should grow the most austere of all mental qualities. I mean the sense of style . . . the love of a subject in itself and for itself. Style is the ultimate morality of the mind." [56]

He believes that each school must develop its own curriculum and that the sequence of subjects should be determined by readiness, interest, and ability of the learner, and the use he will make of it.

It is not true that the easier subjects should precede the harder. On the contrary, some of the hardest must come first because nature so dictates, and because they are essential to life. . . . The first intellectual task which confronts an infant is the acquirement of spoken language. . . . What an appalling task . . . . We all know that the infant does it and the miracle of his achievement is inexplicable. . . . All I ask is that we should cease to talk nonsense about postponing the harder subjects. . . . The uncritical application of the principle of the necessary antecedent of some subjects to others has, in the hands of dull people with a turn for organization, produced in education the dryness of the Sahara.[57]

[52] *Ibid.*, p. 26.
[53] *Ibid.*, p. 18.
[54] *Ibid.*, p. 13.
[55] *Ibid.*, pp. 14–15.
[56] *Ibid.*, pp. 23–24.
[57] *Ibid.*, pp. 27–28.

"The process of mental development is essentially periodic. . . . I would term them [the stages of development] the stage of romance, the stage of precision, and the stage of generalization." [58] He describes these stages as romance, the stage of first apprehension, of vividness, of novelty; precision, the stage of grammar, of language, and science, where width of relationships is subordinated to exactness of formulation; and generalization, a synthesis, a return to romance with the advantage of classified ideas and relevant techniques, the fruition, the final success of precise training. Education should repeat such cycles. For example, when the study of languages has progressed to the stage of precision, the sciences may be introduced on the romantic level. He further warns that although mentality develops in rhythmic cycles, the distinction between the three phases of the cycle should not be exaggerated. "The university course," he concludes, "is the great period of generalization." [59]

About formal discipline, he remarks that the mind never remains passive long enough to be "sharpened." He rejects the idea of deferred values in education and maintains that whatever interest, power, or mental life the teacher wishes to develop in the pupil must be exhibited here and now. This is the golden rule of education.

He is much concerned with liberal, scientific, and technical education especially on the college level. Of liberal education he observes: "In its essence a liberal education is an education for thought and for aesthetic appreciation. It proceeds by imparting a knowledge of the masterpieces of thought, of imaginative literature and of art. The action which it contemplates is command. It is aristocratic education implying leisure." [60]

He continues:

A technical education is not to be conceived as a maimed alternative to the perfect Platonic culture: namely as a defective training unfortunately made necessary by cramped conditions of life. No human being can attain to anything but fragmentary knowledge and a fragmentary training of his capacities. There are, however, three main roads along which we can proceed with good hope of advancing toward the best balance of intellect and character: these are the way of literary culture,

[58] *Ibid.*, pp. 28–29.
[59] *Ibid.*, p. 37.
[60] *Ibid.*, p. 55.

CHART 6: POST-HEGELIANISM AND THE CENTURY OF DARWIN

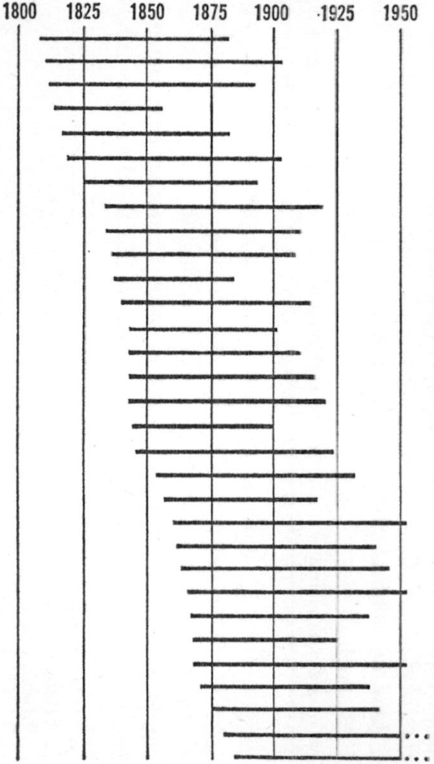

CHARLES DARWIN	1809-1882	"Origin of Species"; evolution
POPE LEO XIII	1810-1903	Return to scholasticism as basis for Catholic thought
NOAH PORTER	1811-1893	Followed Kant; everyone must assume existence of God
SOREN KIERKEGAARD	1813-1855	Opposed Hegel; modern existentialism
KARL MARX	1818-1883	Dialectic materialism; "Das Kapital"
HERBERT SPENCER	1820-1903	Followed Comte, J. S. Mill, Darwin
THOMAS HENRY HUXLEY	1825-1895	Darwinism; epiphenomenonalism
WILHELM WUNDT	1832-1920	Academic psychology
WILHELM DILTHEY	1833-1911	Positivistic idealism
WILLIAM T. HARRIS	1835-1909	Hegelian; idealistic tradition in American education
THOMAS HILL GREEN	1836-1882	English idealism
CHARLES S. PEIRCE	1839-1914	Pragmatism
JOHN FISKE	1842-1901	Applied theory of evolution to history
WILLIAM JAMES	1842-1910	Pragmatism; psychology
HERMAN COHEN	1842-1918	Modern idealism derived from Plato and Kant
GEORGE TRUMBULL LADD	1842-1921	Studied German idealism; pioneer in experimental psychology
FREDERICH W. NIETZSCHE	1844-1900	Will to power; the master race
F. H. BRADLEY	1846-1924	Only the Absolute Whole is strictly real
HANS VAIHINGER	1852-1933	Idealistic positivism; an interpreter of Kant
JOSIAH ROYCE	1855-1916	Absolute idealism
JOHN DEWEY	1859-1952	Instrumentalism
HENRI BERGSON	1859-1941	"Creative Evolution"; vital force
ALFRED NORTH WHITEHEAD	1861-1947	Panpsychism
GEORGE SANTAYANA	1863-1952	Critical realism
FERDINAND C. S. SCHILLER	1864-1937	Humanist
JOHN M. E. MC TAGGART	1866-1925	English idealist
BENEDETTO CROCE	1866-1952	Idealist; Minister of Education
WILLIAM MC DOUGALL	1871-1938	Hermic psychology; supported mind-body dualism
GIOVANNI GENTILE	1875-1944	Hegelian; reformed schools of Italy; fascist
... JOHN B. WATSON	1878-	Behaviorism
... JACQUES MARITAIN	1882-	Thomism

the way of scientific culture, the way of technical culture. No one of these methods can be exclusively followed without grave loss of intellectual activity and of character.[61]

The antithesis between a technical and a liberal education is fallacious. There can be no adequate technical education which is not liberal, and no liberal education which is not technical: that is no education which does not impart both technique and intellectual vision. In simpler language, education should turn out the pupil with something he knows well and can do well.[62]

With regard to higher education he writes:

During the school period the student has been mentally bending over his desk; at the University he should stand up and look around. . . . Your learning is useless to you till you have forgotten . . . the minutiae which you have learned by heart for the examination. The function of a university is to enable you to shed detail in favor of principles.[63]

The task of a university is to weld together imagination and experience. . . . Prolonged routine work dulls the imagination . . . . Imagination is a contagious disease. It cannot be measured by the yard, or weighed by the pound and then delivered to the students by members of the faculty. It can only be communicated by a faculty whose members themselves wear their learning with imagination.[64]

The ideal of a University is not so much knowledge, as power. Its business is to convert the knowledge of the boy into the power of a man.[65]

SUMMARY

Our account of the growth of educational thought has shown that most Western ideas derive from ancient Greece. In general, it may be said that idealism (a theory of innate ideas) began with Plato, realism (a theory of forms) with Aristotle, naturalism (an atomic theory) with Democritus, and pragmatism (a theory of activity and change) with Heraclitus and the sophists. Plato's theories were developed by his disciples in the Academy, expounded by Plotinus, and blended with Christian doctrine by St. Augustine. Aristotle's Lyceum existed to the third century A.D. His

[61] *Ibid.*, p. 64.
[62] *Ibid.*, p. 58.
[63] *Ibid.*, pp. 37–38.
[64] *Ibid.*, pp. 98–101.
[65] *Ibid.*, p. 39.

works were well known in Africa, especially among the Arabian scholars, but suffered a temporary eclipse in western Europe until the eleventh century when the great dispute between the Platonic realists and the Aristotelian nominalists began, ending in the synthesis of St. Thomas, scholasticism, and the triumph of Aristotelianism as the official philosophy of the Western Church. But Platonism was not dead. The battle cry of the Renaissance was "Back to Plato." Luther and Calvin valued St. Augustine above St. Thomas.

The Garden of Epicurus and the Stoa of Zeno produced the philosophies of Epicurianism, hedonism, skepticism, and Stoicism, the last of which became the official religion of Rome under Cicero, Seneca, Epictetus, and Marcus Aurelius until the time of Constantine. Naturalism became dormant because of the otherworldly emphasis of Christianity until the sixteenth century when Sir Francis Bacon and his group became interested in studying the world empirically and developed what has since been known as the scientific method.

These three philosophies, Platonism (idealism), Aristotelianism (realism), and naturalism, have developed side by side in the modern world, each receiving new interpretations. The British spirit, with notable exceptions such as the idealism of Berkeley, has been empirical and realistic. Idealism developed to the greatest extent in Germany. France and the Low Countries have developed various types of naturalism and realism. Pragmatism is said to be a philosophy particularly indigenous to modern America, but its antecedents can be traced from Heraclitus, through the sophists, Quintilian, certain aspects of Bacon, and Comte, to William James.

Some philosophers are hard to classify. Spinoza, while generally considered to be a realist, has certain idealistic characteristics in his pantheism, while Kant, conceded to be an idealist, is realistic in aspects of his epistemology. Terms such as logical-empiricist and critical-naturalist are used to describe many modern thinkers, indicating that each has constructed a philosophy of life of what seems to him to be harmonious points of view. This is much different from the eclectic approach which chooses pleasing bits of theory from here and there without any thought for the total pattern.

All of these philosophies are current in American education. The philosophy of idealism dominated American education of the nineteenth century and stemmed from the Americans who had studied with Kant, Fichte, and Hegel in Germany. But the realism of Herbart, Pestalozzi, and Comenius has also had considerable influence on methods and the curriculum. Although differing in many respects both idealists and realists believe in fixed values and in a subject-matter centered curriculum. The term "essentialist" is sometimes used to describe both groups.

Non-essentialist educators have a harder time finding a blanket term for their philosophies. Those at the extreme right differ from the essentialists principally by insisting that the chief responsibility for learning belongs to the student, and that school subjects are instruments to accomplish desired ends, not ends in themselves. One studies a subject for its own sake after he has studied it for the use he can make of it. On the other hand some progressivists insist that subjects, grades, and all other familiar marks of traditional education can be abandoned for the free and natural self-development of the individual. Experimentalists believe that education can favorably affect the on-coming generation by improving their present quality of living, while reconstructionists believe that the schools can and should build a new social order through "frontier thinking," and by organizing adult action-groups in labor, politics, and other phases of social and economic life.

Some of the foregoing schools of philosophy claim to have the only solution to the problems of life. Such ideas are not in keeping with the pluralism of American life and thought. Some philosophers believe that there must be different types of education for fixed upper and lower classes of citizens. This doctrine is also quite un-American, for although the existence of social groups in America must be recognized, the surprising mobility with which many Americans pass from group to group makes a fixed pre-World War I European system of education singularly inappropriate.

Actually, most educational philosophies in America are not too far apart in the statement of aim: to prepare good citizens. Some believe that citizenship involves only the brotherhood of man, others that it involves also the fatherhood of God. Some are concerned only with a "temporal city," others with an "eternal." For each there must be a right way, but it is not the same for all. In a pluralistic society, each should be permitted to pursue his own plan, path, and pace toward this consonant end, providing he does not prevent another from doing the same.

Recent attempts have been made to create a synthesis, to effect a reconciliation between the old and the new. These are highly commendable endeavors so long as they purport only to make men appreciate their similarities and their differences. But when they are offered as *the* pattern for American education they must be looked upon with suspicion.

BIBLIOGRAPHY

Dewey, John, *The Child and the Curriculum* (Chicago: The University of Chicago Press, 1902).

———, *Democracy and Education* (New York: The Macmillan Company, 1916).

———, *Experience and Education* (New York: The Macmillan Company, 1938).

Edman, Irwin, *John Dewey* (New York: The Bobbs-Merrill Company, Inc., 1955).

Geiger, George R., *John Dewey in Perspective* (New York: Oxford University Press, 1958).

James, William, *Essays in Pragmatism*, ed. Alberney Costell (New York: Hafner Publishing Co., 1948).

———, *Talks to Teachers on Psychology and to Students on Some of Life's Ideals* (New York: Henry Holt and Co., 1924).

Johnson, Allison Heartz, *Whitehead's Theory of Reality* (Boston: Beacon Press, 1952).

Maritain, Jacques, *Education at the Crossroads* (New Haven: The Yale University Press, 1943).

———, *Man and the State* (Chicago, Ill.: University of Chicago Press, 1951). A Phoenix Book.

———, *The Rights of Man and Natural Law*, trans. Doris C. Anson (New York: Charles Scribner's Sons, 1943).

Schilpp, Paul Arthur (ed.), *The Philosophy of Alfred North Whitehead*, 2nd ed. (New York: Tudor Publishing Co., 1951).

Spencer, Herbert, *Education, Intellectual, Moral, and Physical* (New York: D. Appleton & Co., 1912).

Whitehead, Alfred North, *Adventures of Ideas* (New York: The Macmillan Company, 1940).

———, *The Aims of Education and Other Essays* (New York: The Macmillan Company, 1929).

———, *Essays in Science and Philosophy* (New York: Philosophical Library, Inc., 1947).

Part III

THE EDUCATION OF MAN

Chapter VIII

Nature and Nurture

PREVIEW

In Part II we have studied the contributions of the great philosophers to the theory and practice of education. It is now our purpose to examine, contrast, and compare their theories in relation to the professional study and practice of education. First we shall consider theories relative to the nature of man and the integration of his personality, after which we shall consider man in society and the nature of his values. Our final study will be concerned with the aims of education and their implementation.

In the present chapter we shall consider the nature of man in its several aspects. We shall draw freely from philosophy, and from the biological and social sciences to collect the data upon which conclusions can be made. Our method will be historical, comparative, and analytic. The author believes that the conclusions of educational theorists must be based upon that which can be empirically or logically demonstrated to be valid. He also maintains that the individual is a complex organism interacting with a complex environment, and that, therefore, it is invalid to reach a conclusion about one aspect of an individual or his environment without taking into account all other pertinent aspects of both. In other words, the author's point of view is holistic and organismic.

Accordingly, it is not until much pertinent evidence has been presented that the author allows himself to express a personal point of view. This he presents as a hypothesis because he believes in cultural and intellectual pluralism. While we live in a world of private absolutes, each holding his own opinions, we must not deny a similar right and existence to others, but since we also live in a pluralistic social and intellectual world, we must be able to integrate these views into a workable social pattern of individual respect and social concern. We are faced here with the eternal problem of the self and the other, the one and the many, the individual and the group. Let us proceed.

THE NATURE OF MAN: DATA

THE BIOLOGICAL NATURE OF MAN

Although dates are highly speculative and subject to constant revision with the disclosure of new evidence, archeologists estimate that the present world on which we live took some 4,000 million years to evolve. The earth was formed in a lifeless Azoic age. About 1,550 million years ago under fortunate circumstances, by chance or by design, unicellular life began. The protozoa came into existence during the Archeozoic age. It took some 700 million years for the earliest living forms to emerge during the Proterozoic age. During the Paleozoic era from 520 to 220 million years ago, fishes, the amphibia, insects, reptiles, and land plants appeared. It took 80 million years more for the birds and mammals to develop. During the Cenozoic era, from 70 to a million years ago, the first primates appeared, culminating in the origination of man in the Pliocene period and developing into the genus "Homo" in the Holocene period in which we are now living.

This basic pattern for the development of life on our planet is generally agreed upon. The length of the time periods and the method by which each genus came into existence, whether through special creation or a process of natural development, is still in dispute. It is also generally agreed that man is somehow continuous with nature. Honigmann credits man's origin to the first animal-like plants which probably arose about one and a half billion years ago, and sums up his position in the animal kingdom as follows:

Kingdom: Animal
  Subkingdom: Metazoa (multicelled)
    Phylum: Chordata (chordates)
      Subphylum: Vertebrata (animals with backbones)
        Class: Mammalia (mammals)
          Subclass: Eutheria (placental animals)
            Order: Primates (the first)
              Suborder: Anthropoidia (manlike)
                Family: Hominidae (human)
                  Genus: Homo (from Greek word "same")
                    Species: *sapiens* ("wise") [1]

Two important conclusions can be drawn from the preceding discussion, namely, (1) the biological structure of man is similar in many respects to that of other living organisms, and (2) it has taken man a very long time to attain to his present imperfect state of development. For education, we may infer that a careful study of lower forms of animal life will yield important insights into man's biological structure and functioning; also, that the process of human development is slow and that educators should not be disturbed because changes cannot be effected too rapidly. Man has only yesterday, according to the above time scale, entered upon his spiritual, intellectual, social, economic, and political development. Perhaps we should not be impatient with his halting steps.

We should, however, not lose sight of what Eisley calls "a small soundless concussion," the emergence of man's brain.[2] It has been since this development, a little more than half a million years ago, that all of the distinctly human characteristics of man, social and intellectual alike, have come to pass. In contrast to one-and-a-half-billion years when animal life began to be differentiated from plant life, the half million years since man began to be human is a very short time. What, then, are the unique characteristics which make man so distinct from all other creatures? The answer seems to lie in the brain and what man has been able to do through the use of it. Scientists and philosophers have set for themselves the task of describing this uniqueness. Man is the animal that stands

[1] John J. Honigmann, *The World of Man* (New York: Harper and Brothers, 1959), pp. 798–801. This classification has been adapted.

[2] Loren Eisley, in *Adventures of the Mind*, ed. Richard Thruelsen and John Kobler (New York: Alfred A. Knopf, Inc., 1959), p. 9.

erect, that turns his head, that turns his thumb in. He is the animal that laughs, that thinks, that remembers, that makes tools including language, writing, laws, and social institutions.

It is this complex of insights, memories, and abilities which constitutes man's mind and which sets him apart from nature and gives him control over it. To a very considerable extent the lower animals are more or less successfully adapted to their environment, both physically and instinctively. Although his erect posture and his brain have caused man to lose some of his physical power and the keenness of his sense organs, and have left him with fewer hereditary instinctive conduct patterns, it is the mental curiosity, restlessness, and ingenuity which have enabled him in large measure to adapt his environment to himself. To the biological heredity which is slow to change, as we have seen, and which sets limits to his activities, he adds the cultural and social heredity which he has fashioned for himself and which opens limitless vistas of growth and improvement.

What then is man? Or should we rather ask: "What then are men?" We have seen that the biological sciences cannot help us very much, aside from showing the affinity of man with nature, particularly living organisms, and the long, slow, tortuous way up from the slime where the first germ of life came into existence. In the course of his long development man has acquired many selves as James points out (see Chapter VII, p. 156). Besides his physical self, he has a mental self, an emotional self, a social self. And somehow he must seek, largely through education, to integrate these selves into a consistent personality.

MIND AND MATTER

The nature of man has been a perennial problem in philosophy. One of the knotty problems has been to describe exactly the nature of mind, the nature of matter, and the relationship between them, if indeed such a relationship can be said to exist. It will be well for us at this point to review the preceding chapters and to piece together the theories dealing with the mind-body relationship.

We have seen that Heraclitus (a naturalist) taught that the basic substance of existence and its cause were all one, which he called *fire,* while Parmenides laid the basis for idealism by suggesting that being and thought are one and the same thing, and that thought creates being. The sophists believed that what a man's mind told him was true, *was true* for *him* and that the mind of man was the measure of things and superior to them. All these groups, therefore, recognized mind and matter as fundamental to a concept of reality. For Plato mind and matter were entirely distinct, and mind impressed the reality upon matter. For example the table you see is not a real table; what is real is the idea of table which your mind impresses upon it. For Aristotle, on the other hand, mind was in matter as its formative principle. Mind is everywhere, in everything, but there is a progression in clarity to abstract forms. Both mind and matter exist, but mind must dominate matter and must give it form. Epicurus and the other early Greek atomists believed that objects threw off images which are received by the senses and thus impress the organism. The Stoics believed that mind and matter were both real but the mind was of a much finer texture since it represented the rational part of the soul. St. Augustine taught that mind and matter existed independently, and that the mind can discover truth through revelation as it exists in the mind of God. Thus belief precedes reason. On the other hand the nominalists, Rocellinus and Abelard among them, held that reason preceded and was the source of truth. St. Thomas Aquinas showed the rationality of the universe as revealed by God through the Church, thus championing the rational power of the mind to arrive at truth.

Impatient with scholastic thought, Sir Francis Bacon urged men to discard the idols of thought and begin anew by careful empirical observation of data and the treatment of these data by an inductive method. Hobbes, a materialist, believed mind to be motion in the head, a more subtle material than body. For Descartes the universe is made up of two irreducible substances: mind and matter, a view partly accepted by Locke. Spinoza taught that mind and matter were two aspects of the same reality, God. Berkeley started by accepting the dualism of mind and matter, but considered that matter could not exist without being perceived by mind. Hume went beyond his contemporaries by declaring that all one could prove was a constant succession of impressions. Leibnitz believed that he had reconciled the disagreements by maintaining that matter was not inert but was dynamic and self-motivating.

Kant held that while there is an external world from which the mind received impressions, the mind cannot know it-in-itself, but only according to its organizing or structuring categories. Therefore, the mind is the only source of knowledge. Fichte added to Kant's concept a universal mind or ego which creates the outside world through a projection of itself. Thus matter is a creation of the mind. Hegel followed in the same tradition of absolute idealism and found that this absolute mind is continually creating and realizing itself in objects and institutions.

Following in the tradition of Hobbes, Descartes, and Locke, Herbart held that things exist independent of our ideas about them, and that experience is the only source of knowledge. Positivists, pragmatists, and naturalists like Comte, Dewey, and Santayana, while not in agreement on all points, look upon mind as a kind of behavior.

THE PROBLEM OF KNOWLEDGE

We now come to the problem of knowledge and how it is acquired. This problem is crucial for education, because unless we know it we cannot hope to construct a systematic formula for schooling nor develop methods for its implementation.

Many modern thinkers believe that all knowledge begins in experience. Naturalists maintain that something in the object moves by a physical impulse toward the knowing subject where it is made known by the sense organs and the nervous system. Bacon, Comte, Herbart, and Spencer, as we have seen, believed that the scientific method is the only method for acquiring real knowledge and that the method of induction should displace deduction.

Idealists believe that the validity of knowledge depends upon the validity of the process by which it is known. Berkeley insisted that "to be is to be perceived" and that Ultimate Mind puts meaning into experience. Kant, in his *Critique of Pure Reason,* made no conjecture beyond the phenomenal world. He taught that the confusion of perceptions was ordered by the categories of thought. (See p. 120.) Fichte and Hegel believed that *to exist and to be known* was to be in relation to the Absolute Ego in which ultimate truth lies.

While many critical idealists accept Santayana's doctrine of essences existing apart from the realm of being, as do critical realists, they differ from them in demanding that the verification of phenomena be in terms of Absolute Mind, and that all experiential knowledge is necessarily incomplete. The idealist takes a slightly skeptical attitude toward the findings of empirical science. Reality for the idealist is a logically unified system, rooted in existence, a Universal Mind.

For the realist, to know an object is to perceive the identical object as it exists in the external world and as presented to consciousness. Mind is a relationship between the organism and the object. For the critical realist the quality that the object has in the mind is different from what it is in the object. There is a realm of essences which represent the object to consciousness and give content to experience. For the pragmatist experience is specific and particular. Only facts organized into patterns of successful action may be considered knowledge. While pragmatism begins with sense perceptual experience, such experience is constantly interacting with the knower and his world. Pragmatists are, therefore, not willing to accept verified knowledge of the past as absolute truth as do neo-realists, nor are they willing to admit that absolute truth can be found in predisposed principles of reason as do the rationalists. Qualities become known as we are actively engaged with them in experience. Experience, as viewed by pragmatists, is the area in which individuals and things intermingle. Knowledge is, therefore, always public and objective, it is a process of doing, knowing, living; it is always fractional, contingent, and relative.

The content of science is important as a starting point for thought, but it must never be considered as absolute. It provides hypotheses for experimental action, and a scientific method for problem solving. While many idealists might accept the term "experiential" to describe knowledge, the pragmatists would use the term "experimental" since they hold that verification of knowledge depends upon practical consequences.

THEORIES OF LEARNING

From the foregoing discussion it appears that many modern thinkers believe all knowledge begins in experience. But, we may ask, what happens to the initial experience of the newborn child, to the original booming, buzzing, and confusion? Theories of learning are often grouped into two schools, namely,—the connectionist or associationist theories and the gestalt or field theories.

The associationists maintain that the individual first recognizes simple sensations, stimuli, and effects such as hot-cold, sweet-sour, hard-soft, rough-smooth. Learning takes place according to the frequency, primacy, recency, vividness, similarity, and duration of the stimuli. The philosophical basis for this school of psychology can be traced through Herbart and Hume to Locke's "tabula rasa" and the sense realism of Comenius. It is mechanistic and realistic. It had its first formulation as a science under Wundt at Leipzig. Among its earlier exponents in America were Titchener and Thorndike. To this group belong the behaviorism of Watson and the dynamic psychology of Woodworth. Its chief idealist exponent was McDougall.

The field theorists, sometimes known as gestaltists, are primarily interested in problems of perception. Philosophically field theory has its basis in Plato's theory of ideas and Aristotle's theory of forms. It is implicit in Froebel's theory of the young child's unfoldment through education. Field theorists maintain that the earliest mental states are general non-localized experiences of warmth, hunger, and pain. Mental life begins with these primary undifferentiated wholes out of which specialized forms are differentiated. Persons, objects, events, processes are first perceived in their entirety; they are not built up or composed of simple elements, but exist as wholes in their own right. With experience and maturity the learner differentiates parts and details. These parts in turn become wholes which may be transposed into new situations. On entering a room one first perceives a group of people. The group is differentiated into men and women which in turn become units for further differentiation. For example the head is such a whole which can be differentiated into eyes, mouth, etc., each of which in turn becomes a unit for further differentiation. A tree is first perceived as a unit which can be further differentiated into roots, trunk, branches, and leaves, each of which may become a separate unit for differentiation and may be transposed to an entirely new situation. For example the root system may become an integral part of an experience about soil erosion, or the trunk may be transposed to situations dealing with fuel or cabinet making. In the same way sport skills may be transferred to other sports, or generalizations in mathematics may find wide application in scientific study. The above theory of gestalt psychology had its beginnings in Germany under Wertheimer, Koffka, and Kohler. It is implicit in the organismic panpsychism of Whitehead (see p. 173). In America it was embraced by experimentalists, notably Dewey and Bode, in their emphasis on the education of the whole child. Connectionism tends to be atomistic and mechanistic; the field theories are organismic and tend toward vitalism. In connectionism the idea or object is primary; in gestalt the situation or experience is primary. Both schools are valid methods of describing human behavior, and many psychologists are of the opinion that further research will show how these seemingly opposing schools complement each other.

THE KNOWER AND THE KNOWN

With regard to the process of knowing it is well to remember that inanimate matter, that is primitive matter, can be known, but there is no evidence that it is knowing. Mechanical devices, such as computing machines can recall and manipulate data, but as the term suggests, these data are knowns given to the machine by a knower. This fact takes on added significance with the development of the science of cybernetics, which tries to predict and regulate human behavior, in an era of automation.

All animate objects, even the simplest structures, may be said to be aware, which is possibly a very elementary type of knowing. This type of knowing with its appropriate response is built into nerve structure and into the voluntary and involuntary muscles in the form of instincts or tendencies toward action, so that it may be called determined response. In the higher animal forms below man, the responses of the voluntary, and sometimes of the involuntary muscles also (e.g., the Pavlov experiment on canine salivation), may be modified or conditioned by training. Man, like his distant animal relatives, bears in his physiological functions and anatomical structure many "instinctive" patterns. Like the higher forms of animal life these "instincts" may be used to build habits through conditioning. It is well to recall here that Aristotle called habit "man's second nature" (see p. 51). Certainly habituation of the multitudinous lower level and routine responses is necessary so that man can be free to exercise judgment for decision making on a higher and more complex action level. In addition, as we have seen, man has developed a verbal or symbolic memory along with his physiological memory. Therefore, in addition to his biological inheritance, and possibly more significant, man has a cultural heritage which affects the program of education which the human society provides for the rearing of its young.

HEREDITY AND ENVIRONMENT

Man, then, like his animal cousins, is born with certain physiological structures and certain tendencies toward behavior which adapt him to function successfully in his physical environment. This physical heredity is of great importance, because within it is the entire physical potential of each human being. It is made up of the assets and liabilities bequeathed to him by his ancestors. Beyond the limits of this potential he cannot go. This potential, then, determines all of his actions and responses. Practically all of his responses, however, are subject to modification by some form of external or environmental control, but whereas the lower animals are for the most part confined to their environment and must adapt to it, men can change their environments by removing to another more friendly place or by adapting their present environment to their needs or purposes. Men can modify all aspects of their environment except one, the time in which they live.[3] A man's conduct, then, is conditioned by the interplay of external forces, both natural and societal, and internal forces physiological, mental, and intuitive.

We have seen above that man belongs to the subclass of mammals which not only bears its young alive, but which carries them for long periods before birth and, because they are born helpless, cares for them for long periods after birth. In man this period of infancy extends over many years. This formative period of extended infancy is perhaps the greatest asset of Homo sapiens, because it is the period of plasticity in which modifications in conduct patterns are effected. The chief instruments which man has

[3] Psychotics who live in the past are usually excluded from society. "A normal man" is defined as one whose outward or observable acts are in conformity with the norms of the society in which he lives.

made to pattern the conduct of the individual are the cultural heritage, and, more immediately, the mores or customs of society. Even such basic physiological functions as feeding and elimination are thus conditioned. The process of patterning in man is called education, and the instrument which society has devised to insure the speedy and effective acquisition of essential and approved patterns of knowledge, skills, and attitudes is called the school.

FATE VERSUS FREE WILL

The nature of the school will be determined by what a given social group believes to be the nature of man. So far we have explored the relation of man to nature, the relative influences of his biological and cultural heredity and his environment upon his conduct, and the method by which he obtains knowledge. We have introduced the terms "patterning" and "conditioning," and now we must raise the important issue of fate versus free will.

Determinism versus indeterminism is crucial to a discussion of learning. If individual man has no free will, then society must condition him to act according to fixed social laws through the operation of fixed natural laws. If man has the ability to make his own decisions, then instead of breaking the will, education must strengthen it and help it to discover standards of right conduct. How much freedom should be allowed to each individual is one of the most important questions in education. It will be well for us now to recall some of the ideas developed in the historical study in Part II.

Both the Pythagoreans and the Heraclitians believed that the universe, including man, was a closed system, and that the cosmic process operates according to law. On the other hand, the sophists held that man possesses unrealized potentials, is not bound by inescapable laws, and can mold his own destiny. Socrates, believing that man's highest achievement is knowledge, held that its acquisition would lead him to desire the good and thus to influence his future. Wrong knowledge he thought led to wrong choices. Plato also believed that freedom was a necessary basis for the good life. Aristotle pointed out that virtue as well as evil lies within the power of man and that morality demands the freedom to make a real choice between them. In the Roman world the Stoics held that the world is ruled by Fate which is the will of God.

Philo, Plotinus, and the early Christian apologists agreed that the soul of man is free when in God, but when in matter it partakes of the evil of matter. Freedom consists in the return of the soul to God. Man cannot be blamed for his sin if he did not have the power of choice. St. Augustine, on the other hand, denied individual freedom. God, he said, chooses those he will save. St. Thomas Aquinas took a medial position when he asserted that man's will is free, but that God, forseeing that some men would not accept the offer of His grace, had predestined punishments for them.

At the beginning of the scientific movement, Galileo and Newton observed that the events of the universe followed definite laws into which man must fit by necessity, while Hobbes declared that to hold that man has free will is absurd. Spinoza was also of the opinion that man's actions are absolutely determined, for God alone is free. Descartes distinguished mind from matter and believed that mind is free while the body must act according to natural laws. The will of man is, therefore, independent of the body.

Locke and Hume both supported the idea of free will. Locke believed that man has a will because he can prefer one action to another, but that God has endowed him with tendencies toward right action. Hume asserted that so long as man's actions arise from his own character, nature or desire, they are free. Leibnitz attempted to mediate the positions of Newton, Hobbes, and Spinoza on the one hand and Locke and Hume on the other, by advancing the theory that man is not free in an absolute sense, but strives for the realization of his strongest desire.

Kant held that freedom of the will cannot be proved by pure reason or by experience, but in transcendental ideas. Freedom of the will, he wrote, is an idea which man erects because of the demands of his moral nature. This intuitive or transcendental truth of the moral nature of man is higher than the truth of science. Fichte believed that each individual ego or will is a part of the Absolute Ego or God and derives freedom therefrom, while Hegel maintained that man is free to realize himself to the fullest.

Herbart joined the determinists in denying freedom to man. Believing that everything followed fixed natural laws, he attempted to build up a system of psychology and educational method which would follow the method of the physical sciences. John Stuart Mill believed that human actions are the result of many factors which if fully known and understood would enable one to predict an individual's future action. He admitted that praise and blame implied the ability to make a choice and so included freedom as a fact in human existence.

In America, William James found in man a "will to believe" and freedom to build his ideals and to strive for their realization. John Dewey also held that man is a free agent in a world in the making. He must, therefore, be free to make decisions, and his wants and desires must count ultimately in determining the nature of the universe.

Most educators, with the possible exception of personal idealists, believe that man's actions are bound by the "laws" of his physical and social environment, but that he has the power to use these laws for ends which he determines for himself. In this power lies his freedom of will. The problem of free will is important for the motivation and control of conduct in school and society. Determinists will set up rules and laws and promote conformity to them by a system of rewards and punishments. Idealists will attempt to instill high ideals by which the individual will motivate himself to "right" conduct. Humanists and experimentalists will insist that "right" conduct is not determined by a priori standards, but rather by the results of action, that man has the ability to choose the action leading to the best results for the greatest number in the long run, but that he also has the obligation to evaluate existing standards of conduct in terms of a constantly changing world.

GOD, THE SOUL, AND IMMORTALITY

The Nature of God

Closely allied to a discussion of fate and free will is the nature of God, the soul, and immortality. Here again we shall apply the knowledge gained in Part II to our present consideration.

Plato equated God with pure idea or universal mind while Aristotle designated him as Pure Form and the Unmoved Mover. Philo considered God so great and good that he could not be comprehended by man. In much the same vein Plotinus believed that God was the source of everything in the universe, that man cannot understand him perfectly, and that the more man is concerned with things the farther he is from God. This is the position of the early Christian apologists who identified pure reason with a person. St. Augustine considered God so good, powerful, perfect, and knowing that he had predetermined (predestined) the control of the universe forever. St. Anselm, in his ontological proof for the existence of God, maintained that God is the necessary Existence of which all other existences are parts. Influenced heavily by the thinking of Aristotle, St. Thomas Aquinas reasoned that God is pure form and the First and Supreme Cause, the Unchanged Principle in a changing world. He is absolutely perfect, the source, creator, and motivator of all things. Meister Eckhart, a fourteenth-century mystic, believed that God can be revealed to man only by mystical experience. Many branches of Protestant Christianity hold to this point of view. Francis Bacon and many subsequent philosophers have divided theology into natural and revealed. Natural theology is that which man can learn through a study of nature. Revealed theology, on the other hand, is that which comes from God himself by mystical experience.

Spinoza reasoned that God is the sole independent substance of the universe and that mind and body, thought and extension, are attributes of him. Locke, who discarded the theory of innate ideas, believed God to be a summation of certain of man's experiences extended to infinity. Bishop Berkeley believed that God is the supreme spirit and that everything exists in the mind of God. Hume believed that the existence of God could not be proved by reason, but that such a belief was a necessity for man and arose from human misery, fears and hopes. Like Philo and Plotinus, Leibnitz associated God with clarity. In his monadology he maintained that monads existed in varying degrees of clarity, and that the greater the clearness, the nearer they were to God who was the clearest and most perfect monad. Hume's theories inspired Kant to differentiate pure and practical reason. There is inherent in man a categorical imperative, a standard for moral conduct. This standard must spring from a perfect being, God, who is all-good, all-knowing, wise, and powerful. The idea of God and goodness cannot be proved by pure reason, but is transcendent in that it goes beyond reason and experience.

Fichte maintained that God was universal reason or intelligence, and Hegel, that he was Idea, that is, the entire process of historical evolution. Spencer held that all that can be known is finite and limited, but that we can relate this knowledge to a problematic infinite, while Comte declared that all speculation about God and infinity are signs of immaturity in man. Like Hume, James held that a belief in God is necessary to a satisfaction of man's nature. While we cannot prove his existence, we have a "will to believe" in him and we must satisfy this will. Dewey does not find the concept of God useful, but rather takes solace in a "common faith" that men may strive together for a more perfect society. Some modern theologians, Martin Buber and Paul Tillich for example, seem to believe that God is constantly seeking man (not man seeking God) and confronting him with situations to which he must respond for the good or harm of himself and others. Man cannot hide from God.

The Soul and Immortality

In the following discussion of the soul and immortality it will be important to note the close correspondence between the ideas of God described above and the concepts of soul and immortality. The soul of man is often conceived to be of the same substance as the stuff of the universe. Among the early Greek atomists the soul was considered a part of the vital principle of the universe. Democritus considered it to be composed of the finest, purest, and most perfect atoms. It was in the world and of the world, had no immortality except as matter, which was indestructible, and existed in a variety of forms. For Plato it was part of the realm of pure, perfect ideas, temporarily imprisoned in the body. The goal of the soul was to free itself from the body and live in a realm of pure abstractions.

Aristotle taught that the soul exists throughout nature. After death it returns to God of which it is a part and loses its identity therein. Like Aristotle the later Greek atomists could not admit of personal immortality. The Stoics on the other hand, held that the soul is a spark of the divine and is the source of all our knowledge; and some taught that all souls live on after the death of the body until the end of the world. Early Christian apologists taught that the soul and the body were different entities and that the soul most nearly represented the good in the universe. St. Augustine taught that the body is the prison house of the soul. After the death of the body it lives on immortally. St. Thomas Aquinas formulated the view of the soul most acceptable to Christianity. According to him the intellectual soul enters the body at birth; at death it forms a new spiritual body which endures throughout eternity.

Hobbes, Comte, and Dewey all follow Aristotle and the early Greek atomists in denying the immortality of the soul. Bacon, Locke, and Descartes all subscribed to the concept of a rational and an irrational soul, the former of which they believed to be immortal. Berkeley believed that mind is all that exists and that man's soul is a part of the mind of God which is the beginning and end of the universe. According to Leibnitz the soul is a unit of spiritual force. Kant insisted upon belief in the existence of an immortal soul because there are values in doing so. Herbart taught that the soul is one among many reals established within the brain of man, and that the soul continues after the body disintegrates.

For many modern philosophers "soul" is a name applied to spiritual activity. The mind and the soul are not extraphysical properties of men, but are descriptions of his actions, either intellectual or spiritual. Since many modern thinkers find no certain proof for the existence of an afterlife, they find within the life span of man all they need to understand him.

THE RHYTHM OF GROWTH

Our last excursion into the nature of man will deal with the rhythm of growth. For the purpose of our discussion we shall divide the life span of the individual into three periods, namely: childhood, youth, and adulthood. Each of these periods can be further subdivided, and other five- and sevenfold groupings are useful. Comenius described four schools: the mother's knee, childhood, boyhood, and youth. The purpose of such classifications has always been to group certain characteristics and tendencies which differentiate one period from another. There are two dangers in making such groupings. The first lies in the assumption, that there is a hard and fast line between each class and that a certain point of chronological age separates one from the other. All individuals do not wake up on their twelfth birthday to find that they have left the cocoon of childhood behind to venture into the world as adolescents. Second, all descriptions in each period represent averages which have wide deviations from the mean. For example the child at six varies in height from forty to fifty-three inches and in weight from thirty-six to sixty-six pounds. Since these data represent only a sampling of six-year-olds in a certain area it is quite possible that normal six-year-olds might measure above or below these limits. However there are enough similarities within each group and enough differences between each group to make the above classification useful to education. Realizing that the more general the description, the more open it is to fallacies, we shall venture to classify each age as: childhood, the age of wonder; youth, the age of revolt; and adulthood, the age of responsibility. During childhood, the child is becoming acquainted with his world and is learning his place in it. He grows rapidly until about the age of five. At this point, growth slows down until the adolescent spurt which marks the beginning of a new period of development. He is constantly active, an explorer. There are literally thousands of things he must learn, so he is constantly feeling, squeezing, sniffing, listening, noise making, and manipulating. One of his most difficult coordinations is that of speech, so he must be at it constantly, testing, combining, sometimes enjoying sheer sounds and nonsense syllables. He must learn to accept the conventions of an adult world with regard to colors, sizes, shapes, temperature, and the like. Our brief consideration of perception made it quite clear that what we believe about objects in the external world is largely determined by the traditions of the adult community in which we live. As Whitehead points out, all learning begins in a period of romance, which might be better described as a period of wonder. For the young child, "The world is so full of a number of things, / I'm sure we should all be as happy as kings." Emotional, social, and moral developments occur along with the physical and mental. By five the child has begun to control his emotions and to make an adjustment to the world of adults. He learns to curb his imaginations and to do and say what is expected of him. Girls seek the companionship of a special girl friend, while boys like to associate in groups. If there is any time that boys and girls could be separated in school it is between the ages of nine and twelve. Between the ages of five and twelve there is a tendency to accept adult authority, and there is not too much concern with the basis for moral action. Reasoning develops slowly. This age is a good time to develop what Herbart called "clearness" and his interpreters termed preparation and presentation. In other words it is a good time for the child to learn about his physical and social world in terms of the conventions in which he lives.

Youth, the second stage in our classification extends roughly from ages thirteen to twenty. We have characterized it as the period of revolt. It begins with marked physiological changes seen in a spurt in physical growth and in the appearance of secondary sex characteristics. Many of the adjustments which the child has made are undone. The tight little world of childhood is shattered. The adolescent begins to discover himself as a person. His questions are not so much on the physical level as in the realm of values. There, he must test values in experience, actual or vicarious, just as his younger self tested his first associations with things by manipulating them. How he will react to his strangeness in a world with which he has at one time been familiar, how he will respond to the feeling of loneliness which is the price we pay for individual freedom will depend on the experiences of his childhood. Many young people devaluate their parents as being behind the times especially so far as social conventions are concerned. They want to walk alone; yet they are afraid. They want to feel that there is support which they can rely on if needed. Some seek this support among their peers, others in some other adult for whom they have high regard; still others find security in organizations with ready-made slogans, high ideals, and promises of security. Youth becomes increasingly aware that he has a life to live. He thinks seriously of the purpose of life, his future vocation, and often of that one with whom he will share his greatest intimacies. Education in this period might well be concerned with the systematization of knowledge, with the techniques of arriving at generalizations, and with the application of methods of problem solving to the many vital issues which confront newly discovered selves in a newly discovered world.

Our last grouping, adulthood, makes the transition from the period of revolt to the period of responsibility. Responsibility, both directed and self-directed, begins in the earliest periods of childhood. For example, at two most children will be able to take care of many of their own physical needs. Adult responsibility is related to that just described, but it differs in that the adult now assumes responsibility for the fulfillment of his own personality. Maturity means the choice of a vocation, the will to pursue it at the highest level, the assumption of the maintenance of a home and family, and the active participation in social and civic affairs. This care for oneself and others will last throughout life or until one ceases to be an adult and enters "second childishness and mere oblivion, / Sans teeth, sans eyes, sans taste, sans everything," as the melancholy Jacques in Shakespeare's *As You Like It* describes it.

Educationally, young adulthood is the time for vocational and professional training and for those types of guidance which will help the young adult to realize his potential in the vocational, social, political, and spiritual world in which he finds himself.

SUMMARY

From our study of the biological nature of man, we see that all philosophers and scientists agree that man is a part of nature. Idealists and religionists believe that there is a supra-sensory or transcendental quality in man which makes him a unique creation. Man's knowledge is rooted in experience. Naturalists and realists maintain that objects in the external world are real in themselves. Idealists believe that there is no knowledge without a knower and that there is an a priori disposition in the mind which determines the method and the relationships by which knowledge is realized. Pragmatists declare that knowledge is fractional and situational and that knowledge of ultimate truth is impossible. Concerning heredity and environment, each individual has both a biological and a cultural heredity which is the starting point for his education and behavior. Man has the advantage of a symbolic memory in language and literature, ritual, and the arts, which, together with certain physical adaptations, makes it possible for him to adjust his environment to himself. Habituation in man takes on, not only physical, but also cultural aspects such as customs and codes of law, conduct, and tradition.

Regarding fate and free will, there is no agreement. Naturalists and many realists believe that there is a purpose in nature which determines all actions. Idealists agree that there has been purpose in the universe since the beginning, expressed in innate ideas, in absolute form, in the Mind of God. There is no general agreement as to whether this purpose predetermines all of man's actions, or

CHART 7: Metaphysics of

	IDEALISM	PRAGMATISM
The Nature of Reality	Ideas, minds, or selves—is in the inner experience of man. Ultimate reality is spiritual.	A liquid process which is constantly changing and in which there is no abiding Spirit.
Man's Nature and Destiny	The self is a soul, a spiritual being which has the power of self-determination in striving or not to achieve the perfection of the absolute Self.	Man is neither free nor determined, but can delay some responses long enough to reconstruct a total response which gives a new direction to subsequent activity.
The Mind–Body Relationship	Mind is more fundamental than body. The body depends upon mind.	Man is a part of Nature and is continuous with it. Reason is a disclosure of Nature by the evolutionary process. Our thoughts and the events of Nature are not two different substances, but constitute a continuity.
The Nature of God	Ultimate reality is Spirit. Three views: general and diffused in form; a composite of selves; a personal unity within whom there is multiplicity and unity.	Is no abiding Spirit. Knowledge of ultimate truth is impossible. There are no unchanging substances and no unchanging relations. The summation of the highest ideals man has so far conceived.
The Place of Purpose in the Universe	Has been a purpose in the universe since its beginning as can be discerned in history.	Purpose is not inherent in the cosmos but by purposeful activity man can impose purpose upon it.
The Meaning of Existence	To exist means to be Mind or Spirit or to be dependent upon Mind or Spirit.	Existence is a category which is not valid. Everything is flux or change and there is nothing which fits into category in any ultimate sense.

whether man can be a partner with the Supreme Mind in making choices of his own within limited areas. Pragmatists believe that man has free will and by it imposes purpose on a purposeless world.

Much disagreement centers about the soul and immortality.

Four Leading Philosophies

NATURALISM	REALISM
Reality is in the external world, the world of Nature. The physical universe is all that there is.	The objects of our experience are regarded as real things and are not dependent upon any mind for their existence.
The self is essentially the same as the body, an offshoot of Nature. Man may develop a degree of self-consciousness in adult life which is his one hope of salvation.	Doctrines range from the idea of a physical to a spiritual constitution of man. Man is a child of the natural order and a mixture of good and evil and any attempt to better him must recognize this fact.
Mind exists in Nature as essentially the same as the body.	Mental life is rooted and grounded in bodily existence.
No recognition of the supernatural. Religion is an affair of men adjusting themselves to the forces and processes of Nature.	An independent reality beyond the consciousness of man and whose dependable working is evident in man's contact with the world.
There is order in Nature and this order can be depended upon. "Let Nature take her course."	Some form of determinism as opposed to the anything-can-happen kind of world, a certain orderliness in the universe.
To exist means to occupy time and space, to be matter or physical energy. Space-time or Nature is conceived as identical with existence.	To exist means to occupy time and space, to be matter or physical energy.

Naturalists will admit of an immortality so far as the indestructibility of matter is concerned. Idealists believe in the eternal existence of mind, but disagree whether the mind or soul retains or loses its identity when it returns to the Supreme Mind. St. Thomas Aquinas stated a Christian view in declaring that after death the soul creates a spiritual body in which it lives immortally. Pragmatists view the doctrine of immortality practically. Those who find the concept useful and satisfying, will to believe it; those who do not find it useful discard the idea for a concept of social and cultural immortality which man and society create for themselves. The ideas expressed are compared in the following chart.

HYPOTHESIS AND IMPLICATIONS

What follows is a position taken by the author on the topics described above. It has only a present and personal validity and is stated not to be accepted, but because the author feels that a teacher's obligation to his students is not fulfilled when he has presented all sides of a question. He feels that the teacher is under the necessity of demonstrating how an individual who has given con-

CHART 8: Epistemology of

	IDEALISM	PRAGMATISM
The Nature of Knowledge	A priori, self-evident. Mind, which is replete with all the qualities, meanings, and values which experience yields us.	Hypotheses tested by experiment. Experimental knowledge which carries forward experience satisfactorily.
The Possibility of Knowledge	True knowledge of ultimate knowledge is possible, but process by which it has been discovered must be approved.	Knowledge of ultimate truth is impossible and of little practical value. An affirmation of functional knowledge.
The Instruments of Knowledge	Formal logic—induction as well as deduction. Dialectical method. Revelation; self-observation; intuition.	Experimental reasoning or problem solving. A form of reason largely inductive but using deduction as well.

siderable study to such subjects as are here discussed has gone about formulating a theoretical basis for his educational procedures. The student should note points of agreement and disagreement with the material presented and should attempt to formulate his own position.

THE BIOLOGICAL NATURE OF MAN

From the evidence of the biological sciences it seems clear that man is coextensive with nature, that is he is related in structure and function to other living forms, that he is composed of the same inorganic material as the physical world about him, and that he is a part of a universal system of energy which motivates and is the universe. Man, however, differs in two important respects. First, he has developed a brain which not only increases enormously his mental coordinations, but also develops symbols whereby he can transfer his own ideas and feelings to objective codes which can be communicated to others and preserved out of his own time span. In the second place, man has extended the period of infancy, or comparative dependence and helplessness, over many years. This long period of plasticity and flexibility provides time for the

Four Leading Philosophies

NATURALISM	REALISM
Observable reality—abiding, objective, and external realities comprising a fund of scientific information.	The objects of the external world are real in themselves and are not dependent upon any mind for their existence.
Unchanging, objective, external realities can be revealed by science and accumulated as an abiding fund of knowledge.	Composite of percepts and concepts constituting knowledge can be discovered by man through perceptual and conceptual transactions.
Science is the method of knowledge.	Methods of science—sense-perceptual experience and conceptual functions.

acquisition of knowledge, attitudes, and skills consonant with the environment in which he lives.

Since man is a part of the natural world he cannot be educated apart from it. Education must give him opportunities to become familiar with the world in which he lives, how it operates, and how he can use it to his best advantage. Education should be according to nature. This implies growth through active participation. Society must take advantage of the extended period of infancy by establishing educative agencies which will develop special programs and techniques by which the student may acquire specially selected and approved knowledge, attitudes and skills. Since plasticity and adaptability are the factors which have allowed man to progress beyond other animals, education must make every effort to continue the willingness and capacity to make adjustments in a changing world. Finally, since man's brain power and verbal ability are among his most distinctive characteristics, education must give considerable attention to their development.

MIND AND MATTER

The stuff of the universe is described in a number of ways. Modern science refers to extended substance as a system of energy. That part of an individual which engages in thought processes is referred to as thinking substance, psyche, or mind. The function of mind may be further differentiated into knowing and judging. The human organism is then not three substances but an organic unity of process with a trinity of inseparable functions: being, knowing, and judging. The term "panpsychism" has been used from Thales to Whitehead to describe the life or soul which pervades the universe. The author accepts this term as valid in this connection.

Every educational enterprise must combine the three elements described above: the knowing, the thing known, and the judgment of the thing known. The emphasis on each element will vary considerably, but they cannot be separated and every complete educative experience will include them in some degree. One cannot, therefore, educate the mind apart from the body, the body apart from the mind, or the process of evaluation apart from either. Education then is concerned with a sound body, a sound mind, and a sound judgment.

THE PROBLEM OF KNOWLEDGE

All knowledge begins in experience, but there is in the mind a method of knowing, selecting, classifying, and organizing experience. This method, however, is not infallible and is developed and refined through use. There is also a method of forming extra-sensory hypotheses, which is sometimes called intuition. It is possible to know the external world through sensory experience, the rational world through reason, and the supra-sensory world through intuition. Knowledge is tentative and fractional. The surest way to arrive at the most valid conclusion is to submit empirical data gathered by the scientific method to logical analysis. There are still areas of knowledge for which appropriate methods of observation, description, and analysis have not been devised. Until such time as accurate instruments are made, this vast area of knowledge can be discussed only in intuitive and transcendental terms.

Since all knowledge begins in experience, all learning situations must begin with personal, present, sensory experience, either actual or vicarious. Experience must precede generalizations, rules, and and abstractions. It is well to cultivate a thirst for knowledge, but a slightly skeptical attitude toward information or data. All methods of gaining knowledge (see Ch. I, p. 9) should be employed, and techniques for validating the methods as well as the knowledge gained thereby should be constantly employed.

THEORIES OF LEARNING

In agreement with his holistic theory of reality, the author belives that the initial experiences of the individual are undifferentiated wholes and that through experience the individual begins to differentiate these wholes into parts which become independent wholes subject to further division, analysis, and clarification. For example, the person is a closure of which the head is a part. The head is a configuration of which the oral cavity is a part, and the oral cavity is a gestalt of which a tooth is a part. This differentiation of wholes into constituent parts is a convenient device for detailed study and analysis, and is a posteriori to the organic whole which is the original perception. The interrelationship between wholes and their parts is one of the most important tasks of education. Therefore early educative experiences should deal with whole immediate situations, including especially their emotional tone, and the intrinsic impulse which motivates the individual to be interested in them. Systematization, analysis, and transfer of identical or similar elements should follow. Last, an attempt should be made to synthesize fragmented experience so that the individual may see the relation between the whole and its individual parts or elements. Thus generalizations such as rules of grammar should follow experience rather than initiate it.

THE KNOWER AND THE KNOWN

With regard to the knower and the known there is an "I–it" relationship and an "I–Thou" relationship. The former is between man and things and is objective and scientific. The latter is between man and man and is subjective and personal. In the former the mentalistic and emotive response is that of the knower to the object known; in the latter, the responses are reciprocal. Such a theory as that stated above would preclude any animistic or purposive qualities in things or in the purely physiological function of living organisms. One cannot blame a door for blowing shut when driven by a strong gust of wind, or punish an individual when his tonsils are inflamed or when he becomes restless after sitting too long in an uncomfortable chair listening to the drone of a flat voice discussing an uninteresting topic. On the other hand the employer should not treat his workers as so many "hands"; the administrator, his staff as so many teaching machines; or the teacher, his pupils as so many piggie-banks into which daily deposits of the coins of the realm of culture are to be inserted. It is also well to remember that in addition to its high degree of complexity the "I–Thou" situation is not only mutual but is constantly changing. A repetition of button pushing may produce a ringing of a bell each time, but a repetition of the same type may elicit from the individual a desired predictable response, a violent emotional reaction, or complete indifference, depending upon the emotive overtones which have been built up between each repetition and the circumstances in which the experience occurs. Each "I" strives for recognition as an individual. The teacher should remember this in dealing with his pupils and his associates. It is the recognition that one is known that differentiates the animate from the inanimate. It is the degree of recognition, communication, and communion between individuals which determines the genuineness of the "I–Thou" situation. It is the degree of this genuineness which tests the integrity of a democratic society.

HEREDITY AND ENVIRONMENT

Man and his environment, physical, intellectual, and social are one and are constantly interactive. Heredity determines what a man can be and environment determines what he will be. Although man cannot exceed his hereditary potential, the environment determines which of these potentials will be realized and to what degree. "Potential" as here used does not imply an innate tendency, but rather the power to control and manipulate the physical organism, including the brain.

Heredity is of two kinds, biological and cultural. In animals the process of manipulating biological heredity is called genetics. In animals and plants there is, besides the process of natural selection, the process by which man combines and propogates desirable characteristics and eliminates less desirable ones. This process is called breeding. In human beings, it is called eugenics and is usually accomplished by the control of the social heredity over several generations.

When we consider the cultural heritage we can see clearly the relationship between heredity and environment. The cultural heredity may be looked upon as the accumulated cultural experiences which make up the infant's initial environment. The longer the individual remains in this environment the stronger are its influences upon him. What we are indicating here is basic to psychoanalysis and to what anthropologists call "patterning." When man becomes conscious of his cultural heritage and learns to manipulate it, the cultural heritage becomes the cultural environment, in exactly the same way as man has learned that he is able to use climate, altitude, diet, rest, exercise, and the like to bring about changes in the physical organism. A seedling palm can develop only into a palm tree; this is its biological inheritance. It will grow most successfully in a tropic isle, whereas it will be stunted and perhaps die in a frigid climate unless protected from the weather during the severest part of the year, or grown in the simulated tropical atmosphere of the conservatory. This general situation for growth may be likened to the cultural heredity of man. The pruning and shaping of the tree, watering and fertilizing it, protecting it from insects and disease, are like the physical and cultural environment of man. A tree may be transplanted from one location to another, but unless the new location is similar to or more favorable than the old, unless there is enough of the root structure and the soil in which it grew, and unless the transplantation is done in a relatively short time, the possibility of the plant's thriving after transplantation is problematic.

From the schoolman's point of view, the individual is limited by his biological inheritance. By the time he reaches the school he can be said to have become acculturated into a social pattern which may be called his cultural heritage. All education must constantly keep these factors in mind. The biological environment can modify the biological heredity by such things as diet, rest, exercise, and medical care. During his earliest years the child forms many of his habits and attitudes, which become his second nature, his cultural inheritance. These can be modified by changing his cultural environment, but the more deep seated are these habits of speech, manners, and attitudes, the more difficult it is to change them. The school is an especially selected and controlled environment designed to bring about certain desirable patterns of conduct.

The process of bettering the physical conditions of persons and increasing their educational and social opportunities is called "euthenics." Formal education is a part of this process.

In any discussion of heredity and environment, what has been said above about the I–Thou relationship must constantly be borne in mind. The sculptor must think of the innate structure of the stone while carving it. Sometimes he talks of the figure emerging from it. The horticulturist must take into account the nature of the plant he would cultivate. So also the educator must consider the nature of the man he would educate. But the pupil is himself a knowing and self-motivating being who can not only bring about modifications in his own development, but can influence the development of others including his teacher. Both teacher and pupil are influencing each other, both are learning, but each is learning different things.

FATE AND FREE WILL

Problematic situations where several alternatives are presented demand that the individual make a choice. The fact that he can make such a choice suggests that he has the ability to do so. This ability to choose is called "free will." Free will is restricted by natural laws and often by tradition, custom, habit, dogmas, and other conventions among which an individual lives. A person cannot change natural laws, but he can manipulate them. He can defy tradition or bring about change by revolution or by the democratic process.

Education for the exercise of free will consists of six parts:

1. The individual must become aware of the limitations placed upon his free will by natural law and traditions.
2. He must develop an understanding and appreciation of accepted conventions and how they came about.
3. He must come to realize his responsibility in having the use of so powerful and instrument entrusted to him.
4. He should develop valid standards for evaluating present conventions and for developing new objectives for himself and society.
5. He must will to be free, since responsible exercise of free will requires considerable courage.
6. He must have practice in decision making, beginning with simple decisions for which he will examine pertinent facts and circumstances and then compare the actual outcome with his projected objective.

THE SOUL AND IMMORTALITY

Physical immortality, that the individual lives on in his descendants, is easily demonstrated. That one lives on through transmission to one's cultural heirs is also apparent. That the individual lives on bodily or spiritually after death has not been demonstrated empirically to the satisfaction of a majority of investigators. There is no good reason, however, to believe that what cannot be demonstrated empirically does not exist. Such belief must come through intuition or some other transcendental means. There must be a will to believe. The author finds belief in immortality satisfying and useful and, therefore, accepts it.

Since public secular education is concerned with the improvement of present society, the question of immortality does not affect it directly. The school should encourage students to accept whatever points of view their tradition dictates and to respect the points of view of others.

THE RHYTHM OF GROWTH

It has been amply stated that within the continuous process of maturation there are many individual differences, but that there are three distinct groups which can be recognized: childhood, youth, and adulthood. In the face of the wide variation in background, experience, and physical and mental maturation it is quite evident that not any one of these can be taken as a basis for homogeneous grouping. Identical chronological age merely means that persons have lived through the same number of tickings of the second hand in a conventional system of seconds, minutes, hours, days, months and years. When we consider variations in rate of metabolism, blood pressure, and pulse beat within the same chronological time span, the inaccuracy of this measure for determining similarity in age becomes apparent.

The classifications childhood, youth, and adulthood are based upon configurations which determine certain characteristic responses to life situations, while allowing for considerable individual differences within each class. The author advances the theory that if formal education could be so arranged, with perhaps several subclasses within each group, problems of readiness, method, subject matter, and control could be seen in organic relationship and could be more intelligently resolved.

THE INTEGRATION OF PERSONALITY

Our study of the nature of man has shown him to be a complex of many factors. Not only is he a biological organism, but a reasoning being, and, as Rousseau has said, "a feeling heart." He seeks self-realization and identification and at the same time longs for recognition and acceptance. He is the tool maker, the precise investigator, the system maker, and the storyteller.

As he passes through the rhythm of growth he retains some of the wonder of childhood and the rebellion of youth. Assumed responsibility of childhood foreshadows the development of this capacity as an adult.

Socially he is many selves simultaneously. He is a son, a husband, a father, a citizen, a patron of the arts, a religionist, a follower of a profession or trade, or perhaps a leader of men. Each of the roles he must play requires a separate setting, lines, and trappings. The scenes may be brief. He will need to skip from one role to another, and perhaps he will play several simultaneously, or he may be asked to judge among them. He is full of paradoxes that he must resolve. He must choose purposes and ends which are acceptable to himself and to society, and the means by which he attains them must be agreeable to him. There must be internal harmony between means and ends of life and education if we are to form integrated rather than schizophrenic personalities.

We will remember that Socrates admonished men to know themselves, that Plato insisted that the intellect should rule over man's basic passions, and that St. Augustine recommended the rule of faith. These are some of the means by which man integrates his personality. Each man must be able to live with himself; otherwise how can he live with and respect others. A well-conceived plan of education will help man perceive this complex situation and reconcile it for himself.

BIBLIOGRAPHY

Brown, Francis J., *Educational Sociology* (New York: Prentice-Hall, Inc., 1947).

Crow, Lester A., and Alice Crow, *Human Development and Learning* (New York: American Book Company, 1956).

Gruber, Frederick C. (ed.), *The Emergence of the Modern Mind* (Philadelphia: The University of Pennsylvania Press, 1958).

——— (ed.), *Foundations of Education* (Philadelphia: The University of Pennsylvania Press, 1957).

Havighurst, Robert J., and Bernice L. Neugarten, *Society and Education* (Boston: Allyn and Bacon, Inc., 1957).

Honigmann, John J., *Culture and Personality* (New York: Harper and Brothers, 1954).

Meltzer, Bernard N., Harry R. Doby, and Philip M. Smith, *Education in Society* (New York: Thomas Y. Crowell Company, 1958).

Robbins, Florence G., *Educational Sociology* (New York: Henry Holt and Co., Inc., 1953).

Rodehaver, Myles W., William B. Axtell, and Richard E. Gross, *The Sociology of the School* (New York: Thomas Y. Crowell Company, 1957).

Skinner, Charles E. (ed.), *Educational Psychology* (Englewood Cliffs, N.J.: Prentice-Hall, Inc., 1959).

Stanley, William O., B. Othanel Smith, Kenneth D. Beene, and Archibald W. Anderson, *Social Foundations of Education* (New York: The Dryden Press, 1956).

Thorpe, Louis P., and Allen M. Schmuller, *Contemporary Theories of Learning* (New York: The Ronald Press Company, 1954).

Chapter IX

Society and the Individual

PREVIEW

Having discussed the nature of man and its implications for education, we now turn our attention to the individual and the society in which he lives. We shall first review the main theories of the state as described in Part II, after which we shall consider aspects of American society as they relate to problems of American education, among which are the development of the democratic ideal, freedom to teach and to learn, equality of educational opportunity, public and private education, and the organization and support of education in America and certain European countries.

MAN AND THE STATE: A HISTORICAL REVIEW

Anthropologists tell us that man, being gregarious, is usually found in groups and that hermits are exceptions to this general rule. Since men live in societies and in political units called states, it is important to ask whether the authority for government lies with the people or with the rulers. Is the state formed by the power of man or the power of God?

The ancient Greeks and Hebrews claimed a divine origin for the law. Absolute monarchies, especially those which claim that the king rules by divine right, also look to God as the author of the state and the laws which govern it. Modern totalitarianisms which base their political doctrine upon German absolute idealism believe that the authority for the state and its laws rests with the Absolute evolving through history.

Although each citizen possesses a conscience which dictates the moral imperative, all do not obey this imperative. Therefore, it is necessary for a great lawgiver to arise from time to time to teach his people which of their traditions conform to the divine will. Thus, Moses gave the Hebrews ten fundamental laws, and Lycurgus codified the customs of ancient Sparta so that all could understand and obey them. These basic laws were elaborated into intricate legal systems which the individual had to obey or be destroyed. Pythagoras and Democritus rationalized the legal systems of the Greek world.

The sophists, on the other hand, led the movement toward freedom of the individual and independence of thought by declaring that laws were instituted by weaker members of the group to subjugate the stronger.

Socrates held that the state was the mother of civilization, and that any breaking of the law by an individual weakened the state. He advocated reform from within rather than revolution. Plato agreed, but added that the state should have complete control over the other members (as does present-day communism). Aristotle's idea was much like Plato's, but neither was able to solve the problem. Epicurus taught that all social life is based upon individual self-interest and that there is no "good" except what men call "good." Since happiness is the greatest good, each man should shun public responsibility and seek happiness for himself. The Stoics taught the opposite: that all men belong to a universal state whose laws are to be obeyed as the laws of nature. All should participate in public affairs as universal citizens in a great society.

Early Christians acknowledged the City of God to be superior to the secular state whose laws were to be obeyed only as they accorded with God's laws. St. Augustine believed that the ruler of the City of God, the Church, was infallible since it was the representative of God on earth. Medieval nominalists believed that man was the true reality while the state was a mere aggregate of men, while realists believed that the state was the reality and that men were merely units of this reality.

St. Thomas Aquinas taught that man is naturally a social and political being, that the supreme purpose of the state was the good of the group, that governments were of divine origin, and that the best form of government was the one which was most strongly centralized. The Church was supreme over the State.

During the later middle ages, groups with a common language, interests, and traditions formed themselves into states and opposed other groups. Machiavelli wished to establish an Italian nation independent of the Church by setting up an absolute monarchy in which the ruler could use any means necessary for the good of the state. This condition he considered an intermediate step toward the establishment of a free, independent nation where the rights of each individual would be guaranteed.

Thomas Hobbes believed that, since man in a natural state can do anything he pleases, governments are necessary to preserve him from a condition of chaos. Men gave up their rights for the protection of a strong ruler whom they agreed to obey; therefore, absolute monarchy was the best form of government. This argument strengthened the theories of the divine right and the infallibility of kings.

Locke maintained that man's original state was one of perfect freedom and equality. Therefore, no one has a right to take away another's life, liberty, or possessions. Man is by nature peaceful and of good will. He is naturally attracted to social living, and enters into a social contract with laws mutually agreed to and with an impartial judge to uphold them. Unlike Hobbes, who held that the individual freedoms once surrendered were irretrievable, Locke maintained that these powers can never be legally taken away from the people who can never give them up. Rousseau would do away with all representative governments in favor of direct citizen participation. Sovereignty rests with the people who at times have the right to abolish and reconstruct governments.

Hegel believed, on the other hand, that the individual should surrender his freedom to Universal Reason. Prussia adopted the Hegelian system and justified war as the means by which progress is made. Auguste Comte, the father of modern sociology, constructed a logical positivist philosophy of the state based upon a society governed by laws of group living. At the same time, in England, Mill believed that through a study of particular instances in history and of current societies, laws with wide applicability could be formulated. Social well-being, he declared, was necessary for individual well-being. Herbert Spencer saw in mankind a struggle for the survival of the fittest and the dependence of this struggle upon group life for success. He rejected Mill's socialistic thesis for one in which the state is greatly restricted. As a disciple of Hegel, Nietzsche believed that in the struggle for power the weak should be destroyed to make room for the strong.

Dewey considered society at its best to be a group of individuals sharing their experience and growing thereby. The individual is free, but through incorporation into the group he shares in its responsibilities as well as its benefits. According to Dewey, the individual is of supreme worth, and society must never use him as a mere means to accomplish its ends.

DEMOCRACY AND TOTALITARIANISM

The weight of tradition and thought during the long period of the history of the western world has been in favor of an absolutist, authoritarian, or totalitarian organization of the state. From Plato, who viewed democracy as the seed of anarchy, through the Church fathers, notably St. Augustine and St. Thomas Aquinas, through Erasmus and Machiavelli in the Renaissance, down to Hegel and his disciples, Marx, Neitzsche, and Gentile, who were respectively the "fathers" of modern communism, national socialism, and fascism, we find an insistence on the domination of the weak by the strong by means of a well-ordered political structure.

We Americans cannot subscribe to the theory that the citizen is a pawn of the state. We believe that he has freedom of choice especially regarding where he will live and what occupation he will pursue, but that while he has the right to exercise individual freedom, he may not infringe upon similar rights of others. He also has a responsibility to the body politic of which he is a part and which is the group that guarantees his freedoms.

"Democracy must be nurtured and guarded. There is no evidence in history to support the thesis that democracy is natural. Democracy is a vast and complex cultural achievement in the sphere of human relations and social values. Like all of man's finest achievements, it is extremely delicate and fragile, difficult to maintain at the highest level of excellence and easy to let follow a course of gradual degradation. Democracy exists only in the patterns of behavior, feeling, and thought of a people."[1]

THE CASE FOR DEMOCRACY

The case for democracy can be traced to its origin among the sophists of ancient Greece, through the nominalists of the later middle ages. Democracy accompanied the growth of nationalism and the rise of the middle class. In England it is related to the revolt of the barons at Runnymede where King John signed the Magna Charta in 1215. It is reflected in the rise of Cromwell and the establishment of the Commonwealth in England, the government of the free cities in northern Germany, in the Dutch Republic, and in the free Swiss Cantons. American democracy traces its philosophical origins to the Puritan divines in England and Scotland, to John Locke and other English empiricists, to Rousseau, and to the French Encyclopedists.

On November 11, 1620, forty-one Englishmen attached their names to an agreement in the form of a Separatists Church covenant known ever since as the "Mayflower Compact." The signers promised all due submission and obedience to "such just and equal laws, ordinances, acts, constitutions, and offices from time to time as be thought most meet and convenient for the general good of the colony."[2] This was not a revolutionary document, but an agreement among Englishmen to govern themselves. It was legal under the common law. It is, however, the first known example on the North American continent of what Lincoln later described as a "government of the people, by the people, and for the people."

Over a century and a half later, when the colonists were aggrieved over the oppressive commercial restrictions of the rule of George III, they again, like free Englishmen, stated their grievances to the world and justified their stand according to the political theories of John Locke in the Declaration of Independence in Congress on July 4, 1776.

When in the course of human events it becomes necessary for one people to dissolve the political bands which have connected them with

[1] Educational Policies Commission, *The Education of Free Men in American Democracy* (Washington, D.C.: National Education Association, 1941), p. 48.
[2] Quoted in Edward Channing, *A History of the United States* (New York: The Macmillan Company, 1925), I, 308–309.

another, and to assume among the powers of the earth the separate and equal station to which the laws of nature and of nature's God entitle them, a decent respect for the opinion of mankind requires that they should declare the causes which impel them to the separation.

We hold these truths to be self-evident—that all men are created equal; that they are endowed by their Creator with certain inalienable rights; that among these are life, liberty, and the pursuit of happiness. That to secure these rights governments are instituted among men, deriving their just powers from the consent of the governed; that whenever any form of government becomes destructive of these ends, it is the right of the people to alter or abolish it, and to institute a new government, laying its foundations on such principles and organizing its powers in such forms as to them shall seem most likely to effect their safety and happiness.

The implications of this document are so far-reaching that it will be well to consider it further. Here a group of free men catalog their grievances openly to justify their course of action. Free men have entered into a contract to secure, that is to make sure, to guard, or to guarantee, the integrity of certain rights which cannot be taken away or alienated from them. These rights include life, liberty, and the right to possessions—the pursuit of happiness. These are the inalienable rights of free men, not opportunity, intelligence, or other physical or intellectual endowments. Free men have a duty to defend these rights and to appeal the justice of their cause to the court of human opinion.

The belief that sovereignty rests in the people is made even more explicit in the opening words of the Constitution: "We the people." Here again a company of citizens mutually agree to certain laws in order to form a better government and to assure certain benefits to themselves and succeeding generations. These benefits are as follows: justice, domestic tranquility, common defense, general welfare, and the blessings of liberty. Article III, Section 2, within the body of the Constitution guarantees to the citizens of each state the privileges and immunities of citizens in the several states. Even before the Constitution went into full operation as the supreme law of the new nation, the rights of the citizen were further guaranteed in the first ten amendments, the Bill of Rights, two of which, the first and the last, are particularly applicable to our system of free public schools. The first guarantees freedom of speech and of religion and the tenth reserves to the individual and to the states the regulation of such matters as concern them, and them alone.

WHO ARE OUR CITIZENS?

Who are "the people," or who is "the citizen" about whom the Constitution speaks? The answer to these questions furnishes a key to our understanding of some of the issues regarding the equalization of educational opportunities. The concept of "the citizen," "the voter," has been an evolving one, historically and legally. During the federalist period he could be described as a free, white male of property, over twenty-one years of age, native-born, naturalized, or a citizen of the United States at the time of the adoption of the Constitution.

In 1868 the Fourteenth Amendment made male members of the Negro race full citizens and the Fifteenth Amendment, adopted in 1870, gave them the right to vote. In 1920, the Nineteenth Amendment extended the right to vote to women. Recent federal legislation has extended voting privileges to members of other races, and certain states have lowered the voting age of citizens. The qualification of being a man of property or paying a poll tax has been removed in most states. Every child living in the United States is a potential voter with all the privileges and responsibilities adhering thereto. Every citizen is guaranteed equally the rights and immunities of citizens of the several states. Public education must take this into account when it sets up a program for the education of all the citizens.

POPULATION CHANGES WITHIN THE UNITED STATES

The census of 1790 revealed that the population of the United States scarcely exceeded four million. Statisticians tell us that according to present trends we shall soon exceed 200 million. The implications of this phenomenal growth are tremendous. In 1790 most of our population was found along a narrow coastline extending from New Hampshire to Georgia. Our culture was oriented toward Europe and largely in the Anglo-Saxon tradition. English was the predominant language.

By purchase, treaty, and conquest we acquired an area of enormous natural resouces extending to the Pacific Ocean. This vast area needed to be developed. Pioneers were urged to seek their fortunes to the west of the mountains. They were spurred on by promises of free land and by the chance to exploit natural resources according to the economic philosophy of "rugged individualism" of Adam Smith's *Wealth of Nations*.

It was on the frontiers that the egalitarian spirit was fostered and the ideals of democracy enriched. It was here, amid common hopes, common tasks, and common dangers that the blending of social, racial, and economic backgrounds took place.

Western expansion, transcontinental railroads, and the industrialization of America needed initiative, imagination, venture capital, and, above all, workers. From earliest times America has been a land of opportunity and an asylum for the religiously and politically oppressed. Waves of population came to our shores. These new citizens had to be oriented to American life and to American ideals. So long as their backgrounds were in the Anglo-Saxon tradition the process was not too difficult, but when, after about 1850, large numbers came from other parts of the world, the problems of Americanization became more acute.

There never was a time when the American population was economically, socially, or geographically static. The industrial revolution changed the character of the American people from agrarian to urban. Within the last generation there has been a marked movement toward suburbia. Many industries are decentralizing their plants and locating them at places where labor is plentiful, where there are better living conditions for their employees, and where there is room for physical expansion. Large national corporations frequently transfer their technical experts and managerial forces from place to place, and the role of the traveling salesman and company representative has expanded considerably in our contemporary society. There are also large numbers of migrant agricultural workers. There are relatively few American communities that can boast of a continuity of population over three or four generations. Truly we are a nation on wheels.

Social mobility is also a determining factor in American life. Studies by Havighurst, McGuire, and others show that about one-quarter of our population is constantly moving up or down the social scale and that about one-fifth of the population increases its status by one step each generation.[3] There are possibly greater crowds of lonely confused individuals in the United States than anywhere else in the world.

Building operations, model villages, radio and television advertizing, coupled with the great desire of the newcomer to belong, to be accepted, produce a great amount of uniformity. This uniformity does not only apply to split-level homes, sports, cars, fashionable colors, styles, and cocktail parties, but also to patterns of thought and to social conduct. The social and economic conditions which produced the individualist have largely disappeared, but in this age of the lonely crowd and the gray-flannel mind, society and education must give due consideration not only to the adjustment of the individual to his social environment, as important as this is, but, as Whitehead points out, to the development and maintenance of that individual initiative and imagination without which there can be no intellectual advance.

THE DEVELOPMENT OF THE DEMOCRATIC IDEAL

Having examined the documents from which the basic patterns of our democratic society are formed, it will be well for us to sketch briefly what are the more obvious characteristics of American democracy. We must be careful to remember that the term democracy has been variously interpreted at different times and in different countries. In our present discussion, when we speak of the democratic spirit we mean, of course, that which is attributed to the United States of America.

For the present writer there are seven characteristics of American democracy, and they can be conveniently combined into four groups. The first two are *change* and *optimism*. Perhaps the only certainty in the physical world is change. This possibility has been recognized for a long time. Heraclitus maintained that one could not step across or into the same river twice. However, in the past,

[3] Reported in Robert J. Havighurst and Bernice L. Neugarten, *Society and Education* (Boston: Allyn and Bacon, Inc., 1957), pp. 51–54.

change has been observed in resignation or with dismay. Change and decay, as in the old hymn,[4] were often linked together. But American democracy welcomes change, because it sees within change the possibility of growth and improvement. American democracy values change as the condition within which man has the chance to mold his own destiny. American society is organized to promote change.

The next three characteristics are also closely related. They are *majority rule, the protection of minorities, and respect for the individual.* American democracy has a fundamental faith in the ability of the majority to make the right decisions in the long run. Europeans are often at a loss to understand the psychology of an American election, especially the custom which requires the defeated candidate to send congratulations and a pledge of loyalty to the victor. But this act is closely related to our concept of the genesis of leadership and group aims of which we shall say more later.

Although Americans are committed to majority rule, they insist upon the protection of minority groups and of the individual because they are the agents who evaluate the rule of majority and develop new ideas and new outlooks. The framers of our Constitution went to great pains to safeguard these rights. We should be careful, however, that the minority does not usurp the prerogatives of the majority and rule in its stead.

In our democracy the individual is of supreme worth, because through him new sights can be raised and leadership can be exercised. Leadership in our democracy is not by force or by birth. It arises from the group. The individual possesses, theoretically at least, the right to express his ideas. As their ideas gain common acceptance they become the will of the majority who carry them into action.

Closely connected with the value which American democracy places upon the individual is the *ideal of equality.* We have seen that the framers of the Declaration of Independence declared that all men are created equal, and that the Constitution guarantees these equal rights to all citizens. In our discussion of the expanding concept of the citizen it was shown that over the years certain qualifications for citizenship have been removed and the base has been broadened considerably. While many Americans accept these

[4] Henry Francis Lyte (1796–1847), "Abide with Me," stanza 3.

newer citizens in theory, many do not accept them in fact. At least they are not willing to extend to them the same rights, privileges, and immunities once guaranteed only to the freeborn white man of property. This unwillingness to recognize the equality of free men retards equalization of educational opportunity, of voting, and of other traditional American guarantees.

The last characteristic of American democracy to be discussed is that of *participation.* Intelligent participation requires dedicating oneself to the ideals of American democracy and assuming responsibility for their realization. Democratic education will, therefore, provide the basic knowledge of the origins and meanings of democracy. It will provide exercises for the development of attitudes leading to a dedication toward its realization and opportunities for acquiring and perfecting the skills necessary to its effective operation.

OUR PLURALISTIC SOCIETY

"E Pluribus Unum," the motto on the Great Seal of the United States, "out of many, one," serves as a fitting text for a discussion of America's pluralistic society. The face of America: the diversity of its landscapes, the variety and richness of its natural resources, the divergence of national and cultural origins of its people, are basic to the pluralistic philosophies of its great poets and thinkers, notably Whitman, James, and Dewey. But as these men and others have pointed out, it is not the heterogeneous nature of America which is its distinguishing characteristic, but heterogeneity within homogeneity, or obversely, it is the unity within diversity which characterizes American society. Thus through living together we actualize our motto, "E Pluribus Unum." The pattern of American life might then be likened to a fine oriental rug in which the individual and the cultural strands are woven into a consistent pattern, but with infinite variety, as each individual and each group adds to the richness of the fabric of American life.

SUMMARY

There are two main points of view with regard to the foundation of human society: the authoritarian and the democratic. Authoritarians maintain that man realizes himself fully through close association with the state and its aims. On the other hand, those who take the democratic viewpoint believe that individual man is the real and basic unit, and that states are aggregates of individual men voluntarily and mutually agreeing to band together for the realization of certain aims which they hold in common.

Democracy is a delicate and intricate relationship between men. It is of slow growth, but when once established it is the most stable form of government. It is a way of social behavior, having seven characteristics: change, optimism, majority rule, protection of minorities, recognition of the worth of the individual citizen, the ideal of equality, and participation. Democracy is a way of life. Social-civic behavior is regulated by laws arrived at by common consent and administered by leaders chosen by the group from among its own members. American society is pluralistic and denies any political authority other than the voice of the people.

A pluralistic society poses many problems for education. We shall examine three of these in some detail under the headings, "Freedom to Teach and to Learn," "Education for Leadership," and "The Organization and Support of American Education."

FREEDOM TO TEACH AND TO LEARN

It is a comparatively easy thing to prove yourself right, but to prove yourself wrong is another matter. Yet this is the basis of all scientific advancement. If we always took *what is* to be true, we would still be living in the Stone Age. Hence advancement depends upon a "divine discontent." But how few of us are willing to venture into the untried and the unknown or to risk the disapproval, even the enmity, of our contemporaries.

The history of censorship is very old. Socrates drank the hemlock for corrupting the youth of Athens. The Church had its Inquisition. To burn a man's body was an act of charity if by doing so one could save his immortal soul. Works of Copernicus and Galileo were placed upon the Index. Calvin burned his heretics in Geneva. As president, John Adams tried to suppress freedom of speech through the Alien and Sedition Acts. Toward the close of the eighteenth century a group of radicals produced a document which has been called subversive by very respectable organizations. The principal writer was called a dangerous radical, an atheist, a liar, an assassin.

If he and his companions should succeed, declared the President of Yale College, American wives and daughters would be the victims of legal prostitution. The man was Thomas Jefferson, and the document the Declaration of Independence.

Totalitarian nations abroad have a different idea of freedom from ours. They believe that one is free only when one is able to give up one's liberty for the good of the state which gives him his citizenship and his manhood. "Soviet writers condemn pragmatism and relativism, and insist that there is an absolute and knowable truth. They also insist that the basic content of objective truth is revealed through Marxism-Leninism. Where there is class conflict, so the theory goes, truth is obscured by class interests; under Soviet socialism the Communist party as the vanguard of the proletariat can perceive the truth pure and unadulterated through its Marxist-Leninist glasses." [5]

Freedom consists in voluntarily obeying the will of the party, or the will of a higher authority, possessed of absolute truth, whomever this may be. We are not without our totalitarian groups in America who go upon the proposition so well parodied by Lord Macaulay: "I am in the right and you are in the wrong. When you are stronger, you ought to tolerate me, for it is your duty to tolerate truth. But when I am the stronger, I shall persecute you, for it is my duty to persecute error." [6]

Many British and continental intellectuals view communism as a social theory with limited appeal and likely to gain few adherents. They say that schools should be neutral because there is little cause for alarm. Most Americans believe, however, that communism is a philosophy, a religion, a way of life, not only different but actively hostile to ours, and that it has penetrated deeply into American life. We believe that education for democratic American citizenship should have priority in our program of studies.

While we recognize the dangers of communism, the fact that a person has once been interested in communism should not disbar him from teaching. It is said that since 1919 more than a million persons have gone in and out of the Communist party in the

[5] Harold J. Berman, "The Right to Knowledge in the Soviet Union," *Columbia Law Review*, LIV (May, 1954), 762.

[6] Quoted in David Spitz, *Patterns of Anti-Democratic Thought* (New York: The Macmillan Company, 1949), p. 283.

United States. For the majority of young people, communism has been weighed in the balance and found wanting. Those who *now* maintain membership in the Communist party, however, should not be allowed to teach, for by retaining membership in the party they have relinquished their intellectual integrity. Persons whose basic assumptions are determined by the organization to which they belong are no longer free to think for themselves, and this freedom is basic for all who prepare American youth for the arduous duties of citizenship in a free society.

ACADEMIC FREEDOM AND TEACHERS' OATHS

Academic freedom involves both the teacher and the learner. While the teacher should be free to express his considered opinion in the field of his academic competence, and while he should not be denied any of the privileges of a citizen with regard to political and social action outside the classroom, he should always remember that during the time he is in school he has a captive audience and must not impose personal views upon his pupils.

According to the American Association of University Professors:

> The teacher is entitled to full freedom in research and in the publication of the results, subject to the adequate performance of his other academic duties. . . . The teacher is entitled to freedom in the classroom in discussing his subject, but he should be careful not to introduce into his teaching controversial matter which has no relation to his subject . . . he should at all times be accurate, should exercise appropriate restraint, should show respect for the opinions of others, and should make every effort to indicate that he is not an institutional spokesman. . . . Public opinion . . . is at once the chief safeguard of a democracy and the chief menace to the real liberty of the individual. . . . One of the most characteristic functions of a university in a democratic society is to help make public opinion more self-critical and more circumspect, to check the more hasty and unconsidered impulses of popular feeling, to train the democracy to the habit of looking before and after.[7]

A free society cannot avoid an element of risk. It will search in vain for absolute security. It is based on the assumption that people can be trusted to be free, that a majority of them will not in the long run per-

[7] *American Association of University Professors Bulletin,* XXXVI (Spring, 1950), 46–47.

sist in acting to their own disadvantage, that, given freedom to think, to act, and to influence each other, they will on the whole do better for themselves than if their direction were entrusted to a few, however wise, not subject to popular control. This is the traditional faith at the heart of our political society.[8]

Freedom of thought and speech is vital to the maintenance of the American system, and is essential to the general welfare. We must have freedom of speech for all or we will have it for none.

"Ideally," writes Laing, "there is only one oath any teacher in a democratic society should ever need or wish to take: 'In all my efforts to comprehend what truth is, and to teach what is true, I shall follow only the guidance of my own conscience, without fearing or favoring any creed, or doctrine, or person.' "[9]

There is no reason why the teacher should be separated out from other citizens and held suspect so that he must take a special pledge of loyalty. Forcing a teacher to take an oath is a most degrading and useless practice for it lowers his status in the eyes of the community. Further, oaths do not screen out communists from the profession, because they feel no moral compunction against swearing falsely. As has been shown above, there has been a decided trend over the last century and a half to reduce discrimination and increase equality among our citizens according to the guarantees of our federal Constitution. Teachers' oaths are a reversal of this trend. The loyal teacher, as well as all other loyal citizens, should, of course, be willing at all times to show his loyalty to the laws of the nation, the state, and the locality of which he is a citizen, and to pledge faithfully to carry out the duties of the office and the public trust to which he has been appointed.

FREEDOM TO LEARN

We have seen above that one of the characteristics of democracy is participation in determining the purposes and aims of American life and in the selection of its leaders. We have shown that the vitality of our pluralistic society depends upon the contributions

[8] Report of the Committee on Academic Freedom and Tenure, *American Association of University Professors Bulletin*, XXXVII (Spring, 1951), 73.

[9] Alexander Laing, "The Three Ways of Swearing," *New Republic*, December 28, 1953, p. 9.

of individuals and minority groups. We have observed that among other freedoms our federal Constitution guarantees freedom of speech and religion. Our children must be given a chance to be free and to exercise these freedoms, because it is only by exercise that they become strong. Democracy cannot be learned where it is not lived. Neither can one learn to exercise judgment without being given a chance to do so. Freedom to learn requires that the student be given sufficient facts in as unprejudiced a manner as possible, and that he be given methods of validating them for himself. He may well cultivate a skeptical attitude toward knowledge, realizing that much of what is "known" is only partial, and that future investigations and circumstances may modify it considerably. Freedom of the individual involves beliefs and actions which are private and those which are public. A pluralistic society allows the greatest amount of freedom in thought and action in the private concerns of the individual. Our democratic society permits much freedom in the public aspects of conduct within the pattern of American life and its guaranteed freedoms.

It is the duty of the school to educate the student to examine social and political problems with a considerable degree of objectivity, to gather data representing more than one point of view, and to examine these data with a critical, penetrating, unprejudiced mind. He should also be permitted to give considerable thought to the possible effects of his conclusions before putting them into operation. Every individual is entitled to his private beliefs, opinions, and prejudices, but he should recognize the same right for others. In dealing with controversial issues, all would agree that the public school should give the student a method for collecting and evaluating data and also a method of critical judgment.

The position of the Catholic Church toward academic freedom may well be set forth here because its system of private and parochial schools from kindergarten through the university constitutes one of the most important and influential educational activities in America today.

The Catholic Church approaches the problem of man's right to knowledge with the realization that in settling concrete problems relative to human freedom two fundamental principles must be observed: First, liberty is a most precious possession, based on the dignity of every human person as a creature of God destined to everlasting existence; hence it must be respected and protected. Second, for the good of society as well as for the welfare of individuals, personal liberty must be curtailed in certain circumstances. . . .

The notion that people should be allowed to read everything they wish is quite common in our land, for we are a freedom-loving people, resenting any restriction of our freedom. . . . People can be influenced to evil as well as to good by what they read. And while we justly uphold the ideals of freedom, we must admit that freedom has its limitations. Catholics believe that the laws of their Church in regard to censorship and the prohibition of books represent a reasonable limitation of their freedom. . . . The Catholic Church believes that the chief purpose of man's earthly life is to prepare for an eternal life after death. . . . Whatever advantages may accrue through the exercise of personal freedom, they can have no real value if they impede or imperil the attainment of one's eternal destiny. Hence, it is not an evil but a good when those in authority, whether parents, civil rulers, or ecclesiastical authorities, regulate the exercise of freedom by those subject to their jurisdiction so as to aid them to observe God's law and to reach the eternal happiness which the Creator has appointed to every human being. . . . Naturally it will be asked by what authority the Church claims the right to do this. The Church replies that it has received from God Himself the right to teach officially the truths of religion and morality and the right to legislate on matters pertinent to the spiritual welfare of those subject to its jurisdiction.[10]

Sometimes our students are not free to learn because discussion of certain topics may disturb the vested interests of certain powerful groups. This should not be. There should be no forbidden subjects. The very foundation of education must be the study of the actual problems and controversial issues of our people. There is no other way by which the democratic principle of consent can be implemented. Consent based upon knowledge of only one aspect or side of a problem, upon the avoidance of controversy, is a travesty of both knowledge and democracy. To keep issues out of the school is to keep thought out of it; it is to keep life out of it.

While we advocate freedom of thought and speech for both the teacher and the student, we must constantly guard against unprincipled demagogues who will use the right of free speech to

[10] Rev. Francis J. Connell, C.S.S.R., "Censorship and the Prohibition of Books in the Catholic Church Law," *Columbia Law Review*, LIV (May, 1954), 699–709 *passim*.

provide a refuge for subversive groups, to disseminate anti-American propaganda, and to undermine the very freedom we cherish. Such small but well-disciplined groups will formulate a grandiose and idealistic program, will prey upon the idealism of youth and the common weaknesses of men to gain adherents, and will exploit the virtues and processes of democracy. What we need, as Whitehead points out, is freedom balanced by discipline, and this disciplined freedom must be based upon a thorough understanding of the principles of American democracy. Two ways in which the school can guard against the encroachment of totalitarianism and promote the democratic way of life are, first, to raise the general level of education for all, and second, to train youth for leadership.

EDUCATION FOR LEADERSHIP

Any discussion of education for leadership must immediately raise the questions, "What kind of leadership?" "Who are the leaders?" "Where do they come from?" "Where do they get their authority?" "In what direction and for what purpose do they lead?"

There is a fundamental difference between the American concept of democratic leadership and leadership in the democratic states of Europe, South America, or almost any other part of the world. In Europe, education aims to make men different. In America, education aims to make them the same. Let us look at these two statements.

From the earliest times, the peoples of Europe have been divided into classes. There are those who rule and those who obey. There are the few who think and the many who work. There is the emperor and the subject, the master and the servant, the clergy and the laity. There are the intellectuals and the toilers. Europeans will tell you "Happy is the man who knows his place and remains in it." A society in which every man stays on his own acre is proud to carry on the trade of his fathers, knows his place, and is respectful of his betters, they will tell you, is the best kind of society in which to live. Useless ambition, vain strivings, jostling for position, make a nation of neurotics. Long ago, Erasmus of Rotterdam, when describing what he considered to be a perfect system of government and education, advocated that the king own all the land

and wealth of the nation and administer it in a truly paternalistic spirit for the benefit of his loyal and obedient subjects.

For the most part, the same relationship between rulers and those ruled exists in Europe today. European education reflects this social system by maintaining a dual system of education—one for the upper classes, the intellectually elite, and another for the lower classes who will do the work and carry out orders. It is extremely difficult to pass from one type of school to another: Very few attempt it and fewer succeed. Since World War II, England has developed what is called "the comprehensive high school" with its three streams—college preparatory, commercial, and general education. This high school, although fashioned on the American model, bears very little resemblance to our comprehensive high school. Other countries have attempted to liberalize the curriculum and to equalize educational opportunities with some small measure of success.

We have often been told of the effectiveness of the European school, of how much the students learn, especially of the fundamentals, meaning reading, writing, and arithemetic. Yes, students, some students at least, do learn to read. In some countries, illiteracy is almost non-existent. But for what purpose do they learn to read?

In all too many European secondary schools, especially those which prepare for the universities, successful learning is the ability to memorize vast amounts of facts and to repeat them exactly as they have been given by teacher or textbook. For the most part, critical reading and thinking are reserved for the very few who attend the universities.

Such a system which trains leaders apart from followers is appropriate for a society which wishes to preserve a rigid class system. It is also grist for the mill of totalitarian states where a strict censorship multiplies the output of printed material but restricts the content to views approved by the ruling group.

Totalitarian education believes there are many ways to tell the same story. Democratic education believes there can be different views about every topic. Totalitarianism uses the printed page to reinforce a single point of view; democracy, for enlightenment.

A good example of the misuse of education from an American's point of view is Orcutt's description of the Soviet press:

We were conducted through the great printing establishments of Leningrad. We saw tens of thousands of books coming from the press. We saw school books in languages and alphabets that never before had been used for such purposes. There were books in Armenian, Ukranian, White Russian, Tataro-Bashkir, so that the Soviet peoples might learn to read. But to read what?

To read, of course, what they were told to read—to read the Soviet gospel of the party line. They were to become literate in order that the power of the party might extend its grasp to the remotest worker in this gigantic realm, so that children might be conditioned down to their very reflexes, so that this to-be-literate population would be orthodox and safe under the direction of the leaders in the Kremlin.[11]

Reading, writing, and arithmetic are, indeed, most important for they are the fundamental tools for learning. But American education must go beyond reading to get information or to follow instructions and must stress reading to make judgments.

America started out with the same class distinction and the same social organization as Europe, and, so long as the Appalachians shut out our view to the west and so long as we looked to Europe for cultural and intellectual inspiration, we continued in the same tradition. As was pointed out above, the wagon trains to the west promoted a new kind of fraternity—the fraternity of the common danger and of the common purpose. Blood, rank, and wealth did not matter too much on the frontier. The leader was he who could do and had concern for the welfare of the group. He possessed ability to understand the job at hand, to work with people, to inspire them to work together for the common good and, very important, willingness to serve under another leader when a new purpose developed or a better leader appeared. These were the qualities of leadership developed on the frontiers of America.

LEADERSHIP AND FOLLOWERSHIP

In our discussion of the characteristics of citizenship we maintain that a citizen is not only the man who votes on election day or pays his taxes, but is one who bears a real responsibility for his government. This includes participation in the making of policy,

[11] Reginald Orcutt, *Merchant of Alphabets* (New York: Doubleday, Doran & Company, 1945), pp. 158–159.

selection of leaders, and the evaluation of the effectiveness of these leaders. In American democracy, initiative arises from within the group and not from the specially educated leaders or those who have been born into positions of responsibility. The group sets its own objectives, having determined where it wants to go or what it wishes to accomplish. It searches its own group for that individual who possesses all the qualities it deems necessary to lead it in the direction of the accomplishment of its objective. Having chosen the leader, members of the group may not sit by complacently and wait for its goals to be accomplished, but, like the pioneers on the great plains of the middle west, they must share in the toil and the responsibility of accomplishing their purpose. A most important responsibility is the constant evaluation of the quality of the leadership of the man they have chosen, and to remove him from his position if he is not able to lead them toward the accomplishment of their objective. New objectives may require new leadership in which case the former leader will become a follower, and a member of the group who has been a follower will become the leader. Thus, it is possible that everybody in America at some time and under certain circumstances will be both leader and follower according to his talents and his willingness to use these talents for the benefit of the group. This idea is very precious to Americans but is extremely difficult for Europeans to understand.

This reciprocal relationship between leader and follower is basic to the concept of American democracy. What America needs, then, is loyal followers and a loyal opposition. What America needs is leaders—many leaders, not a single leader, whether he be king, Führer, duce, or any other totalitarian dictator. Training, then, for intelligent, democratic leadership and followership is the most important aim of American education.

THE GENIUS OF AMERICA

When our ancestors established the first permanent settlements on these shores, they brought with them the heritage of a culture well over two thousand years old. We have built upon that cultural heritage. Some say we have exploited it. This point of view deserves examination. It is quite true that America has a derivative culture but so did the barbaric Britains, Gauls, and Germans, according to the Romans, and, in turn, so did the Romans according to the Greeks. We, in America, have produced no Galileo or Copernicus, Newton or Einstein. We have no Descartes, no Spinoza, Hegel, or Marx. Europeans tell us that this is the result of our education, that we do not detect leaders soon enough or give them a separate and challenging education, that our educational system encourages mediocrity, that it produces a nation of chauvinists and Babbitts. They ask, "Who discovered the law of the Golden Mean? A Greek." "Who discovered the theory of the rotation of the earth? An Italian." "Who discovered the law of gravity? An Englishman." "Who discovered the theory of relativity? A German."

But, wait! Newton did not invent the law of gravity nor did Copernicus set the world revolving around the sun. These phenomena had existed long before man made his appearance on this planet. The great contribution of such men to the modern world was that they fomulated these so-called laws and were able to demonstrate them. The steam engine was a play toy, electricity a laboratory phenomenon, psychology a university discipline, until another kind of genius saw the practical application of these theories and made them operative in the world of men and to their benefit. Such is the genius of America. Such was the genius of Thomas Alva Edison and John Dewey. There are many points of similarity between ancient Rome and America. Just as Rome applied, organized, and spread the culture of Greece to all corners of the then-known world, so America has been called to assume the leadership of bringing the benefit of centuries of European thought to the world of today.

CHARACTERISTICS OF LEADERS

With this background, we can perhaps see more clearly what is required of education for leadership in America. First, and most important, we must raise the level of knowledge, action, and social responsibility of every citizen if we want our kind of democracy to continue. If we must make a choice, and I do not think we are called upon to do so, between a working level of active and free citizens or a few highly-trained experts with many blind followers, we must unhesitatingly choose the former. This point cannot be made too vigorously or too often. Then, since America believes in the freedom and integrity of the individual, and since American education is dedicated to give each student an opportunity to develop his gift to the utmost, we must be constantly on the lookout for the gifted child. Here we might well take St. Paul's text about the diversity of gifts but the same spirit (I Cor., 12:1–11). Within the universal spirit of democracy, there are uses for the greatest diversity of gifts. Myopic professors with thick-lensed, horn-rimmed spectacles often tell us that the only gift worth cultivating is the intellect. This is the most important and perhaps basic gift, and here the accusation that American education tends to promote mediocrity is largely justified, because, by and large, we have done a very poor job of late with our intellectually brilliant. Too often, they have gone unchallenged. Too often, they have developed bad habits of study, laziness, and lack of responsibility. Too often, a brilliant intellect has been hammered into dullness by having to drag along with the crowd. We may have built our prosperity on an economy of waste of material things, but we cannot waste intellect and not pay for it dearly.

Some educators advocate segregating the intellectually gifted in separate schools. The creation of such a brain-trust will be a retreat over territory we have fought so hard to gain. Any kind of segregation develops class distinctions and tends to promote artificial feelings of superiority and inferiority. Fundamentally, all Americans are the same. They may possess more or less of certain qualities, but they must all live and work together and use their abilities for their own legitimate satisfaction and for the welfare of the group. Educationists have developed very effective progams to take care of individual differences and it is this method and this organization which we must follow. Our American coins bear the motto, "E Pluribus Unum," "out of many, one." It is this unity in diversity that American education must strive to promote.

A DIVERSITY OF GIFTS

On the other hand, the genius of America is more pragmatic and social than intellectual. We have a flair for organization, for promotion, for getting things done. This means that we must discover and develop these gifts. Among them is the artistic gift. We have many talented young people in the various art fields. The time is long since past when we need to send our young people to European art schools or conservatories for training, or when they must assume foreign names in order to get recognition at home. Many of our students do study abroad, and we should endeavor to give every worthy young person an opportunity to enrich his experience in this way, but it is true that we grow up artistically and develop an indigenous art of our own out of our own folklore, our own traditions, and our own people. Imitative art is always second rate.

When we consider questions of art, we must take into account the producer and the consumer. So far, we have considered only the producer but we need leaders in the appreciation of art as well. We need trained consumers. We shall never develop an art worthy of America until we train the great mass of Americans in the appreciation of music, painting, literature, and the other arts. American education must develop audiences for American artists or, to use a crass expression, we must "create a market for art."

Our contribution in the entertainment field is second to none. Here, too, in radio, television, and moving pictures, we must develop standards of excellence in performance and standards of good taste among listeners and viewers. The entertainment industry declares that it gives the public what it wants. American education has a duty to develop a discriminating audience. We come back again and again to our original theme—*We, the people*—or in American democracy, our ideal is that the American people themselves set the standards.

Then there is the physically gifted, the athlete. By and large, he receives recognition and excellent training because the American people are sports minded and athleticism has often been taken to extremes in America. Here again, it is more important to have an intramural sports program from which all students benefit than it is to have a championship basketball or football team.

Social competence needs also to be developed. The socially gifted girl and boy should be given an opportunity to use his or her gifts within the high school social and activities program. Until recently, the American public high school has been singularly remiss in this respect. Socially-minded youngsters have joined high school and college fraternities which, in many cases, have formed cliques whose activities and influence have not always been in the interest of the entire student body. Knowledge and familiarity with the amenities of life are badly needed in America. Many students are awkward because they do not know what to do. The student with the social gift should be given every opportunity to use it for the benefit of all.

Then there are spiritual gifts. We have had no St. Augustine, St. Francis, or St. Thomas. We have produced no Martin Luther, John Calvin, John Wesley or Søren Kierkegaard. We have had, to be sure, our early New England divines and nineteenth-century transcendentalists, and we can name such important figures as John Woolman, Joseph Smith, Mary Baker Eddy, and Reinhold Niebuhr. Such evangelists as we have had have been of the promotional, big-business, showmanship type. Such writers in both Protestant and Catholic camps are for the most part superficial and sentimental. We probably go to church in greater numbers and spend more money on church budgets than ever has been spent before, but is this a true index of our spirituality? When we consider our hospitals, orphanages, homes for the aged, and other welfare projects, perhaps it is. Maybe here again we are practicing what St. James called "pure religion—to visit the fatherless and widows in their affliction." Or is our foreign aid program really selfish and economic while we talk glibly of the brotherhood of man? Here is an area of leadership to which we have given too little thought or attention.

Leadership in business has received its fair share of attention. Such educational institutions as the Wharton School of the University of Pennsylvania have long been in the forefront of training men for responsible posts in business. Industry itself has played an important role in training its own leaders while on the job, but unfortunately school counsellors often encourage pupils with considerable mental ability to go into the professions instead of showing them the possibilities for service in business. On the other hand, much business training, both on the secondary and college levels, has been almost totally lacking in cultural subjects. It is one thing to organize business to make vast profits, but it is more important to use these profits with a full knowledge of the social needs of our people and a general love of the humanities. Only a liberal education can give this.

LEADERSHIP TRAINING IN INTERNATIONAL RELATIONS

We have fallen down most in leadership training in the field of international relations. Although there has never been a time that we have not been directly or indirectly involved in European politics, it is only within the last sixty years that we have begun to assume the role of leadership in international affairs. Among the causes for our singular unpreparedness in this field are our geographical isolation and our economic sufficiency, and it is these two factors which greatly influence the teaching of history, international politics, and foreign languages. In the United States, one can travel three thousand miles from east to west and two thousand miles from north to south without the necessity of using any other language but English. Foreign language in the school became an academic discipline, a frill, or, at most, an accomplishment to permit the individual to read foreign literature and scientific works in the original languages.

Before World War I, the great majority of Americans never left the shores of the continental United States. American history was often taught without reference to the history of other countries. The expression "the old world" gave the impression that Europe was decadent, culturally and economically burned out. The Orient was a place to which to send missionaries, and, aside from familiarity through the Bible, the Middle East was an unknown area. Africa was the dark continent; South America the land of revolutions. Discussion of international politics was suspect and always began with the premise that America was right.

Today all this is changed. Two world wars and their political and economic aftermath together with the rapidity of travel and communication have made the whole world one whether we are willing to accept this fact or not.

Aside from a few brilliant examples on the college or postgraduate level, American education has done very little to train career diplomats and politicians. Senate investigating committees discouraged rather than encouraged young men and women from going into the foreign service. Here again, an effective leadership depends upon a responsive and informed followership. Many people do not understand the difference between politics on a local level—citizens dealing with citizens within the body politic—and international politics, where America deals as a sovereign power with other sovereign powers. Wendell Wilkie as a practical politician, Jacques Maritain as a great philosopher were right in maintaining that the future peace and welfare of the world will depend eventually on men talking to other men. But, until such time as world government can be effective, we must play the game according to the rules now enforced with our diplomats receiving support from a well-informed, alert citizenry. The training of such an alert citizenry is within the province of the public school.

RESPONSIBILITY FOR TRAINING LEADERS

The first responsibility of our schools for training leaders is to the mass. We must raise the general level of understanding of the place of America in world affairs. We must teach our people not only to make a living but to make a life full of purpose, to make the world a place in which men can live together. Second, we must raise the general level of practical proficiency so that we are prepared for the age of automation and, most important, we must seek out leaders and encourage them to emerge from the group. We must fill them with a social purpose for leadership and we must give them the finest training the world has ever known.

We shall need thousands of scientists in the years to come. The making of a scientist begins in the arithmetic classes of the elementary school and continues through the science classes of the high school. Many boys and girls are repelled from scientific careers by the poor quality of science instruction. We must strengthen such instruction by selection, training, and compensation for teachers. Research laboratories which are stockpiling Ph.D.'s will have to share them with the classroom. The benefit of the National Science Foundation in strengthening science teaching by providing advance training plus adequate financial support for science teachers cannot be overestimated.

We must strengthen our internal governments. We must elevate the profession of politics to its proper dignity. Public servants should offer knowledge, skill, experience, and integrity as qualifications for office, rather than attempt to lure votes by baby-kissing, rabble-rousing, and graft. Institutes of local and state government, notably the Fels Foundation, are offering services and trained personnel to these governmental units. We need wide interest and understanding of governmental units. We need to train more intensively a larger and better-selected personnel. Little is being done on a national level for the training of legislators. There is need here for a sound understanding of the philosophy of government and wisdom in seeing local problems in the light of national and international situations. Foundation and governmental support for such training is badly needed. We need to promote international understanding. We need to give every boy and girl a second language at an early age. We need to teach foreign language as communication. We need to free teachers of current problems of the fear of persecution by vested interests. We need to bring our students into contact with other countries, other customs, other modes of thought. We need to pick out our best students and teachers and make them our unofficial ambassadors while they study and teach abroad. We need to support such movements as FLES, Foreign Language in the Elementary School, in order to correct the entirely erroneous impression that Americans cannot learn foreign languages. We need to support programs of exchange of teachers and scholars from the secondary to the post-doctoral level. Various foundations and governmental acts, for example, the Fulbright and the Smith-Munt Acts, have done much to make America known and respected abroad. We need not be ashamed of the quality of our scholars and professors who represent us at foreign universities.

We need to promote the arts. We need to build a broad base of appreciation. We need to be ever so much more selective of would-be artists, actors, and musicians. We need to support the really talented through their apprenticeship and productive years. We need to give opportunity to every talented young person to get the technical, collegiate, or professional training he needs. These men and women who will soon be our leaders should not be barred from advanced training because of social and economic pressures. The GI Bill has given many men and women opportunities to receive advanced training which would otherwise have been denied to them. We must raise the educational level by establishing more and more municipal junior and senior colleges, by making more funds available for scholarship. We must make it possible for young people to earn their way through school. It must be recognized as a noble thing to do to go it on your own.

We must raise our spiritual sights by supporting those with highly creative and reflective minds to do research and to write in the arts and the humanities. We must make it possible for our universities to carry on research in pure science as the foundation for applied science. Government and industry have been most generous in providing funds for university researches, but too frequently these have been of a practical nature. Universities should always include a generous overhead for pure research in such contracts. We must establish more institutions like the Princeton Institute for Advanced Studies. We must give scholars and scientists the freedom they need to go as far as they can go in their investigations, research, and experimentation. We must raise the general cultural level of men who control the economic and political destinies of America so that more and more funds can be spent to promote the general welfare of the arts and the sciences. We must encourage the general public to recognize ability and leadership, while we must make it possible for the emergent leader to receive the training he needs. We must never educate him out of his group.

Finally, we must encourage every man and woman in America to embrace a vocation, that is, an occupation to which he has been called. We must insist that our leaders are dedicated to their vocations, and that, in the pursuit of them, they are involved in the destiny of mankind.

SUMMARY

Our study so far has shown that the ideals of American democracy derived from Locke and from the French Encyclopedists. Fundamental American political documents define certain inalienable rights of man and vest the authority of government in the people. Universal education is a necessity in America because the perpetuation and the advancement of our democratic way of life depends upon the active participation of all of our citizens. Education must provide opportunities for individuals and groups to learn and to teach, to investigate and to appraise all phases of American life. American education must develop intelligent leadership and followership within the tradition and organization of American society. American education must provide every opportunity for those who are gifted intellectually or talented in other ways to develop qualities of leadership, so that no talent will be wasted. American society must provide for intelligent adjustment and co-operation among all its people without regard to their intellectual, religious, social, or economic status.

THE ORGANIZATION AND SUPPORT OF AMERICAN EDUCATION

In America we have fifty independent school systems. The Constitution of the United States makes no direct reference to education, but we have read federal participation in education into the general welfare phrase in the preamble. In addition, we have assigned the control and direction of education to the states, because the Tenth Amendment declares that what is not specifically mentioned in the Constitution is delegated to the states themselves. Because of this arrangement, there is the widest possible diversity among educational opportunities within the United States.

There are, of course, many advantages to local control of education. For one, school districts may develop educational programs to fit their individual needs. Second, the decentralization of educational authority tends to prevent the seizure of this very important instrument by a small group to further its own interests to the detriment of the people of the entire country.

THE FINAL EDUCATIONAL AUTHORITY IN AMERICA

The final authority for government and education within the United States resides with the people, or as Maritain rightly describes this group, the body politic. *We the people* are the government; we are the United States. These are our children and it is the duty of the body politic on local, state, or national levels to provide a proper education for them, and the wherewithal to do so.

It should be pointed out, however, that these conclusions, while supported by a large majority of Americans, are not universally agreed to. For example, the Catholic author quoted below states a different point of view, and since his book bears the imprimatur of high ecclesiastical authorities, it may be inferred that it has the approval of the Roman Catholic hierarchy in America.

> In the very nature of reality any agency or person that is directly commissioned to perform a function takes precedence, *caeteris paribus,* over one that is indirectly commissioned. Likewise, a superior agency or person takes precedence over an inferior. We may deduce from the first principle the fact that if an organization or agency should receive directly from God a commission to teach, it would, all else being equal, be the primary and supreme educator of men. From the second principle we may infer that a supernatural educator enjoys a more basic educational function than a merely natural one. Because the Catholic Church has received from God a direct commission to teach and because her function is a supernatural one, it follows that she is the primary and supreme educator of men.[12]

Father Dubay states in a footnote that "this truth . . . is immensely distasteful to some non-Catholics." He claims that such a point of view is "unthinkable" and "decidedly unscientific." He then presents some thirty volumes by Catholic authors as "irrefragable evidence" to support his position.

The above statement notwithstanding, we take the position that it is the responsibility of the American people through their local, state, and national governments to provide, regulate, and support appropriate education for citizenship for all, and to see that no potential talent is wasted for lack of educational opportunity. So far as government and education for citizenship, with all the term implies, is concerned, *we the people* are the highest authority.

WEAKNESSES OF AMERICAN EDUCATION

On the other hand, unfortunately, the distribution of wealth and the funds available for education are not everywhere the same nor is the interest in promoting education nor the competence of educational leaders and school board members everywhere of the highest quality. As a result, there are many weaknesses in our present system. For example, there are no uniform compulsory

[12] Thomas Dubay, S.M., *Philosophy of the State as Educator* (Milwaukee: The Bruce Publishing Company, 1959), p. 55.

attendance laws. The school-entrance age varies from six to eight and the school-leaving age anywhere from twelve to eighteen. There is no general pattern with regard to the number of days per year nor the number of hours per day included in the educational program. Although there are compulsory education laws on the books of every state in the union, they are not always diligently enforced. Over two million children in the United States, from six to fifteen years of age, are not in school, and unless they are in school, we have no chance to influence them or educate them in any way.

Another weakness is that there is no uniform pre-elementary school offering. Modern educators believe that the elementary school should be extended downward to include at least the kindergarten and, if possible, the nursery school. England, France, and Russia all follow this pattern and find that such a program helps the students to be ready to undertake the more formal work of the elementary school and provides for a better social adjustment. In France, for example, sixty per cent of the children from three to six attend pre-elementary school. In England, forty per cent do so. In the United States, the richest country in the world, that boasts of its program of free public elementary education, only eight per cent of our three- to six-year-olds are enrolled in either public or private pre-elementary school programs.

There are, in America, inequalities in educational opportunities for minority groups. Not only is this true among the Negroes in the South but, to a less degree, the Mexican population and the Chinese and Japanese populations of the Pacific Southwest do not have the educational opportunities they need.

One of our great weaknesses in America is the illiteracy rate. We are considerably below Scandinavian countries in regard to literacy. At the present time, approximately three million persons in the United States have had no schooling whatsoever and approximately ten per cent have completed only the first four grades. During World War II, more than two hundred thousand men of draft age were rejected because of illiteracy alone. Much of this illiteracy is found among the southern Negro, but by no means is it confined to this group alone. It is, of course, definitely traceable to the inequalities of education throughout the various sections of our country.

DIVERSITY OF ORGANIZATION AND OPPORTUNITY

In America, there is no unified system of education even with regard to minimum essentials. With the mobility of our population, this presents quite a problem when school children transfer from one school district to another. While a uniform program of studies or uniform administrative procedures is undesirable, it would be well for educators to make use of the great amount of scientific evidence now available to show what can reasonably be expected of students at certain periods of their development.

There is the greatest divergence in teacher preparation, teacher certification, and salary. Although theoretically school board members only appoint state-certified graduates of teacher-training institutions approved by the state, there are so many loopholes that literally hundreds of school boards in districts having only one-room schools hire the person they can get for the least money without concern for his professional training or competence on the job.

FINANCIAL SUPPORT FOR EDUCATION

There is no uniform distribution of financial support for the public schools. Our schools have three principal sources of revenue: the federal government, the state government, and the local school district. About two per cent of the total school budget is provided by the national treasury, about forty-two per cent from the state funds, and the rest, about fifty-six per cent, from the local school districts.

Since the contribution of the federal government at the present time is rather small, let us see what happens to the state appropriations, including both state and local support, in some of our states. New York spends about 1.5 per cent of its annual income on the schools. Mississippi spends 1.6 per cent, but, because of the inequalities in wealth, with less effort, New York provides five times as much for the support of each pupil in its public schools. Arkansas spends slightly more of its annual income on its schools than California but has only one-third the budget. For over twice as much effort and expenditure, West Virginia can provide less than two-thirds as much money for the support of public education as can the state of Washington.

Because of inequalities in financial resources, there is the greatest variety in the types of instruction, in school buildings, facilities, and other equipment. States which have much money to spend can provide higher education at public expense, and wealthy school districts frequently offer many scholarships to the best colleges. Scholarships go begging in some areas, while in less-favored areas, brilliant students are denied opportunities for acquiring higher education.

These same inequalities exist to a considerable extent within the states themselves. It took a long time for wealthy school districts, for example, in Pennsylvania, to be willing to help to support the educational offering in a small mining village. Thirty-eight state departments of education are now dedicated to equalizing educational opportunities within their own borders. This is good, but it is not enough. All fifty states should so resolve. But, even if they did, the lack of financial resources among the states themselves makes it impossible for the poorer states to offer anywhere near an adequate educational program.

EDUCATION FOR ALL

In America, we have undertaken to educate all our children at public expense and we must be willing to pick up the check. The very nature of our democracy demands that we develop a high level of education, for "an educated people moves freedom forward." [13]

But how can we provide such education without funds? States and local school districts cannot go it alone. The time must come when the wealthy New Yorker will help to pay for the education of the boy in the backwoods of Tennessee. We need federal aid.

In considering federal aid to education, two problems are generally involved. The first is the relationship between federal aid and federal control of education: The second is the support of private education or independent education by the federal government.

[13] Slogan of the National Education Association National Convention, 1957.

FEDERAL AID AND FEDERAL CONTROL

We cannot have federal aid to education without some measure of federal control or regulation. In fact, the reason we want federal aid is to set up some kind of minimum standard. There should be minimum standards with regard to school buildings. There should be minimum standards with regard to safety and sanitation. Schools should be provided with enough equipment to do a good job. Our boys and girls should go to schools in which teachers are properly trained and certified. We should see to it that there is an adequate school year so that there is enough time to ensure the accomplishment of the objectives which we set. We should have compulsory attendance laws that are actually enforced so that we can be sure that all children profit from the offering of the schools. There should be equal opportunity for all children and youth without regard to race, creed, or color. There should be minimum essentials in the arts of communication and computation, in health and in citizenship.

These aims should be stated in very general terms. They should be developed by groups of competent educators who are actually representative of the school personnel throughout the country. The funds for carrying out these objectives should come through the Office of Education so that it will not be necessary for a school superintendent to approach a half-dozen or more governmental agencies in order to take advantage of the funds which the federal government provides for various educational purposes. The implementation of these objectives should be entirely up to the local school boards and the local school personnel who should have the widest choice of materials and method.

Federal Support of Educational Programs and Institutions

The federal government began its active participation in educational affairs back in 1787 when it passed the Northwest Ordinance which provided the sixteenth section of land of every township for the encouragement of school and school organization. The federal government has been interested in the training of officers for the armed services. West Point was established in 1802, Annapolis in 1845, and more recently, the Coast Guard Academy and the Air Force Academy. During the Civil War, the Morrill Acts provided for the establishment of land-grant colleges. These colleges have been able to extend their activities and educational programs throughout the state by subsequent congressional acts. Beginning in 1917, government funds were made available for vocational education, home economics, distributive education, and apprenticeship training on the secondary school level. Beginning in 1944, the federal government took an active part in providing higher education through the various GI bills. There is scarcely a department within the President's cabinet which does not carry out some type of educational program.

What we need now is a further extension of these programs and a better type of coordination and administration of them. Much can be learned about the relationship between federal support and federal control of education from the development of education in Great Britain since the Education Act of 1944. England established a number of local educational authorities, generally referred to as L.E.A.'s. Each L.E.A. raises whatever funds it can to support its own educational program, and the Crown supplies sufficient additional funds to provide a standard type of education. These funds are given to the local authorities to be used and administered by them. The Crown assumes no control over the local schools and school districts. The Ministry of Education owns no buildings, appoints no teachers, selects no textbooks or any other kinds of materials used in the classrooms. In this way, initiative and authority remains with the local school unit. Wealthy local educational authorities receive little governmental support while the poorer L.E.A.'s receive generous subsidies from the government.

Cooperation in Financing Education

Financing public education in the United States should be a cooperative enterprise, involving the local school district, the state and the federal government. The proportion of the cost of education assumed by each of these units will depend upon the ability of the local school district and the state to pay the bill. Obviously, some school districts will receive little or no governmental support while others will have to be subsidized to a very considerable extent.

Besides equalizing education, such a program might have certain desirable social and economic effects. In general, at present young people are moving from the farm to the big city. If education were of a high level in our rural areas, the adjustment that these young people would have to make when coming to a big city would be considerably less, and the social, economic, and health problems which are of such great concern to our big cities at the present time would decrease. On the other hand, good educational opportunities, not only for formal schooling, but for the use of the school plant and the school personnel for adult education and out-of-school education in our rural areas, might encourage young people to stay in farming and related occupations.

The American public schools are the bulwark of democracy. They are the training grounds for the battle of ideologies which we face in the years ahead. We must use them as effectively to promote our philosophy and way of life as the Russians are now doing to promote Communism.

The American public school is the greatest unifying agent in America. We come from many lands, from many economic backgrounds. There are many racial and religious differences. Our new Americans have different languages, different customs, different social systems, and different political organizations, and it is the public school, both in its regular program for childhood and youth, and also in its adult and citizenship programs, that opens vistas of the good life in America, inculcates the duties and responsibilities of citizenship, and welds us into one people. Everything must be done to maintain and to strengthen it.

PRIVATE EDUCATION IN AMERICA

Finally, with regard to the second question, public support for private education, there have been isolated attempts within the United States to insist that all boys and girls attend the public school. The most famous case of this type is the Oregon case. In 1922, the Oregon legislature attempted to abolish all private schools and to enroll all its boys and girls in public institutions. This law was declared unconstitutional by the Supreme Court in 1925, and the Supreme Court's decision is in line with the traditional policy of pluralism in American life.

Private education in America has had a long and distinguished history. In colonial times, we can distinguish three types of educational organization. There was, first, the theocratic organization of the New England colonies which supported public education at public expense. Second, in the middle colonies, which were largely proprietary, we have the development of parochial types of education by the various national and religious groups that came to this part of the country. The Friends, the Reformed, the Lutherans, the Moravians, the Catholics, and later the Presbyterians, the Baptists, the Methodists, and others established private schools, academies, and colleges for the general education of their children and youth, for the perpetuation of their language and tradition, and for the inculcation of their religious beliefs. Third, the southern colonies, made up largely of members of the Church of England, established some schools and colleges after the English model but, for the most part, sent their boys to England to be educated. If it were not for the parochial systems of education in the middle colonies, education there would have lagged far behind New England. As it was, however, newer types of education, especially the academy of a more modern and practical nature than the traditional Latin School, were developed, and these institutions set the model for the program of the public high school when it was established in the beginning of the nineteenth century.

We in America believe that parents have a right to educate their children in the schools of their choice provided that these schools adhere to the basic doctrines of American democracy and maintain the minimum standards, at least, which the states set up for them. On the other hand, we believe that no parent has a right to deny his children the right to public education or to some education appropriate to the American citizen.

We must be careful in America to preserve the integrity of the independent schools because they do serve the needs of certain types of boys and girls and because the more progressive and experimental of them are frequently proving grounds for new methods, new techniques, and new forms of organization and administration which, when proved to be good, can be adopted by public education. These schools, both on the secondary and collegiate level, can also maintain high standards of scholarship and intellectual endeavor.

I believe that the parent who chooses to send his boy or girl to an independent school should pay for it, and that it is a privilege for him to do so. We must preserve this privilege. But I also believe that it is the duty of those who believe in a particular type of education, which meets the needs of certain classes or religious groups, to support it for themselves.

Holland has a system of state subsidies to private educational enterprises, and those who think that the federal government should support independent education in America often point to the glowing reports of the system of education in the Netherlands as an example we should follow. Having spent some time in the Netherlands and having been a rather close observer, I can safely maintain that there is considerable discrepancy between the reports and the way the system actually works out. In the first place, all types of educational ventures must receive governmental support if the funds are to be dispersed equitably. In the section of Amsterdam where I lived, there were seven secondary schools within two blocks of my home. The schools were small and their programs restricted. For the most part, faculties were part-time and there was very little relationship between faculty members or faculty and students. Schools established on this basis are divisive. In Holland, there is little movement into the country. There is a great deal of emigration. Families have lived in the same area for many generations, and there is a fierce Dutch patriotism born of the soil and also the common enemy, water.

In America, we cannot afford such luxuries, and we must have the public school as a unifying agent in our society. The public school must be the school for the majority, the independent school, the school for the minority. The majority of the American people should not be asked to support, with their tax money, the education of such groups.

As Americans, we must do everything to allow parents to educate their boys and girls when, how, and where they will. But our sole concern, so far as federal aid to education is concerned, must be with strengthening the system of public education which unifies our people, helps them to live the good life, instills a love for democracy, and moves us forward to the free and peaceful world in which we all want to live.

BIBLIOGRAPHY

Berman, Harold J., "The Right to Knowledge in the Soviet Union," *Columbia Law Review*, LIV (May, 1954), 748–764.

Channing, Edward, *A History of the United States*, Vol. I (New York: The Macmillan Company, 1925).

Connell, Rev. Francis J., "Censorship and the Prohibition of Books in the Catholic Church Law," *Columbia Law Review*, LIV (May, 1954), 699–709.

Dubay, Thomas, S.M., *Philosophy of the State as Educator* (Milwaukee: The Bruce Publishing Co., 1959).

Educational Policies Commission, *The Education of Free Men in American Democracy* (Washington, D.C.: The National Education Association, 1941).

Gruber, Frederick C. (ed.), *Education and the State* (Philadelphia: The University of Pennsylvania Press, 1960).

Orcutt, Reginald, *Merchant of Alphabets* (New York: Doubleday, Doran & Company, 1945).

Spitz, David, *Patterns of Anti-Democratic Thought* (New York: The Macmillan Company, 1949).

Chapter X

Education and Value

PREVIEW

In Chapter VIII we studied the relationship of education to the nature of the individual. We found him to be co-extensive with nature but possessed of unique functions which distinguish him from other living creatures. Among these is intelligence, which is the way man deals with experience. Through the symbols of liturgy, language, and the arts he has preserved certain selected experiences by which he interprets and reconstructs the present, and through which he stretches the bounds of the present and vicariously lives alternatives for future action. This ability to delay action, to "stop and think" as Dewey says is one of man's most valuable assets.

In Chapter IX we considered men in relation to society. We made a brief for democracy as the best kind of social organization and control and showed the importance of a system of free public schools for initiating young Americans into the ideals and practices of democracy.

In both studies we found that individuals and groups were constantly under the necessity of making choices. Science gives us a wealth of reliable information upon which choices can be made. A study of history and of literary criticism gives us an insight into past experiences of the culture. Methods of philosophical analysis and verification give us a clearer understanding of the meanings and relations of terms. Yet none gives us a formula for making choices.

Should desegregation in the South be brought about immediately by force or by a long term educational program? Psychologists and sociologists can predict what will happen in each instance, but neither can tell us which course to pursue.

Should juvenile delinquency be looked upon as a social illness to be cured by appropriate means, or as an offense against society to be rooted out at all costs? In either case what should be the role of the school regarding the delinquent? Moving directly into the field of education, we may ask:

Should higher education be reserved only for the intellectually elite?

Should everybody in America be educated at public expense?

What education is of most worth?

What ought to be the outcomes of American education?

Should religion be taught in the public schools?

Is it moral to give full credit for work half done because the learner is capable of only that much?

Should children of the lower classes be made to accept the moral standards of their middle class teachers in the public schools?

VALUE THEORY—A HISTORICAL SKETCH

There was a time when society knew the answers to many of these questions, when values were fixed and sure and regulated by a higher power. Plato had a very low opinion of the common man. In *The Republic* he stated that people would not do right except for the fear of getting caught and punished, and that *justice* is a compromise between doing unjustly and not getting caught and suffering injustice without the power of retaliation. He had great faith in the power of reason to set moral standards when used by the upper class, and even advocated a separate standard of morals.

The early Christians had much the same idea. The Church officially maintained that men were by nature selfish and evil, and that morality could not exist without the fear of hell or the hope of heaven. St. Augustine and St. Thomas both taught predestination.

St. Augustine believed that although God made Adam and Eve free, he knew in advance what they would do, and St. Thomas maintained that man is free in a general sense, but that his actions are determined in particular situations. Even as late as the mid-seventeenth century, Thomas Hobbes held that in a state of nature, men were constantly at war and needed to surrender completely to a stronger power to be saved from chaos and destruction. Thus all matters of relativity were settled by a Divine Will or by a king who ruled by divine right.

ETHICAL THEORY SINCE COPERNICUS

From the publication of the *De Revolutionibus Orbium* in 1543 through the Enlightenment and Darwin's *The Origin of Species* of 1859 to the present day, much has transpired to shake man's faith in a fixed order of things and morals. The development of the sciences and the scientific method, and the philosophies of democracy and utilitarianism reduced dependence upon authority to a minimum. Unlike Hobbes, Locke believed that men formed governments by mutual consent and for their convenience and welfare. Jefferson added that by nature all men are free and equal, and Rousseau insisted in *Emile* that "all is good as it comes from the hand of God."

The psychologies of Descartes and Spinoza reduced altruism to enlightened self-interest, and the utilitarians from Gay through Mill reduced ethics to a pleasure-pain continuity with which the positivism of Comte was in sympathy.

On the other hand, both David Hume and Adam Smith recognized such characteristics as pity, kindliness, good will, and moral sense as human capacities not connected with self-interest. Kant and the transcendentalists believed that morals existed absolutely and independently in a real world apart from human experience, and that while right acts might result from such motives as self-interest, kindness, and habit, only those which are motivated by a sense of duty or conscience can be called moral acts. German idealism was interpreted in England by such men as Coleridge and Carlyle. The latter pointed out that what society needs is a sense of social responsibility and unity motivated by a concern for the greatest *nobleness* rather than the greatest *happiness.*

Two other English thinkers need to take our attention here. John Stuart Mill, schooled in the associationist psychology of his father and the individualistic economics of Ricardo, accepted much of eighteenth century hedonism, but believed that individual pleasure was determined by internal sanctions formulated according to the customs of the community. The interest of the community, he said, is the interest of the individual. There are degrees of pleasures, mental pleasures exceeding all others. To do without happiness is often undertaken by the hero or martyr for the good of mankind. With Bentham, he taught the socialistic doctrine that everybody counts as one, and nobody for more than one.

Herbert Spencer followed the hedonistic tradition that life is good or bad as it does or does not bring a surplus of agreeable feelings. As a follower of Darwinian evolution, he believed in the survival of the fittest. Pleasure, he thought, was the state of the static individual. It is only through inequality and pain that the process of evolution takes place. Standards of ethics grow out of man's moral ideals rather than from cosmic forces. The state should keep the individual from interfering with the welfare of others, so that the fittest, not necessarily the ethically best, may survive.

The English idealist T. H. Green, whose disciple G. S. Morris influenced the young John Dewey, opposed hedonism by declaring that man's desires are determined by the nature of his being; that pleasure is the result of attainment, not its motivation; and that the welfare of the individual and society are one. Leibnitz and Schopenhauer represent the optimistic and the pessimistic views of the world-ground respectively, while Hartmann formed a witty synthesis that although this is the best of all possible worlds it would have been better if it had never been.

The reaction to Kant's metaphysical and moral determinism was the boundless individualism of Nietzsche and the complete relativism of James.

A CRISIS CULTURE

Thus, by the beginning of the twentieth century the magnificent theological and metaphysical structure which had constituted European culture for over a thousand years had been severely shaken. As Nietzsche saw, our moral values are simply not compatible with the evolutionary naturalism of Charles Darwin, and as we have seen above, the tide of subjectivism and relativism threatened to destroy all values. Some have maintained that whatever science might do to our notions of the physical world, the old values still remain, but we know that this cannot be so.

When values can no longer be taken for granted, the culture reaches a crisis and there is a feverish re-examination of values: their nature, types, standards, and relation to reality. It is in such a culture crisis that we find ourselves, and the reconstruction of values is, therefore, our most pressing philosophical problem. The twentieth century has seen the development of axiology, that branch of philosophy which examines value systems in morals, the arts, religion, politics, education, and other fields of human endeavor. Our next task will be to examine this new discipline and to discover what help it can give us in dealing with the problem of values in education.

AXIOLOGY AND EDUCATIONAL VALUES

The study of the nature of values began with a study of the psychology of values. It explored such questions as: are values created or discovered? Are they objective, outside the mind—some quality within the object which evokes an appreciative response, or are they subjective, in the mind—a feeling of liking or disliking which an individual brings to a thing or situation which gives it value or disvalue? Do we strive for an object because it is valuable, or do we ascribe value to it because we strive for it?

A subjective approach to values maintains that they vary from person to person, from place to place, from time to time, and from situation to situation. They are relative to the mind which observes them and depend upon the individual's interests, experience, and desires. An objective approach believes values to be "out there" in the world to be discovered. There is something in the object which makes us form a judgment of it. Values reside in objects, just as colors, smells, temperature, size, and shape. A person of good taste recognizes beauty when it is present; a moral person recognizes goodness; a wise person, truth. A pragmatic approach to values insists that values are events, that they are relative, and exist situationally and instrumentally as a complex in which objective and subjective factors are brought into relation with each other. Society sets a standard of value with which an action or a plan of action is compared as to its present and future validity and effectiveness.

All theorists agree that both subjective and objective factors exist in order to create values, and that evaluation is a special kind of relationship which shows which things are true, good, and beautiful. All agree that liking or being interested in an object, or its opposite, is not the basic characteristic of value. All recognize the "naturalistic fallacy" of mistaking what *is* for what *ought* to be; all agree that a value judgment is not merely a disguised factual judgment.

It should be noted here that logical positivism maintains that such a field as axiology is impossible by its very nature and that normative sciences are not knowledge or judgments at all, but expressions of feeling. However, in regard to education and the other social sciences, value theorists believe that there are statements of facts and statements of values, and that these value statements are the life blood of the social sciences.

Possibly all we can say with certainty is that for all forms of axiology values are present in some sense, and that whether they exist or do not exist, they are nevertheless valid. The imperative "oughtness" is a part of their essential being and validity. This leaves us with the question, "Do values exist only for human beings, or do purpose and values for the individual imply purpose and value in the cosmos?" Most humanists reject the latter proposition on the grounds that to admit purpose in the world, humanizes matter and dehumanizes man, but there is a mass of philosophical argument to support the view that value in its elementary nonhuman form is the universal feature of the interconnection of things.

Whitehead's argument is pertinent here. He develops a philosophy of panpsychism which reads value down into the most elementary constituents of the universe. This concept has been made possible by certain notable changes in the fundamental concepts of modern physics, namely: the change in our concept of matter and the status assigned by many physicists to natural laws, which seem to open up a place for values in the scheme of the cosmos. Two difficulties with this theory are, first, how to recognize value in elementary, nonhuman form, and second, to separate value from mind. Whitehead, however, maintains that while value is present in all things, the consciousness of value is a characteristic reserved for human beings. Chart VIII compares the axiology of four current philosophies, namely: idealism, pragmatism, naturalism, and realism.

OBJECTIVES OF EARLY AMERICAN EDUCATION

The public school is the agency which has been entrusted with the task of initiating the young into our democratic society, into what Americans consider to be the good life. Education is not only concerned with what is, but what ought to be. That is, the conduct of American education is concerned with the selection of values and providing the implementation for their realization in the lives of children and youth.

Until about a century ago most value systems were based upon ultimate values. The determination of values was largely an epistemological problem since values as reality itself existed in the idea or in nature. It is only to be expected that early American schoolmasters should express values in terms of the subject matter of literature and later in mathematics and natural philosophy. That education was of most worth which gave the student an intimate knowledge of eternal truth found in the laws of value or of God. "Knowledge is power" was often engraved as a motto over the door of the secondary school. Although the study of great literature, especially the Latin and Greek classics, was originally engaged in to seize upon the ideas of the living past, mediocre schoolmasters soon began to mistake the retention of words for the understanding of ideas, and finally, even the rote memorization of classical phrases was abandoned for the formal disciplinary value of these subjects, for it was maintained that inherent in the forms of the classical languages was a power which sharpened the wits and stretched and toughened the mind. Studies in physiology and psychology, of course, do not support such a claim. Early colonial education was religiously oriented: Calvinistic in New England, sectarian in the Middle Colonies, and Anglican in the South.

In Chapter IX we have seen that the change from colonial to independent status caused a shift of emphasis from citizenship in the world to come, to citizenship in a rapidly growing nation. We saw how the old class structure of the Atlantic seaboard was challenged, and how new ideals of democracy were forged on a rapidly

CHART 9: Axiology of

	IDEALISM	PRAGMATISM
The General Nature of Value	Values are real existents, are what they are because there are individual persons to possess and enjoy them.	Values have their existence by virtue of their relation with individual-social activities. Wise selections must be made under the guidance of a persistent principle.
Determinants of Value Moral and Ethical	Act so that in your own person as well as in the person of every other you are treating mankind also as an end, never merely a means. Kant.	Constituted by the individual-social life process of communication. Ethical value is realized by acting satisfactorily to resolve indeterminate elements of indeterminate situations and to open the way to the most satisfactory control of succeeding situations.
Esthetic	In enjoying beauty we possess two values—knowledge of the Idea which the object represents, and existence for a moment as a well-less subject receiving impressions of the Ideas behind the phenomenal world.	Closely coupled with the nature of experience. The conversion of resistance and tensions into a movement toward an inclusive and fulfilling close. Dewey.
Political	Society is an organism in which individuals participate. The individual realizes selfhood only within society.	The community is one among many and not the one of which the many are subordinate parts. A sharing within and between communities.
Social	The individual must recognize his place as no more than part in the total society and must be willing to grant all other individuals their privileges.	Values are rooted in the individual-social life process. Individual depends upon society; society depends upon the individual.
Education	Education is the eternal process of superior adjustment of a . . . free, conscious human being to God. Horne.	Education is a social function. A general objective could be stated as social efficiency since life is primarily social at the same time it is individual.

Four Leading Philosophies

NATURALISM	REALISM
Values are resident in Nature; are the qualitative aspects of Nature.	Two general theories—values are simple, indefinable elements which are experienced for what they are; values are dependent upon the attitudes of the sentient beings.
Hedonistic—the highest good is the most highly refined and abiding pleasure.	Moral good is "the greatest happiness of the greatest number." Some, who grant reality of the spiritual, define the good as also virtue.
Purely natural in character, not involving any spiritual or supernatural factors.	"Enjoyment results in experience when cognition and feeling blend." Montague.
Individual man is free, but needs some kind of social organization to preserve his freedom, such as democracy.	Men are distinct individual units to whom real incentives must be held out and with whom real mechanics of social organization must be used.
Individual man is Nature's offspring, not a child of society. Social values are synthetic values which result from agreements in which individual men bind themselves together.	Foundations of social values are the physical universe and individual man, not society itself.
Education is a guide and augmentation of natural maturation. Modern view—the school must equip children to cope with the exigencies of a changing order by providing a special environment.	The objective of education is to realize the "good life," attendant on the fulfillment of self-determination, self-realization, and self-integration.

expanding frontier where settlers of diverse languages, cultures, and social and economic backgrounds were being welded into a unified people. The schoolhouse, so to speak, became the temple where the democratic faith was taught and nurtured. Thus the big "C" of citizenship took its place beside the three "R's" of the traditional common school. Religion was by no means forgotten. The founding fathers wrote "freedom of religion" into the fundamental laws, and this has frequently been interpreted to encourage each individual to embrace a faith of his own, rather than to conform to a state church under which many of the early colonists had suffered.

The economic theory of the day taught a doctrine of rugged individualism which encouraged the rapid development of our natural resources and the establishment of native infant industries, safeguarded by a high protective tariff. During the years since the adoption of the Constitution millions of immigrants have come to our shores. Some were recruited for building railroads, and for working the mines, the farms, and the factories. Others came because of economic failures or political upheavals in their native lands, and the prospect of freedom and opportunity which America offered. Each social, economic, religious, and nationality group brought its own standard of values with it. Movements such as the Know Nothing Party and the Ku Klux Klan attempted to force a so-called traditional American standard by violence and intimidation, but the American ideal of the freedom of the individual in such matters prevailed for the most part.

TYPES OF VALUES IN AMERICAN LIFE

At the beginning of Part III we showed the great diversity of the American people with regard to national origins and ideals, race, and economic and social backgrounds; and at the end of Chapter VIII we showed that one of the most difficult problems of each individual is the integration of his physical, intellectual, cultural, spiritual, and social personalities, especially if he is required to play widely different roles simultaneously or consecutively. One of the chief causes of difficulty is that each role has its own set of values generally accepted by the group with which the individual is associated. Thus there are certain outlooks which the religionist holds which are not always similar to those of the nationalist, the business man, the worker, or the intellectual. If one's daily contacts cut across these groups, arriving at a compatible set of values becomes especially confusing and difficult. Chart 10 compares the value systems of five common types of citizens to be found in any community. An examination of the educational values brings out clearly the reasons for the conflicting ideas with regard to the objectives of education such as that between religious education and education for citizenship in a secular state with its interesting combination "For God and Country," and the conflict between the practical vocational education of the working man with the humanistic liberal education of the intellectual. Another source of conflict is the ideals of applied research of the business man and the ideal of pure research of the scholar and scientist.

A RELATIVISTIC ETHIC

Advancements in science and philosophy and the higher criticism in theology maintained that there is no way of proving the existence of absolute values or an Absolute Evaluator except through recourse to faith which is a private rather than a public matter and cannot be domonstrated empirically. According to the writer of "Hebrews," "Faith is the substance of things hoped for, the evidence of thing unseen." [1] Thus the knowledge which comes from revelation is first believed and then known. It is a priori; its verification does not stand upon empirical evidence.

Accordingly twentieth-century man in his daily affairs has learned to live with a certain degree of relativity especially in the field of values. In our pluralistic society social values are likely to be considered as situational and instrumental, as ends in view, rather than ultimate ends beyond man's power to perceive or comprehend. Rather than consider what "good" *means,* we are content to enumerate what things appear to be good for something thought to be desirable under a given set of circumstances. This statement is also true for medicine, law, and the other professions.

Basing a practical social ethic on instrumental values does not deny the existence of ultimate values. However, since ultimate values are beyond human comprehension through the methods of science, and since the philosophical bases for the determination

[1] Hebrews 11:1.

CHART 10: Types of Value

	RELIGIONIST	NATIONALIST	BUSINESS MAN	WORKING MAN	INTELLECTUAL
Ultimate Ends	God, Salvation, Immortality	*Kultur*, Sovereignty, National power, glory, honor, supremacy	Money, Power, Fame, Influence, Possessions	Equality of all as workers—mutuality collective action	Knowledge through science and scholarship. Self-realization through the arts
Life Patterns	Saintliness, Obedience to God, His rule, His representatives, Christian virtues	Soldier, Patriot, Discipline, Honor, mental conformity, ethnocentric	Successful businessman. Shrewd, ambitious acquisitive, aggressive, captain of industry	The little man who does all the work	Toleration, impartiality, urbanity, objectivity, citizen of the world
The Individual	A soul most precious	A tool of the state	A source of human energy with a price tag	The little man with a right to little pleasures and vices	The creative personality
Competition	Competition for souls but not for things	Necessary for individual and national survival eliminates the unfit	Competition is the life of trade	Collective bargaining, group rather than individual competition	Live and let live
Cooperation	The golden rule with reward in heaven	Group cooperation against the common enemy	Corporate action monopolistic	Group cooperation protects the worker	Universality of art, science, culture

Ownership	The Just Steward	Individual achieves greatness through nation's power, possessions, achievements	Prestige value, keeping up with the Joneses. Money buys anything	Enough for simple comforts, pleasures, security	The wherewithal for progress in science and the arts
Social Change	Eternal values; temporal things must change to conform to them	The old ways are the best. Hold the line against change	Social structure sacred. Promotes technological change	Welcome change which improves status of worker	Everything changes but humanist's security and status
War	War necessary to combat heresy and social and political evils	A grand and glorious way to national domination	Good for business	Wants peace but responds to patriotic appeal	Cultural suicide
Education	Other worldly knowledge and conduct judged in terms of dogmatic faith. A means of propogating the faith	An instrument for molding patriotic citizens. My county right or wrong, but first and always my country	An instrument for applied science, for making skilled workers, for preserving the economic status quo	A way of getting ahead, but must be practical and not overdone	The vital connection between Man's past, present and future. The road to Man's advancement and salvation

of values are at such great variance, the "practical schoolman" finds it better to aim at a target he can see.

The ideas of relativism and pluralism are frightening to some. Mankind has, however, been living with them for over two thousand years. We shall now consider some of the characteristics of a relativistic ethic.

SOME CHARACTERISTICS OF A RELATIVISTIC ETHIC

1. Morality is a system of values based upon individual and group habits and sanctions.
2. Morality is a quest for social agreement.
3. Moral codes are determined by a consensus of the mores or customs of the community.
4. The problems of morality are axiological rather than epistemological.
5. The moral value of an act is determined by its results. In this sense what works is true and good.
6. The moralist acts according to what appears to bring the best results for the greatest number, since he cannot determine what is absolutely true.
7. Ends and means should be harmonious; each should justify the other.
8. The highest moral rectitude is that which harmonizes most thoroughly with the most comprehensive view of life of the individual and of the group.
9. Relativism implies a high sense of moral responsibility. It does not imply indifference, irresolution, or that everything is equally right.
10. Certain altruistic impulses, such as pity, kindliness, and other-regarding sentiments, are as valid as selfishness and pride.
11. Morality is essentially subjective; a person's values are assumed to be his own in the sense that he accepts them to live by.
12. Moral conduct demands acceptance of desirable ends in view and a determination to achieve them.

13. Conscience and a sense of duty are a miscellany of moral rules and habits.
14. The standard for individual conduct is that of the largest group in which the individual operates.

These fourteen items can be more succinctly stated as follows:

Morality is that which a society agrees is the most acceptable conduct for producing the greatest well-being for the greatest number.

Since value statements contain elements not verifiable by empirical data, moral judgments cannot be made on the findings of science or reason alone.

A relativistic ethic is instrumental, that is, it bases values upon results rather than intentions. Standards are determined by what appears to be the greatest good for the greatest number. In achieving this "good," ends and means must be harmonious.

There is no reason to believe that selfishness is more basic than altruism. Relativism demands that moral actions be judged with reference to the highest and most comprehensive value to which the individual and the group has aspired. Relativistic morals demand a high degree of social and individual dedication and responsibility.

Since morality is essentially subjective, it demands the individual acceptance of desirable ends in view and a determination to achieve them.

And finally, conscience is the result of social living and decision making and operates within the standards of the largest social group with which the individual is associated.

Before applying a relativistic value system to problems in education it will be well to sharpen further our description of such a system and to point out the paradoxes created by it. A relativistic value system may be said to be instrumental, social, and personal.

1. Values are instrumental. The good, beautiful, and true are thought of in terms of results rather than intentions or absolutes.

2. An individual's values are social. Standards are set by the values which operate in the largest group with which the individual associates.
3. Values demand personal identification, acceptance, dedication, and responsibility for actions and the results of actions.

RELATIVISTIC VALUES AND EDUCATION

The foregoing description poses two seeming contradictions which demand our attention:

1. Individual freedom versus social compulsion.
2. Continuity of experience versus the situational nature of decision making.

A relativistic value system guarantees to the individual much independence of thought and action, while at the same time it insists that moral acts are to be judged in terms of social conventions. The resolution of this dilemma seems to center about beliefs and actions which are public and those which are private. In general, a relativistic value system would allow that all actions and thoughts which affect the individual alone and no other are private and are entirely the affair of each individual. Also those acts of the individual which are public, but which are not detrimental or offensive to the society in which the individual operates, are his own concern. Clothing and food will serve as examples. Within the privacy of his own room, what a person chooses to wear is his own affair. In public, his attire must conform to standards of decency, but he has large latitude with regard to style, color, and other factors. Certain types of costumes are associated with sports, and if he should attend a formal function his dress is further restricted. If he joins the armed forces, his uniform, its care, and the manner in which it is worn are completely prescribed while he is on duty. The choice of food and the manner of eating are the individual's own except as he eats in public, is a guest, or wishes to be identified with a certain social or nationality group. But the manner in which excess or waste food is disposed of is a matter of public health and is therefore prescribed by the community.

Educationally, our society considers competence in the arts of communication to the extent of understanding and being understood by others to be an outcome of the common school. The style of handwriting, the perfection of the calligraphy, the number of colloquialisms, the pronunciation of words, the accuracy of grammatical construction, and the elegance of diction vary according to the intellectual and cultural level of individuals and groups. All that the public school has a right to demand as a universal prescription is that each person of normal intelligence writes legibly, writes and talks intelligibly, follows simple directions, and comprehends simple statements.

This same idea may be applied to the achievement of the student in school subjects. In general education, after the student has achieved the minimum level demanded by society, his advancement will be evaluated in terms of his ability to achieve. Thus the student may be said to set his own standard and to compete against himself. However, when the individual chooses a vocation, his achievement in knowledge, skill, and attitudes will be determined by the vocation he has chosen. Standards of educational achievement, therefore, vary according to circumstance. There can be no single or fixed standard.

So far we have spoken of the relation of the individual to society and the degree of his conformity to the social group. We need now to consider the obligations of a relativistic society to the individual.

A relativistic society encourages its members to develop their own potential and provides an opportunity for them to do so and to achieve personal satisfactions and happiness within the accepted patterns of the social group. Society has no right to prescribe occupations, residence, or social grouping, or to proscribe simple pleasures to any individual if these pleasures are accepted by the social group. The school will provide a guidance program which will assist the pupil to choose those subjects and activities which contribute to his welfare and happiness.

School administration, organization, and method will be such as to encourage the greatest amount of understanding and participation in social living. Life in a relativistic society is one of shared responsibility wherein the individual is concerned with his part in promoting the welfare and happiness of the group, and where the group feels a responsibility for helping the individual to achieve a high degree of well being.

A student talks and promotes a fight with his classmates. His behavior interferes with the welfare of the group. The teacher sends him to the principal who "suspends" him from school. Such action has only considered the welfare of the group. It has alleviated the situation but has not solved the problem. The next step will be to discover through counselling the cause of the misconduct and to take such steps with teachers, pupils, and others which will further the development of acceptable conduct patterns by all concerned.

The second apparent contradiction is found in the continuity of experience versus the situational nature of decision making in a relativistic society. The ancients have told us that all things flow, that nobody can step into the same river twice. On the other hand, modern relativists, notably James and Dewey, declare that we are *always* stepping into the same river.

In his psychology, James, describes the stream of consciousness as continuous and always changing; [2] and in his theory of history, Dewey insists on the continuity of events.[3] The present, then, might be thought of as the place where a selected, remembered past meets an uncertain, projected future. Or again, the present may be described as the process through which the influence of the past may be brought to bear upon the future. It is the sluice through which the past flows into the future. In other terms, the past, like the stream of consciousness is always being reconstructed in terms of present experiences, and the future is a projection of individual and group experiences in terms of present hopes and understandings.

Past and future, then, can be known only in terms of the present. The present itself is a span of time varying in length from the present moment to the present age. It is a configuration in which all the parts are related to a single point of view or to a single purpose. Any change in purpose or point of view will demand a rearrangement and a new selection of parts. Thus, while experience is a continuity in which all parts are interrelated, each individual event is unique, not only in itself but for each person who experi-

[2] William James, *Psychology, Briefer Course* (New York: Henry Holt and Company, 1892), Ch. XI.

[3] John Dewey, *Reconstruction in Philosophy* (Boston: The Beacon Press, 1948), Chs. I and II.

ences it. Each decision is a specific instance dependent upon its particular time, place, circumstance, and purpose.

The following illustration shows the shift which circumstances may bring about in making a decision.

John Brown is very proud of his record. He has a reputation for good work and dependability. He is as good as his word. He has completed all his work for his master's degree, but there are still some corrections which must be made on his master's thesis, and it must be handed in tomorrow morning so that his adviser can read it and recommend him for the degree before sailing for Europe to-morrow night.

Just as he has settled himself to do his work, the phone rings. It is his only brother whom he has not seen since he entered a monastery many years ago. He is at the airport. Only this morning he got word that his request to become a medical missionary to a leper colony in Africa had been granted. He has twelve hours before boarding the plane which will take him to his mission station from which he has vowed never to return. He would like to spend these last twelve hours with his brother.

John Brown must make a decision. Shall he spend the time with his brother or shall he meet the deadline on his thesis and take his degree as planned? If he is a young unmarried man and he expects to remain in his present teaching position, the decision is rather easy. The advance in salary and the degree might well wait until the next convocation. But if the possession of the master's degree puts him in line for a promotion, the problem becomes more complex. If he is married and has a family of small children, and if the possession of the master's degree means that he will receive an appointment to the kind of position which will open up a career for which he has been preparing, and will move the family to a more desirable environment with greater pay and prestige, the decision may be quite different from that in the first situation cited above.

In the first instance the principal considerations are (1) pride and satisfaction in accomplishment, (2) feeling of obligation to meet one's obligations and to keep one's promises, (3) building a reputation for dependability, (4) increase in salary, (5) brotherly affection and desire to be with him under unusual circumstances, and (6) the brother's feeling whether he would "stand in John's way" if he knew. In the second example the possibility of a promotion adds to the complexity of the situation, and in the third instance responsibility to his family, social and financial advancement, career opportunity, and the attitude of his wife and family toward the problem also enter the situation. Which will be the most compelling factor in making a decision will depend on the individuals involved, their sets of values gathered from past experience, and their hopes and plans for the future.

In this sense a person's values may be assumed to be his own. The relativistic test of truth is a transaction or a process of interaction. A relativist cannot say that something is absolutely true or right, but rather he is justified in acting as if it were true. In the illustration cited above it will be noted that the introduction of each new factor changed the whole quality of the situation. This quality of a total experience, this art of living, is what gives value to situations. The quality of the experience lies neither in the object experienced nor in the person who experiences alone, but in the transaction which takes place between them within the continuity of experiencing.

Class size is a problem which has beset administrators for a long time. Some data show that students grouped in large classes perform as well on certain achievement tests as those in small classes. Therefore, some administrators conclude that large classes are as educationally effective as small classes. On the other hand, there is a current feeling that the mystical number for class size is somewhere between twenty-five and thirty. Some of the questions a relativist would need to ask are: "What were the specific items to be learned? What was the nature of the group tested? Under what conditions did the teaching, learning, and testing take place? What were the competencies of teachers and pupils, and how accurate were the measuring instruments. He would then compare his situation with that described in the report, and, if the situations had a high degree of correspondence, he would be justified in accepting the findings of the study and applying them to his situation, under the assumption that "they are right," that is, applicable in a specific instance.

A relativistic approach to the curriculum recognizes the many variations in American life, and the diversity within the pattern of our society. The comprehensive high school with its great variety of class and extra-class offerings on different achievement levels is an attempt to care for the individual needs, abilities, and aspirations of the student while at the same time recognizing his associations and responsibilities within the group. Absolutists, on the other hand, who insist that man is everywhere and at all times the same, and that the acquisition of knowledge is in all cases superior to the acquisition of skills, will insist that each person should be exposed to a prescribed program of "liberal studies" during his school career.[4]

Education is a process of experiences which determines the quality of living. Knowledge and skill are both quantitative. Both lack the emotionally toned reaction that is characteristic of living organisms. A relativist seeks to confront the learner with situations in which these three factors—knowledge, skill, and feeling—are present and interactive.

The relativistic educationalist stresses the need for guidance, especially of the emergent and nondirective type, which equips the person to think through situations as they arise and to make choices upon the best evidence available. The absolutist insists upon a universal curriculum of "liberal education" which instills the "eternal verities" which the individual uses as the basis for his decision making.

The absolutist would consider rules of discipline as universal and would maintain that justice requires that they apply equally to all; the relativist would consider their application individual and circumstantial. Absolutists measure the results of education in terms of knowledge acquired, relativists, in terms of the use to which the knowledge can be applied. Absolutists train persons to conform to universal moral and cultural standards; relativists encourage the individual to cooperate with his group and his times to develop moral and cultural standards applicable to specific circumstances. For the absolutist, the end justifies the means; for the relativist, the ends and means must be harmonious.

EDUCATIONAL VALUES SINCE SPENCER

Enough has been said above to show that during the last century the main stream of public education is turning more and more from the concept of education as the acquisition of knowledge to

[4] See Jacques Maritain, *Education at the Crossroads* (New Haven: Yale University Press, 1943), pp. 64–87.

education as a process of living and learning in a dynamic society. Our previous discussion has provided a background in history and theory for this change in emphasis. A pioneer in the reassessment of what education is of most worth in terms of areas of human conduct was Herbert Spencer. His important work, *Education* began as a series of essays which sought to apply the principles of Darwinian evolution to the social fields, and with the addition of a most significant introductory essay, "What Knowledge Is of Most Worth," appeared in book form in America in 1861. His five objectives, which we can summarize here as: (1) self-preservation, (2) securing the necessities of life, (3) rearing and disciplining offspring, (4) maintaining proper social and political relations, and (5) gratifying the tastes and feelings through miscellaneous leisure time activities, are reflected in every major statement of objectives by American educators, both individual and group, within the last fifty years.

Such a reorientation of educational objectives relegates knowledge to the position of a means through which the ends of education are realized and not as an end in itself. This concept did not originate with Spencer, nor can it be "blamed upon the entrenched professional educationalist." Spinoza considered subject matter to be the least important in the trilogy of objectives, methods, and knowledge; and other similar references among educational theorists, ancient and modern, are not hard to find.

In response to problems arising from the increased enrollment of the secondary schools and the wide diversity in the capacities, backgrounds, and vocational aims of the secondary school population, in 1918, the Commission on the Reorganization of Secondary Education of the National Education Association enumerated seven "Cardinal Principles of Education," namely: health, command of fundamental processes, worthy home membership, vocational efficiency, civic participation, worthy use of leisure time, and ethical character. These, of course, are not principles at all, but rather statements of objectives, or patterns of behavior which are to be induced in young people through the curriculum of the secondary school. The correspondence between these objectives and those of Spencer can be easily seen. Worthy of note is the attempt to reconcile the old and the new by including the command of fundamental processes when such a command is actually a means of attaining the objectives. Another interesting departure from tradition is to include religion, which was a primary aim of colonial education, in the objective of ethical character and to follow Spencer's lead and the demands of a democratic society by including civic responsibility. Goals were stated in terms of activity. Knowledge and skills were to be acquired for use and not for themselves alone. Finally, we should note the positive and optimistic statement of the objectives which reflects the era of self-confidence and technocracy of the "roaring twenties." Other statements of objectives during this decade reflect the same spirit and also the influence of job and activity analysis which had a great vogue in psychology and among the social sciences.

But the depression and the rise of dictatorships in Europe required a restatement of objectives in terms of "economic goals" from 1931 to 1937. "Vocational efficiency" became "suitable occupation," and much stress was laid on mental health, flexibility, freedom, and physical and economic security. These goals went far beyond the province of the school and were evidence of the increasing realization of the need for cooperation among society's various agencies in the education and welfare of the American people.

By the end of the thirties the United States was getting on her feet economically, and the rest of the world was preparing for a war in which many Americans knew we would get involved sooner or later. Much thought was being given to strengthening our democratic faith and to protecting individual liberties. In 1938, the Educational Policies Commission of the National Education Association published a small volume entitled *The Purposes of Education in American Democracy* in which four groups of objectives were set forth under the headings of Self-realization, Human Relationships, Economic Efficiency, and Civic Responsibility. The first of these objectives aimed at making the individual at home in his physical, biological, and cultural environment, and the last three integrated him into the group by developing his ability to understand and to get along with people, to be an intelligent contributor to the nation's economy, and to be a participant in its civic life. Thus, the National Education Association recognized but did not solve what is perhaps an insolvable problem for each person in a relativistic society, the relation between individual freedom and social-civic responsibility.

Social and economic adjustments following World War II sharpened the issues and underlined some of the principal problems toward the solution of which the school might be expected to contribute. As the family came to be recognized as democracy's bulwark against totalitarianism and state ownership of the individual, the school was encouraged to include activities which strengthened family relationships.[5] Since the person makes a life as well as a living it was recognized that there should be a blending of liberal and vocational education. The National Association of Secondary School Principals in their statement of the Imperative Needs of Youth in 1947 declared that the student on leaving high school should possess saleable skills and an appreciation of beauty.[6]

Of vital importance to American life is the individual's responsibility as a citizen. The National Education Association in its discussion of education for citizenship pointed out that the loyalties of free men are to values and processes rather than to persons and institutions, and listed eight of them, namely:

> The free man is loyal,
> First, to himself as a human being of dignity and worth
> Second, to the principle of human equality and brotherhood
> Third, to the process of untrammelled discussion, criticism, and group decision
> Fourth, to the ideal of honesty, fair-mindedness, and scientific spirit in the conduct of this process
> Fifth, to the ideal of respect for an appreciation of talent, training, character, and excellence in all fields of socially useful endeavor
> Sixth, to the obligation and the right to work
> Seventh, to the supremacy of the common good
> Eighth, to obligation to be socially informed and intelligent.[7]

Our brief examination of the statements of objectives in education has shown the shift from knowledge to value and process. We may also observe that while the fundamental needs of mankind re-

[5] The importance of the home has been stressed in a series of White House Conferences beginning in 1940.

[6] *Bulletin of the National Association of Secondary School Principals,* March, 1947, pp. 1–144.

[7] Educational Policies Commission, *The Education of Free Men in American Democracy* (Washington, D.C.: The National Education Association, 1941), p. 55.

main the same, the importance given to each of them and the approved method of satisfying them vary with each generation and each society. The conduct of men has two determinants, the one biological and the other social. The school may be considered a third determinant especially set up by society to bring about the successful development and adjustment of the individual. It follows that such a school will make the learner aware of these biological and social compulsions and his relation to them by a carefully constructed program based upon the "laws" of nature as they are known and the highest standard of values of the society which supports it.

LIBERAL EDUCATION IN AN AGE OF TECHNOLOGY

Having briefly explored the development of value systems with special reference to their relation to the objectives of American education, we are ready to conclude our study with a consideration of what is perhaps the central and most discussed problem in American education today: the meaning and scope of a liberal education in an age of technology. Liberal education is usually thought of as education for free men, but many modern educators have stoutly maintained that it is education to set men free. Perhaps it is a combination of both, and can be more correctly described as education to keep free men free. Let us start at this point.

Many intelligent and thoughtful persons are giving much attention to education now and express widely divergent views. There are those that believe that all education should be bookish and that men and women, especially in their college years, should secrete themselves in a cloisterlike liberal arts college where they give no thought to the affairs of the present workaday world. On the other hand, there are those who consider that all education should be of a practical nature and that anything that smacks of the past or of culture of the Latin and Greek period is inappropriate to our progressive civilization. It is easy to see that many of the critics are biased by the refraction and the tint of the lenses that they wear. Our need in America is for clear glasses and sharp focus.

Let us look at some of the factors in America which necessitate a change in the educational outlook. First of all, there are the effects of mechanical inventions and automation. These have brought about a shorter work day, a shorter work week, and a shorter work year. They are also responsible for shortening the productive period of an individual, for raising the compulsory school-leaving age, keeping young people from going into productive industries and professions at an early age, on the one hand, and on the other, of providing for early retirement. All this adds up to an enormous amount of leisure time. Automation reduces the market for the unskilled and increases the need for the technically trained. Another influence in America is the effect of research and practice in medicine. We are getting to be a nation of old people. In 1900, there were four million adults over sixty-five years of age. It is estimated that in 1980, there will be twenty-two million. This represents an increase of 550 per cent. At the same time, there has also been a phenomenal increase in high school population. In the last forty years, high school populations have increased over 1,000 per cent. There is now in the public high schools of America the widest spread of intelligence, of background, abilities and purposes. Formerly, the high school represented a more or less homogeneous group with regards to population, and ability. High school populations, then, represented a favored socio-economic group, the best brains of the community, and boys and girls who were preparing for college or who wished a finishing education which prepared them for the life of a gentleman or a fine lady. Today the only homogeneity in the modern senior high school is found in the fact that all are adolescents and all will be voting citizens at the age of twenty-one.

We need also to rethink the old work-play dichotomy. "All work and no play makes Jack a dull boy"; "All play and no work makes Jack a fool," is known to all. American society can afford neither dullards nor fools, neither drudges nor playboys. What education must strive for is to activate the individual's inner resources in the direction of socially useful purposes. Certainly, at the present time, and increasingly in the future, men will be free from the drudgery of making a living and will be free to live the good life. Therefore, the student in school should live the life good to live in all its fulness. What shall be the training of these liberated men? What is the appropriate schooling for these free citizens?

What, then, is the modern concept of a liberal education in an age of technology?

In ancient Athens, the education of free men was for the citizen, only a small proportion of the population. There, the men who had wealth and leisure were trained through the seven liberal arts for the duties of citizens of the state. The arts of war and government, the practice of literature and the fine arts were their vocation. To be a good citizen encompassed every phase of life.

During the Renaissance, the secular learning of western Europe had its rebirth. Then the objective was to develop the universal man, the citizen of the world. Classical studies had an extremely practical value. Latin was the universal language and continued to be the language of scholarship well into the seventeenth century. Parents who had ambitions for their sons naturally wanted them to become fluent in the use of Latin and Greek as these were the intellectual passports to culture, business, and advancement in church and state. The Renaissance educator would probably have considered an abstract education utter nonsense.

In early America, our first colonial colleges were established to prepare men for the sacred ministry. A knowledge of the classical languages was therefore essential. It was really their "stock-in-trade" because these languages, together with Hebrew, were the tools with which they examined and interpreted the scriptures. In a very real sense, then, Latin and Greek were vocational subjects because without them no young divine could be considered adequately prepared for his profession. Even the other learned professions besides theology, such as law and medicine, required a good knowledge of Latin, because many of the treatises in these disciplines were written in Latin. It was only at a later period, when commerce, the trades, and the new professions were carried on in the vernacular and when books and other treatises were also written in the language of the country, that the Latinists tried to defend and maintain their positions by claiming a special disciplinary value for their subject. The growth of German idealism in the nineteenth century aided this movement because it tried to demonstrate the value of ideas as contrasted with deeds, maintaining that the abstract idea was superior in every way to the practical application of these ideas in daily life. There is a fundamental fallacy in this separation of ideas from deeds, and education which separates them does not fulfill its complete obligation to the young people of America.

Just before the settlers left for Jamestown, in December 1606, Sir Francis Bacon published *The Advancement of Learning* in which he maintained that knowledge had to be tested through experience. This broke with a century-old tradition going back to Plato and beyond which maintained that few should think while the many worked. In the second spring after the landing, when the Jamestown colonists found that most of their supplies had been eaten by rats, Captain John Smith issued an order: "Every one that gathereth not every day as much as I doe, the next daie, shall be set beyond the river, and forever be banished from the fort: and live there or starve."

The attitude of the men who were loath to work with their hands was deeply rooted in the past. It drew a sharp line between knowledge and action. It associated intellectual enterprise with the privileged classes, above all with priests and scholars. It linked action with those who fought and those who worked. Captain Smith's attitude was more the product of necessity than of philosophical speculation, but it did reflect a departure from the tradition which identified knowledge and thinking with one class and action with the other. Because conditions in frontier Virginia left no alternative, this new idea won out at Jamestown.

It also carried the day on later frontiers, including that of the Pacific Northwest.[8]

Yet many educators are loath to accept this fundamental belief. We are still teaching Latin and geometry and suppose that these subjects contain some mystical value and that knowledge of them sets one apart and above the common herd. On the one hand, these academicians hoard their liberal knowledge as if it were a treasure in a jewel box only to be taken out and admired, while on the other, they look down upon the vocations and would deny those who work with their hands the knowledge of the moral and social implications of their trades in the modern world. For proof of this statement, examine the curriculum of the average American vo-

[8] Merle Curti, *American Paradox* (New Brunswick, N.J.: Rutgers University Press, 1956), pp. 3–5.

cational school, from tailoring to medicine. Dewey appropriately remarks,

> At the very time when an important, perhaps *the* important, problem in education is to fill education having an occupational direction with a genuinely liberal content, we have, believe it or not, a movement such as is sponsored for example by Dr. Hutchins, to cut vocational training off from any contact with what is liberating by relegating it to special schools devoted to inculcation of technical skills.[9]

With what phases and aspects of social life has the whole vocational movement been most closely connected? Today it is most obviously intended to be an aid in preparing young people to get jobs and so to earn a livelihood. It may prepare them quite effectively on the technical side and yet leave graduates with very little understanding of the place of those industries or professions in the social life of the present, and of what these vocations and professions may do to keep democracy a living, growing thing.

Wouldn't it seem as if in a really democratic system of education, in a really democratic society, that the history of labor, the significance of labor, the possibilities of labor, would be an important, integral part of the whole education scheme? Or, turning to another aspect of the matter, how shall we account for the fact that, with some notable exceptions, the medical profession is heartily opposed to the socialization of medicine and to making public health a common public asset? How are we to explain the fact that to such a large extent the lawyers who have had a professional and supposedly a competent professional education seem to be the advocates of the most reactionary political and social issues of the community at any given time?

The people who are active in the direction of public affairs lack prevision because they have no understanding of the scientific technological forces that are actually shaping society. The education of the average scientist and the average technician, on the other hand, is such that he is left indifferent to the social consequences of his own activities. Hence, it is nobody's business to take stock of the resources of knowledge now available for social betterment.

The question I am raising is whether it isn't the educator's business to see that the education given by schools be such that those who go out from them can take stock of the knowledge that is available for social betterment.

[9] John Dewey, *Philosophy of Education* (Ames, Iowa: Littlefield, Adams, and Company, 1956), p. 32.

It might be worthwhile to sacrifice a little of the purity of pure knowledge, to contaminate it here and there with relation to action, if we could save our country from a reaction against those who can talk and argue, but who do not know how to act competently with reference to the social problems that have to be dealt with.[10]

Another great educator, Alfred North Whitehead, whose philosophical background is different from Dewey's, has this to say on the subject: "Education is the acquisition of the art of the utilization of knowledge." [11] "Ideas which are not utilized are positively harmful." [12] "Pedants sneer at an education which is useful. But if education is not useful, what is it? Is it a talent, to be hidden way in a napkin?" [13]

Knowledge, then, should lead to action; it should be put to use in the world of men. And, just as important, action should be based upon adequate knowledge and reasoned judgment. How, then, are our secondary schools and colleges promoting the balance of knowledge and action among our future voters?

We have, in America, a unique institution in the comprehensive high school. Here is an institution of, by, and for all the people. It is a common integrating experience in democratic living. It should be a place where what is learned in the classroom is put into immediate use in the school's other activities. America has extended liberty and citizenship far beyond the reaches of ancient Athens or medieval Paris. Since all citizens are free men, all should receive the education of free men, that is, a liberal education. As Dewey remarked, "A truly liberal, and liberating, education would refuse today to isolate vocational training on any of its levels with a continuous education in the social, moral, and scientific contexts within which wisely administered callings and professions must function." [14]

In the modern public high school, there should be no vocational courses without their social and cultural equivalents. Major subjects should be those which lead directly to social efficiency: health, social studies, communications, computation, science, and the

[10] *Ibid.*, pp. 54–55.
[11] Alfred North Whitehead, *The Aims of Education* (New York: The New American Library, 1956), p. 16.
[12] *Ibid.*, p. 15.
[13] *Ibid.*, p. 14.
[14] Dewey, *op. cit.*, p. 146.

appreciation of the arts. Minor subjects are those which lead in the direction of vocational efficiency: Latin, geometry, welding—and these latter subjects should also be taught with reference to their contributions to the general aims of the secondary school.

In American higher education today, the relationship of liberal studies to vocational education is the subject of much heated controversy. On the one hand, there are the anti-intellectuals who would have all education above the elementary level strictly vocational. America is a young country. We have not got over the growing pains of our westward expansion and our industrial development. Rabblerousers, the self-made businessman, and politicians, even presidents of the United States among them, have boasted of how little they know, how little formal schooling they have had, and how they have never heard a symphony concert, read a poem, or visited an art gallery. Culture is reserved for the ladies and any man found guilty of the same is therefore ladylike. A red-blooded American male might know the name of Robin Roberts but not Robert Browning, and Rocky Marciano is much more of a hero than Rembrandt or Rimsky-Korsakov. Such men have dealt a fatal blow to higher education. They are responsible for crowding out the basic disciplines, for undermining the foundations of the education which leads to social and cultural responsibility. I have no quarrel with vocational training, but I am strongly opposed to the type of training that prevents the student from obtaining a sound understanding of his duties and responsibilities to the culture from which he has sprung and the civilization of which he is a part.

As a reaction to the anti-intellectualism, there are the "great books" enthusiasts. Certainly we should read good books rather than poor ones, but to imagine that all that is worthwhile in western civilization can be encompassed in any list of one hundred great books, no matter how carefully selected, is a little naïve. Such a list is like ready-made clothing—cheap, easily obtained, but does not fit anybody. The great books enthusiasts maintain that they take the student back to the original sources, but I submit that it is not possible to understand Dante without being familiar with history of Florence, with the Guelph and Ghibbeline controversy, and with the tradition and theology of the medieval Christian Church. Similarly, nobody can read *Das Kapital* with complete understanding without knowing the philosophy of Hegel and the German idealists and the social, economic, and industrial conditions of the times in which the book was written. Then, too, events are not always shaped by great books. Had *Hamlet* not been written, we would have been deprived of a great tragedy but, if Luther had not written his ninety-five theses, the whole history of western Europe might have been different. *Huckleberry Finn* is considered to be among America's greatest novels, but the influence of Harriet Beecher Stowe's *Uncle Tom's Cabin* reached much farther.

As Whitehead correctly maintains, "The student of the university should stand up and look around." [15] Up to this time, the student has been largely concerned with acquiring the fundamentals of western culture and the tools of learning and of exploring his capabilities and the adult world of which he will soon be a part. Now he will be called upon to systematize what he has learned, and to develop those generalizations which will guide his further activities and development. Understanding his world is a far more complex matter than it was fifty years ago. That the remotest place on this planet is not more than sixty hours by air from where we are is not compatible with isolationism. That the white race is a minority group so far as the races of mankind are concerned and that many of the other cultures with which we are in daily contact are in many ways older and more profound than ours should give us pause. The very future of the planet depends upon the training of the men and women now in the world's institutions of higher learning. They must know and be proud of their past. They must be dedicated to the welfare of humanity and have the technical and professional know-how to effect it. They must know themselves in a comprehensive way of which Socrates never dreamed. They must be leaders in the cause of universal mutuality so that they and all others may live the life good to live.

What then should be the dimensions of liberal education in an age of technology? In the not unforeseeable future, our technical development will remove much of the drudgery from our daily lives. Man will be possessed of much freedom and of much leisure. In ancient times, liberal education was for free men, the school was a place for the leisure class. In the Renaissance, liberal education developed universal man. Freedom from drudgery and world

[15] *Ibid.*, p. 38.

citizenship have been the dream of mankind for centuries. Today technology has thrust them upon us. Liberal education must be as broad as humanity, as deep as the well of human knowledge. It must equip each man with a vocation in which he can realize his individuality and which he dedicates to the cause of all mankind. It must teach the dignity of all useful work. It must develop the desire of men to work together, yes, even as Maritain says, to suffer together, for the high prize of a united and free world.

BIBLIOGRAPHY

Berkson, I. B., *The Ideal and the Community* (New York: Harper and Brothers, 1958).

Cook, Lloyd Allen and Elaine Forsyth Cook, *A Sociological Approach to Education* (New York: McGraw-Hill Book Co., Inc., 1950).

Curti, Merle, *American Paradox* (New Brunswick, N.J.: Rutgers University Press, 1956).

Educational Policies Commission, *Moral and Spiritual Values in the Public Schools* (Washington, D. C.: National Education Association, 1950).

———, *The Purposes of Education in American Democracy* (Washington, D.C.: National Education Association, 1938).

Gruber, Frederick C. (ed.), *Aspects of Value* (Philadelphia: The University of Pennsylvania Press, 1959).

Hare, R. M., *The Language of Morals* (Oxford: The Clarendon Press, 1952).

O'Connor, D. J., *The Philosophy of Education* (New York: The Philosophical Library, Inc., 1957).

Sayers, Ephraim and Ward Madden, *Education and the Democratic Faith* (New York: Appleton-Century-Crofts, Inc., 1959).

Sprague, Elmer and Paul W. Taylor, *Knowledge and Value* (New York: Harcourt, Brace and Company, 1959).

APPENDICES

Glossary

ABSOLUTISM
The theory that there is always a relevant standard of belief, reality, and action.

AESTHETICS
The study of beauty.

AGNOSTICISM
The theory that the final answer to basic questions is always uncertainty.

ALTRUISM
The theory that the good of others should always supercede one's own good.

ANTITHESIS
The opposite of ideas or statements.

A POSTERIORI
Refers to data of the mind which own their origin to the outside world of human experience, and do not belong to the mind's native equipment.

A PRIORI
A term applied to all judgments and principles whose validity is independent of all sense impressions. Whatever is a priori must possess universal and necessary validity.

ARCHAIC
A style which is primitive and incomplete in comparison with a later or posterior style which is considered perfect and complete.

ATOMISM
The view that there are discrete irreducible elements of matter.

ASSOCIATIONISM
A theory of the structure and organization of mind which asserts that every mental state is resolvable into simple discrete components. A school of psychology based upon mental connections established by a process of learning.

ATHEISM
The belief that there is no God, or that there is no personal God.

AUTHORITARIANISM

The theory that truth is determined by its having been asserted by a certain esteemed individual or group.

AXIOLOGY

The modern term for the theory of values.

CARTESIAN DUALISM

The theory of René Descartes that reality consists of thinking substance or mind and extended substance or matter.

CATEGORICAL IMPERATIVE

The supreme, absolute moral law of rational self-determining beings.

CONSERVATISM

The belief that the school is a restraining and conserving force in the community, which keeps the basic traditions of society healthy and alive.

CONSISTORIUM

The papal senate.

COSMOPOLITANISM

World-mindedness, unprejudiced with regard to other nations than one's own.

COSMOLOGY

A branch of philosophy which treats of the origin and structure of the universe.

DEDUCTION

Reasoning from the general to the particular.

DEISM

Belief that God is a universal principle having no immediate relation with the world.

DETERMINISM

The doctrine that every fact in the universe is guided entirely by laws.

DIALECTIC

For the Greeks, the art of question and answer. For Hegel, a method of reconciling opposites.

DUALISM

The theory that reality is composed of two irreducible elements: matter and spirit.

ECLECTICISM

The principle, tendency, or practice of combining or drawing upon various philosophical or theological doctrines.

EGOISM

The view that each individual should seek as an end only his own welfare.

EMPIRICISM

The proposition that the sole source of knowledge is experience.

ENTELECHY
The realization of that which a thing is by virtue of its form.

EPICUREAN SCHOOL
The school of thought which gave expression to the desire for a refined type of happiness which is the reward of the cultured man who takes pleasure in the joy's of the mind, over which he can have greater control than over those of a material or sensuous nature.

EPISTEMOLOGY
The branch of philosophy which investigates the origin, structure, methods, and validity of knowledge.

ESSENTIALISM
The belief that it is the chief duty of the adult community to transmit the cultural heritage to the oncoming generation.

ETHICS
The study which concerns itself with judgments of approval or disapproval, rightness or wrongness, goodness or badness, virtue or vice.

EVOLUTIONISM
The theory that later things develop from earlier things.

EXPERIMENTALISM
The resort to concrete experience as the source of truth.

EXISTENTIALISM
The theory that existence precedes essence. That the self is the ultimate reality and that its inner struggles are the basic stuff of existence.

HEDONISM
The theory that pleasure alone has positive, ultimate value.

HERACLETIANISM
The view that all things in the universe as a whole are in constant, ceaseless flux. Nothing is; only change is real.

HETERODOX
Belief contrary to accepted opinion or dogma.

HUMANISM
The theory that the human element is of prime importance in the universe.

HYPOTHESIS
A provisional assumption.

IDEALISM
A theory that ideas are the essentials of knowledge; that all reality is of the essence of spirit; that ideas are to be pursued in action.

INDUCTION
Reasoning from the particular to the general. The method of science.

INNATE IDEAS
The power of understanding given in the very nature of mind. Ideas which are inborn and come with the mind at birth.

INTUITION

Immediate, direct apprehension of truth.

INTUITIONISM

Any philosophy in which intuition is appealed to as the basis of knowledge or at least of philosophical knowledge.

KANT'S THING-IN-ITSELF

That which lies beyond human observation and experience.

LOGIC

The branch of philosophy which investigates the structure of propositions and of deductive reasoning; a study of the laws of thought, judgment, and reasoning.

LOGICAL EMPIRICISM (SCIENTIFIC EMPIRICISM, LOGICAL POSITIVISM)

A philosophy which emphasizes the unity of science. Stresses the application of scientific method to all problems of life. Employs method of logical analysis and verification to educational concepts.

LOGOS

A term denoting either reason, or one of the expressions of reason, or order in words or things.

MACROCOSM

The universe as contrasted with some small part of it which epitomizes it in some respect under consideration.

MARXISM

The theory of economic determinism based on the class struggle; sometimes referred to as Dialectical Materialism.

MATERIALISM

The theory that only matter is existent or real.

MENTALISM

The theory of the exclusive reality of individual minds and their subjective states.

METAPHYSICS

The branch of philosophy which deals with the nature of reality: its first cause, its nature, its purpose, and its existence.

MICROCOSM

A world in miniature. Man as an epitome of the universe.

MODALITY

Concerning the mode, actuality, possibility, or necessity in which anything exists.

MONADS

In Greek usage, originally the number one. Later, any individual or metaphysical unit. Leibnitz applied the term to unified, indestructible, self-motivated souls.

MONISM

The theory that there is only one ultimate reality.

NOMINALISM

The theory that abstract or general terms, or universals represent no objective real existence, but are mere words or names, mere vocal utterances.

NORMATIVE

Constituting a standard; regulative.

ONTOLOGY

The study of existence, of the essence of things.

OPTIMISM

The theory that this is the best of all possible worlds, or that everything will happen for the best.

ORTHODOX

Beliefs which are declared by a group to be true and normative.

PANPSYCHISM

The theory that the whole of nature consists of psychic centers similar to the human mind.

PANSOPHIA

John Amos Comenius's plan for an institute of universal knowledge.

PANTHEISM

The belief that the universe as a whole is God.

PARMENIDESIAN

The theory which developed the conception of "being" in opposition to "becoming" of Heraclitus.

PERENNIALISM

The belief in the power of the mind and the patterns of medieval thought as a basis for education.

PHENOMENALISM

The theory that knowledge is limited to phenomena including physical phenomena, the totality of actual perception and mental phenomena, the totality of objects of introspection.

PHILANTHROPINUM

School for boys organized by Basedow in 1774.

PLURALISM

The theory that reality consists of certain irreducible elements.

PLURALISTIC SOCIETY

A society in which many elements exist equally and harmoniously.

POLYTHEISM

The belief that divine reality is multiple; that there are many gods.

POSITIVISM
The theory that man can have knowledge only of phenomena, through the senses, and that only relatively.

PRAGMATISM
The theory that the test of truth is how it works.

PREDESTINATION
The doctrine that all events of man's life, even his eternal destiny, are determined beforehand by a deity.

PROBABILITY
The quality or state of being likely true or likely to happen.

PROGRESSIVISM
The belief that the well-being and the improvement of society lie with the young who must be challenged and trained to accept shared responsibility for its continuing improvement.

PSYCHIC
A characteristic of any mental phenomenon.

PURITANICAL
A term referring, in general, to a purification of existing religious forms and practices. In America, the theological position of the New England colonists.

RATIONALISM
The theory that thought is the clue to nature, reality, and values.

REALISM
The theory that universals exist before things and that things exist independently of the knower. Reality is ultimately independent of any knowledge of its existence.

REASONING
The faculty of connecting ideas consciously, coherently and purposely. Thinking in logical form.

RECONSTRUCTIONISM
The belief that the schools and other agencies of society should plan and work aggressively.

RELATIVISM
The view that truth is relative and may vary from individual to individual, from group to group, or from time to time, having no objective standard.

REVELATION
The communication to man of the divine will.

SCHOLASTICISM
Both a method and system of thought. In its widest sense it embraces all the intellectual activities carried on in the medieval schools. Was grounded on Aristotelianism.

SEMANTICS
The science of the evolution of language and of the phenomena which mark its growth. (C. W. Morris)

SOCRATIC METHOD
A way of teaching in which the master professes to impart no information but draws forth more and more definite answers by means of pointed questions.

SOPHISTS
Those who, in ancient Greece, subordinated purely theoretical learning to its practical usefulness.

STOIC
One who believes that virtue alone is the only good and the virtuous man is the one who has attained happiness through knowledge.

SUPERNATURALISM
The belief in that which surpasses the active and inactive powers of nature.

SYLLOGISM
A certain form of valid inferences which involve as premises two categorical propositions having a term in common—the middle term.

SYNODS
Ecclesiastical councils or meetings.

SYNOPTIC
Giving a general view, often containing identical parts.

SYNTAX
The systematic statement of the formal rules of language.

SYNTHESIS
The general method of deductive reasoning which proceeds from the whole to the part. In Georg Wilhelm Hegel, the resolution of opposites.

TELEOLOGY
The theory of purpose, ends, goals, final causes, values, the Good. Teleology explains the past in terms of the future.

THEISM
The theory that conception of God can be accurately defined and acceptably used.

THEOLOGY
The study of the nature of God and the relation of God to the world of reality.

THEORY OF ORGANISM
That the universe is an integrated and unified whole.

THESIS
An undemonstrated proposition used as a premise in a syllogism. Any proposition capable of being supported by reason.

THOMISM

The official philosophical position of the Roman Catholic church as formulated by St. Thomas Aquinas and derived from Aristotle.

UTILITARIANISM

The view that the right act is the act which will actually or probably produce at least as much intrinsic good as any other action open to the agent in question.

VOLUNTARISM

The theory that reality is of the nature of will.

APPENDIX A: Philosophers and Their Schools

SCHOOLS OF PHILOSOPHY

PHILOSOPHERS	Absolutism	Agnosticism	Altruism	Dualism	Empiricism	Evolutionism	Humanism	Idealism	Monism	Optimism	Pantheism	Pluralism	Positivism	Pragmatism	Rationalism	Realism	Theism	Voluntarism
Plato	X							X		X					X			
Aristotle															X		X	
Augustine	X									X							X	
Aquinas	X									X							X	
Erasmus						X												
Descartes				X											X		X	
Spinoza	X								X		X				X			
Locke				X	X													
Berkeley								X	X								X	
Hume					X													
Kant		X						X										X
Fichte	X							X										X
Hegel	X					X		X							X			
Herbart												X			X	X		X
Comte			X			X	X						X					
Emerson								X										
J. S. Mill			X		X													
Spencer		X				X												
James											X	X		X				
Dewey													X	X				
Whitehead						X		X									X	

Albert E. Avery, *Handbook in the History of Philosophy* (New York: Barnes and Noble, Inc., 1955), pp. 283–292.

APPENDIX B: Modern

	NATURAL REALISM NATURALISM (HORACE KALLEN)	NEW REALISM ESSENTIALISM (HARRY S. BROUDY)	NEO-SCHOLASTICISM RATIONAL REALISM RATIONAL HUMANISM (ROBERT HUTCHINS)
Objectives—Aims—Purposes	The natural development of the child. (Presentism)	To equip man with the exact knowledge and skills which will enable him to compete with nature in the battle for survival. Based upon demonstrable facts—what people do. Impersonal, objective adjustment of individual to society.	To develop the rational powers of man: to reason, to judge, to discriminate. Reason differentiates man from the lower animals. To form an intellectual elite.
Subject Matter—Curriculum	What the child does or wants to do and know.	What human beings do. Adult approved behavior. Known facts about natural phenomena.	The great monuments of thought. A study of philosophy, especially logic.
Method	Children living together.	Experimental acquisition of facts. Memorization. Drill for acquisition of techniques.	Disciplined exercise of the mind in logical processes. Memorization.
Position of the Pupil	All important, an individual to be allowed (encouraged) to enjoy present day life.	A machine to be conditioned.	A mind to be trained.
Position of the Teacher	A servant of the learner.	An agent of Nature and of society.	The umpire between true and false logic.
Evaluation	In terms of the child's freedom and happiness.	Measurement of achievement of learner as compared with objective norms of standardized tests and scientific measuring instruments	Profundity of knowledge. Skill in logical analysis and in abstract thinking.

Philosophies and Education

CATHOLIC SUPERNATURAL REALISM—THOMISM (JACQUES MARITAIN)	IDEALISM (J. DONALD BUTLER)	PRAGMATISM (W. H. KILPATRICK)
To cooperate with Divine Grace to form the true and perfect Christian (Catholic).	Based on tradition, what has stood the test of time, the cultural heritage. Aim to attain the good life of the spirit. Largely intellectual; to form an intellectual elite. Aims distant and individualistic, in terms of knowledge.	Based upon the activities and goals of members of society and the immediate interest of the learner. Objective: to help the individual become a socially efficient member of society.
The Catholic religion and its application to all phases of life. The Catholic church alone possesses Truth. The only representative of God on earth.	Accumulated heritage of the race. Finest in literature, art, music, ethics.	Socially desirable activities. Knowledge and skills of immediate interest and use to the learner.
Conditioning the individual through precept, example, memorization, drill, to live the Catholic life.	Physical, mental, moral discipline. Reading, textbook, lecture, drill, memorization, recitation, controlled discussion.	Activity: mental, manual, physical, appreciative, social. Any method which motivates the learner and catches his imagination.
A Soul to be saved.	Plastic mind to be molded. Much attention to child and to individual differences.	The learner is an individual who grows or develops from within through activity in a social setting.
An instrument of God through the Church.	All important, the representative and purveyor of all culture.	A guide to learner's self-activity. To be in background. A trouble-shooter.
Conformity to the ideal of the Catholic Christian.	In terms of how nearly the pupil has attained the ideal standards established by the best work, achievement and tradition of the past, and specific standards set by the instructor.	Progress of the learner in terms of his own native ability to master the facts, skills, and attitudes demanded by the social group of which he is a part.

Index